T
328

HE

THE CHIEF EXECUTIVES OF TEXAS

Number Fifty-Five:

Centennial Series of the Association of Former Students

Texas A&M University

The CHIEF EXECUTIVES *of*

TEXAS

From Stephen F. Austin

to John B. Connally, Jr.

by Kenneth E. Hendrickson, Jr.

Texas A&M University Press *College Station*

The paper used in this book meets the minimum
requirements of the American National Standard
for Permanence of Paper for Printed Library
Materials, z9.48–1984.
Binding materials have been chosen for durability.

All photographs are courtesy of the Archives Division
of the Texas State Library in Austin.

Library of Congress Cataloging-in-Publication Data

Hendrickson, Kenneth E.
　　Chief executives of Texas : from Stephen F. Austin to John B.
　Connally, Jr. / by Kenneth E. Hendrickson, Jr. — 1st ed.
　　　　p.　cm. — (Centennial series of the Association of Former
　Students, Texas A&M University ; no. 55)
　　Includes index.
　　ISBN 0-89096-641-9 (alk. paper)
　　　1. Governors—Texas—History.　2. Governors—Texas—Biography.
　3. Texas—Politics and government.　I. Title.　II. Series.
　F385.H39　1995
　976.4'0099—dc20
　　[B]　　　　　　　　　　　　　　　　　　　　　　　　　　94-36375
　　　　　　　　　　　　　　　　　　　　　　　　　　　　　　CIP

To

Kirsten, Ron, & Michael

Ken & Kerrie

Bob

&

Carolyn

CONTENTS

ILLUSTRATIONS

FOREWORD

Central to the Texan tribal myth is a simple profession of faith: the Lone Star State has always enjoyed strong leadership. In his 1940 monograph, *They Sat in High Places: The Presidents and Governors of Texas,* James T. DeShields admitted to joining generations of proud Texans in perpetuating that mythic past where "giants" once ruled and legends were born. Not even a hint of contrition may be found in his confession that his book of biographical sketches was little more than an exercise in "hero worship." He even concluded that all men and women who had served as chief executives of Texas were "statesmen . . . entitled to rank high on the scroll of fame" and that "the roll of their names is the register of great and good men." In 1976, Ross Phares was only slightly more realistic in his appraisal of the state's leaders in *The Governors of Texas* as he struggled to find fault or failing with any of his subjects. Although surveying briefly the frustrations and failures of colonial French and Spanish governors, this largely superficial book of biographical vignettes lionizes Anglo leaders as larger-than-life paragons of strength and courage.

Their history as presented in this volume by professor Kenneth E. Hendrickson, Jr., however, is less romantic. To be sure Texans can justly boast of a rich and magnificent heritage, a colorful past that produced a pantheon of heroes with Texas-sized dreams and accomplishments: titans like Stephen F. Austin, Sam Houston, James Stephen "Jim" Hogg, and, more recently, the late John B. Connally, Jr., a genuine legend in his own right. Yet, as Hendrickson reveals in the following chapters, while the Lone Star legacy includes a few individuals of monumental accomplishments, it also leaves us with an even longer list of leaders who failed to measure up to such a vast land as Texas. The corrective lens provided here reflects the modern, revisionist school of scholarship that has essentially reassessed (and in the process) demythologized Texas history.

It has been said that each generation must rewrite the past in light of its own experiences, and so it must and should be. Hendrickson surveys the lives and careers of Texan leaders with a more critical eye than either DeShields or Phares, and in so doing, he offers a volume much more valuable to students, scholars, and general readers alike. Undoubtedly, those who prefer the more mythic past will be displeased to find this candid survey cleansed of anything resembling hero worship. Yet, for those who want to explore and learn more about the Lone Star State, these biographical portraits will provide a welcome breeze of fresh air. Absent in these chapters is the maudlin view and sometimes florid prose of previous works on the subject. In short, here are the leaders of Texas, "warts and all."

As I read these profiles of Texas presidents and governors, I was reminded of the West Texas oil baron and entrepreneur who recently asked me, "Were any of our Texas governors ever sent to prison?" "No," I replied, "but perhaps a couple of them should have been."

Michael L. Collins
Midwestern State University
Wichita Falls, Texas

PREFACE

This book is an effort to establish a semblance of realism in the study of Texas political leaders. Two similar works have previously appeared: James T. DeShields's *They Sat in High Places: The Presidents and Governors of Texas* (San Antonio: The Naylor Company, 1940) and Ross Phares's *The Governors of Texas* (Gretna, La.: Pelican Publishing Company, 1976). Both contain little more than praise for those who have occupied the highest seat in Texas government; in fact, these works contribute more to the perpetuation of Texas' mythology than to a realistic appraisal of Texas politicians.

The present work is offered to establish a more balanced view, but it is not intended to be definitive. It is a collection of biographical sketches designed to accurately place the chief executives in the context of their times and analyze the careers and contributions of each accordingly. Reading this will perhaps whet the appetite of other scholars and influence them to conduct further research, for there are several of these executives who, though worthy of study, have never been the subjects for biographers.

I would like to thank those who assisted me on this project, including the staff of the Moffett Library at Midwestern State University and the Barker Library at the University of Texas. Very special thanks must be given to my colleague Michael L. Collins, who read the manuscript, made valuable comments and suggestions, and saved me from a number of errors; and to my secretary, Kay Hardin, who typed several versions of the manuscript.

For any errors of omission or commission that remain in the text, I take full responsibility.

INTRODUCTION

Since the Revolution of 1836, forty-five men and two women have served as chief executives of Texas, either as president of the republic or governor of the state. Although Stephen F. Austin never served in an elective office, he is considered the "Father of Texas" and deserves special mention in this book.

A summary of the Texas chief executives' lives reveals some interesting patterns. They were a fairly well educated group. Nineteen attended college, thirteen graduated, and twenty-seven held law degrees or were admitted to the bar. Most of them, in fact, made their living as lawyers when they were not in public office, but other professions are represented, including banking, business, farming and ranching, soldiery, and medicine.

The first twenty-three chief executives of Texas were not native born (Anglo immigration did not begin in earnest until after 1820), but most of the early leaders were southerners. Of the first two dozen during the Revolution, Republic, and early statehood periods, only five were born outside the South. More important is that most of the early leaders were attracted to Texas by the Revolution. Of the first twelve men to become president or governor, seven participated in the Revolution and contributed in some measure to Texas' independence. The first four leaders—Austin, Smith, Robinson, and Burnet—came as settlers before the Revolution broke out but were also participants.

Among the next generation of leaders who served from 1861 to 1890, none was a native Texan, but all participated in the Civil War. Eight served the cause of the Confederacy, while two served the Union. Most of them earned reasonably good military records, a few were distinguished, and two, Ross and Sayers were bona fide heroes. The first native Texan to serve as governor of the state was James S. Hogg. But after Hogg came three more, Culberson, Sayers, and Lanham, who were immigrants. Since the days of Thomas M. Campbell, only two governors have not been native Texans. They were Oscar B. Colquitt and W. Lee O'Daniel.

Many writers have perpetuated the myth that Texas has always been blessed by outstanding leadership; but, alas, this is not the case. In the nineteenth century, there were indeed numerous colorful figures who rose to the top in politics, but only three, Sam Houston, Elisha M. Pease, and James S. Hogg, were truly outstanding leaders. Houston stands far above the others for he alone became a legend in his own lifetime. The twentieth century has produced only two leaders of exceptional quality: Thomas M. Campbell and John B. Connally, Jr. Some, like Pat Neff, Dan Moody, and James Allred, had noble intentions for strong leadership but were thwarted by the legislature.

There were, in fact, eight outright failures among the presidents and governors of Texas. These include Henry Smith, Mirabeau B. Lamar, Hardin R. Runnels, Richard B. Hubbard, James and Miriam Ferguson, W. Lee O'Daniel, and Coke Stevenson. The rest fall into a broad and amorphous range between weak and mediocre.

Although the Texas myth of strong leadership does not stand up to scrutiny, it is nevertheless worthwhile and enlightening to examine and compare the careers of Texas' chief executives. This study reveals certain recurring patterns and types of issues in Texas politics, including problems resulting from financial difficulties, extremism, violence, personality cults, race relations, and reaction to the federal system. Many decisions with far-reaching consequences have been made on the basis of these issues rather than on such banal propositions as the "public interest," and the results have not always been positive.

THE CHIEF EXECUTIVES OF TEXAS

Chapter one

COLONIZATION

1821–36

Although a few settlers drifted into Spanish Texas early in the nineteenth century, organized colonization did not begin until 1820, when Moses Austin of Potosi, Missouri, secured a land grant from the Spanish governor in San Antonio. Moses died in 1821, and his son, Stephen Fuller Austin, saw to it that his plan for colonization was carried out.

After separating from the Spanish Empire, Mexico encouraged colonization by enacting the National Colonization Law of 1824, which offered very attractive terms to settlers. They could acquire sizable tracts of land for a small capital outlay, and they were exempted from taxes for ten years and from tariffs for seven. Over the next several years, a number of contracts similar to that enjoyed by Austin were granted to the so-called empresarios, but few were as successful as Austin's.

Nevertheless, the colonization policy was successful enough that several thousand immigrants settled in Texas between 1824 and 1830. Now concerned by the rapid influx of people from a different culture, the Mexican government sought to check the growth of Anglo influence by passing the Decree of April 6, 1830, that essentially prohibited further immigration by Americans. Pressure brought to bear by the Texans resulted in the repeal of the Decree in 1834, and, technically at least, colonization was renewed. By 1835, however, relations between the Texans and the Mexican government had deteriorated so dramatically that conflict seemed inevitable.

Stephen F. Austin was the towering figure of this period. Although he was never to hold an executive office in Texas, he was, as Sam Houston once declared, "The Father of Texas." His was the most successful colonization enterprise. He provided much of the early planning and organization for the settlers, and he performed numerous public services—occasionally at the risk of his own life—that nurtured Texas during some of its darkest hours.

STEPHEN F. AUSTIN ☆ 1821–36

Stephen Fuller Austin was born at Austinville in Whythe County, Virginia, on November 3, 1793. He was educated at home, at his father's old school in Durham, Connecticut, and at Transylvania University in Kentucky. His father, Moses Austin, moved the family to Missouri in 1798 (while it was still Spanish Territory) and took up a lead mining claim. Later, the elder Austin established the Bank of Missouri, the first bank in St. Louis. Stephen assisted his father in his enterprises and entered politics some years after France sold the Louisiana Territory to the United States in 1803. In 1814, when he was only twenty years old, Austin was elected to the territorial legislature, where he remained until Missouri entered the Union as a result of the Missouri Compromise in 1820. He then became a judge in the first judicial district of Arkansas. Meanwhile, his father had suffered crushing financial reverses during the Panic of 1819 and sought to recover his fortunes through a land grant in Spanish Texas. Moses Austin succeeded, but when he died on his trip home in 1821, the contract passed to his son.

Stephen F. Austin led his first band of settlers into Texas in late 1821. On January 1, 1822, they settled near the Brazos River in the area that is now Washington County. Since the original grant, Mexico had

Stephen F. Austin

achieved independence from Spain, and Austin found that his contract was no longer valid. Hoping to reestablish the legitimacy of his venture, Austin set out for Mexico City in mid-1822. He was to remain there for a year, during which time he successfully renegotiated his concession.

Upon his return to Texas in 1823, Austin, now vested with full authority, set out to develop his colony. He established the first company of Texas Rangers to protect the settlers against marauding Native Americans; he founded the first capital of Texas at San Felipe de Austin in what is now Austin County; and he wrote a set of civil and criminal statutes that remained in effect until 1828. In exercising his authority, Austin generated both friendships and animosities among the settlers.

Between 1824 and 1830, thousands of pioneers migrated to Texas to take advantage of the extraordinarily favorable land laws. They settled in and began their new lives, but many were concerned about two issues: slavery and religion. Technically, the Mexican government required settlers to embrace the Catholic faith, but in practice the authorities usually ignored violations, and the settlers retained religious freedom. Also, colonists were allowed to bring slaves into the territory but wondered, as they did about their religious freedom, if Mexico would continue its beneficent policies. Sure enough, with the passage of the Law of April 6, 1830, the relationship between Mexico and the settlers in Texas began to change. This statute forbade the importation of slaves, opened the coastal trade to all nations (whereas it had been previously monopolized by the Texans), placed certain restrictions on immigration, and gave the Mexican government more power to supervise the affairs of the colonists. The central government then proceeded to increase its military presence in Texas.

The initial reaction of the settlers was to demand autonomy based upon their rights under the Mexican Constitution of 1824. They did not want independence. In fact, at their first convention at San Felipe in October, 1832, over which Austin presided, the delegates simply asked for repeal of the more repressive portions of the Law of 1830 and separation of Texas from the State of Coahuila. When no changes were forthcoming from Mexico City, the Texans issued a call for a second convention to meet in April, 1833.

The temper of the second group was somewhat more militant. This time Austin was defeated in his bid for the office of president by William H. Wharton, leader of the "war party." The convention then proceeded to draw up a provisional constitution for the Mexican State of Texas and a resolution asking for modification of the Law of 1830 (specifically, with respect to immigration restriction and tariff exemptions). A committee of three was appointed to carry these proposals to Mexico City.

Austin was a member of this group, but the other two, Dr. James B. Miller and Erasmo Seguin, declined to make the journey. Thus, Austin arrived alone in Mexico City in July, 1833, and filed his petition with the proper authorities. There followed what seemed to him to be interminable delays, and the Texan rapidly became frustrated. Finally, in October, he wrote a letter to J. Miguel Falcoñ, a friend in San Antonio, suggesting that Texas should organize a state government on its own since the Mexican Congress would probably not act favorably on the petition. This letter came to the attention of the Mexican authorities, and in January, 1834, Austin was arrested and imprisoned.

Austin's imprisonment accentuated factionalism in Texas, and for a time it seemed that his enemies cared little for his release and safe return. Finally, however, Peter W. Grayson and Spencer H. Jack, armed with many petitions, arrived in Mexico City and negotiated his release. After more than a year of confinement, Austin was allowed to return home in July, 1835. Meanwhile, relations between the Texans and the government had further deteriorated and soon after he arrived, Austin declared that war was inevitable.

President Antonio López de Santa Anna abolished state governments in 1835 and marched to crush the rebellious colonists. Hostilities in Texas actually began when a detachment of Mexican troops, under the command of Col. Domingo de Ugartechea, attempted to seize a cannon at Gonzales. After a brief skirmish on October 2, 1835, the Mexicans withdrew to San Antonio, and the Texans claimed victory. Now Austin took the lead in preparing for war and created a central committee, which, in turn, set up a general council comprised of one representative from each municipality. This body elected Richard R. Royal of Matagorda as its president and named Austin commander of the Texas Army.

There was considerable disagreement about both how to proceed and who was actually in charge. At last a convention, called the General Consultation, assembled at San Felipe on November 3, 1835. This group was dominated by the moderates, who were not yet ready to declare independence. Austin did not attend this meeting, but he nevertheless exercised considerable influence over it. He sent a proposal calling for recognition of the Constitution of 1824 and the creation of a provisional government. Further, Austin declared that Texas should prepare for war in defense of the constitution and the federal system and that an army should be organized. The Consultation selected Dr. Branch T. Archer as president, adopted nearly all of Austin's proposals, created a provisional government with Henry Smith as governor, and named Austin, Archer, and William H. Wharton as commissioners seeking financial aid from the United States. Sam Houston was appointed commander of the army.

Governor Smith wrestled with his council over the question of whether or not to accept aid from certain elements among the Mexican federalists who favored the Texans' cause. As a result, effective government in the province practically ceased to exist. In the meantime, a force of Texas volunteers under Ben Milam had taken San Antonio, and another group had seized Goliad and Gonzales. Gen. Martín Perfecto de Cós, the Mexican commander and brother-in-law of Santa Anna, was forced to retreat into Mexico.

Amid much dissension, the provisional government all but collapsed; however, a call went forth for a convention to meet in March to debate the question of independence. In January, Austin wrote to Sam Houston from New Orleans, saying that he now endorsed independence. Austin's view no doubt had some effect upon the election of delegates, and when the convention assembled on March 2, 1836, at Washington-on-the-Brazos, it adopted a declaration of independence. With Austin out of the country and Houston in charge of the military, the convention elected David G. Burnet as president of the *ad interim* government and Lorenzo de Zavala as vice president. Meanwhile, Santa Anna massacred the defenders of the Alamo and separated his army into four columns to begin the pursuit of Houston toward the east. Houston lured him but then turned upon his antagonist with a vengeance at San Jacinto on April 21, 1836, and Texas won its independence.

After drawing up a new constitution, the temporary government set a date for elections in the summer of 1836. At first Austin and Smith were the primary candidates for president because Houston declined to run. After literally hundreds of people begged him to do so, however, the Hero of San Jacinto finally consented to candidacy in August. During the campaign that followed, charges were hurled at Austin that he had deserted Texas in its hour of greatest peril and had done nothing of importance to aid the cause of Texas independence while in the United States. Many also were disturbed because he had waited so long to declare in favor of independence and because, in arguing for moderation, he had appeared too sympathetic to Santa Anna. The balloting confirmed that Austin had many enemies: Houston prevailed with 5,199 votes to only 587 for Austin.

Sam Houston appointed Austin secretary of state for the new republic, and the empresario undertook his duties. In the winter of 1836, however, he became ill, developed pneumonia, and died on December 27. He is buried in the state cemetery in Austin.

Sources and Further Reading

Barker, Eugene C. "The Government of Austin's Colony, 1821–1831." *Southwestern Historical Quarterly* 21 (1918): 223–51.

———. "The Influence of Slavery in the Colonization of Texas." *Southwestern Historical Quarterly* 28 (1924): 1–33.

———. *The Life of Stephen F. Austin: Founder of Texas.* Nashville: Cokesbury Press, 1925.

———. *Mexico and Texas, 1821–1835.* Dallas: Turner, 1928.

———. "Stephen F. Austin and the Independence of Texas." *Quarterly of the Texas State Historical Association* 18 (1910): 257–84.

Gracey, David B. II. *Moses Austin: His Life.* San Antonio: Trinity University Press, 1987.

McKnight, Joseph W. "Stephen Austin's Legalistic Concerns." *Southwestern Historical Quarterly* 89 (1986): 239–68.

Miller, Howard. "Stephen F. Austin and the Anglo-Texan Response to the Religious Establishment in Mexico, 1821–1836." *Southwestern Historical Quarterly* 91 (1988): 283–316.

Smithwick, Noah. *The Evolution of a State.* Austin: Steck and Company, 1935.

Vigness, David M. *The Revolutionary Decades, 1810–1836.* Austin: Steck-Vaughn, 1965.

Weber, David J. *The Mexican Frontier, 1821–1846: The American Southwest Under Mexico.* Albuquerque: University of New Mexico Press, 1982.

Chapter two

THE REVOLUTION
1835–36

The underlying causes of the Texas Revolution were similar to those of the American Revolution; that is, the parent country administered its colony with laxity for a considerable period of time and then attempted to tighten its control, thereby creating political resentment on the part of the colonists. After the Decree of 1830, Texans became increasingly disturbed as, in 1831 and again in 1832, Mexico sent more and more troops into Texas to enforce the law. In the Convention of 1832, Texans appealed to the government to modify the Law of 1830; and, in 1833, they requested that Texas be separated from Coahuila and sent Stephen F. Austin to Mexico to plead their case. When Santa Anna came to power in 1833, he planned to ignore the Constitution of 1824 and establish dictatorial rule, but Texans, at first, did not realize his intentions. In fact, even as late as 1835, most people were complacent about Mexican rule, and only a minority of Texans favored war to gain their independence.

During 1835 events played into the hands of the war party as Santa Anna placed increasing pressure upon the Texans. By autumn committees of correspondents were calling for the municipalities to send delegates to a General Consultation in order to decide a course of action, and the creation of this body was the first of a series of provisional governments that would conduct the Revolution. At first, the Texans proclaimed that they were fighting for their rights under the Mexican Constitution of 1824, and in November, 1835, the Consultation named Henry Smith provisional governor of the Mexican State of Texas. Then, as conditions deteriorated further, a convention of delegates assembled in early March, declared independence, and David G. Burnet became *ad interim* president. After defeating Santa Anna at the Battle of San Jacinto on April 21, 1836, Texas won its independence, and the Republic was declared to have existed since March 2, 1836.

The governors during this period were Henry Smith, 1835–36, and James W. Robinson, 1836.

HENRY SMITH ☆ 1835–36

Henry Smith was born at Smith's Station, Kentucky, in 1788. According to legend his father was a companion of Daniel Boone when that hero crossed the mountains of Virginia to settle the area south of the Ohio River. Little is known of Smith's youth, but by the age of twenty-one he had become a merchant in Nashville; afterward, he moved back to Kentucky for a time before heading out to Missouri. His wife died in 1820, leaving him with three children, and two years later he married her sister. Traveling alone, apparently, Smith visited Texas in 1826, and the following year he returned with his family and settled in the municipality of Brazoria. For the next few years he taught school, dabbled in business, and farmed. He became involved early in the independence movement, as a member of the Wharton faction, and was a delegate to the Convention of 1832.

In spite of his connection to the Whartons, Smith was elected provisional governor in 1835 because he was acceptable to the moderates. He soon began to experience such intense difficulties with the council, however, that his administration failed as an effective govern-

Henry Smith

ing body. The problem arose because Smith favored independence while the majority of the council members did not. An example of this discord occurred when Gen. José Antonio Mexia, an opponent of Santa Anna, offered his services to Texans to preserve their rights under Mexican law. The council voted to accept, and when Smith vetoed the resolution, it overrode his action.

Ben Milam's force took San Antonio on December 9, 1835, and in the flush of victory, Smith and the council considered staging an attack on Matamoros. Unfortunately, the governor and the council could not agree upon a leader for the proposed expedition. Neither Sam Houston nor Jim Bowie really wanted to undertake the project. Francis Johnson and James Grant were willing, but neither could raise an effective force. James Fannin was also enthusiastic and attempted to raise a group of volunteers. Amidst the confusion, Smith decided the invasion would be a very poor idea and issued orders that it not be carried out. His orders were ignored, and Houston and others blamed him for ineffective leadership.

In early 1836, Smith's problems intensified when Johnson stole the provisions stored at San Antonio and proceeded south to San Patricio, still hoping to carry out the invasion. Houston demanded that Smith do something, and the governor responded by calling a special meeting of the council at which he blamed that body for all the difficulties. The reaction of the council was to impeach Smith and name Lieut. Gov. James W. Robinson acting governor. At first Smith, outraged by the actions of Robinson and the council, wrote that neither Robinson nor the council could break him and refused to step down. Finally he accepted the inevitable, however, and relinquished the seal of his office to Robinson. As he left he declared that the only hope for Texas now was to make an unequivocal declaration of independence.

After the Revolution and the creation of the Republic, Smith's friends nominated him for president. When Sam Houston entered the race, however, Smith lost heart and withdrew; still, he faired better than Stephen F. Austin when the votes were counted. After the election Houston named Smith secretary of the treasury, and he served in that capacity until 1839. Subsequently elected to the Texas Congress, Smith joined forces there with those who opposed Mirabeau B. Lamar's financial policies. He left after one term and never returned to public life.

Smith was always an adventurer at heart, and in 1849, he joined the gold rush to California. He died there on March 4, 1851, and according to legend was buried somewhere in the mountains of Los Angeles County by his two sons.

JAMES W. ROBINSON ☆ 1836

From January 10, 1836, the day that Henry Smith was deposed, until March 17, the day that David G. Burnet was elected president *ad interim* of the Republic, James W. Robinson served as acting governor. All the officials of the provisional government accepted the change. Robinson attempted a reconciliation with Smith, writing to him that changes in the executive department had resulted from circumstances beyond Robinson's control and that he wished things had been otherwise. Despite these overtures, initially Smith ignored the effort by Robinson to win him over.

The only other significance to Robinson's brief administration was his signing into law an act authorizing the issuance of paper money in the amount of $150,000. He also tried rallying Texans to the cause of independence, and in a proclamation issued on January 19, 1836, he said in part: "March then with the blessings of your household Gods to the western frontier. March then where victory awaits you. . . . Roll back the crimson, the crimson stream of war to its source, and make the tyrant feel the fiery sun of blazing, burning, consuming war – war to the knife, and the knife to the hilt! Let them know how freemen can die, and how freemen will live."[1]

A native of Indiana, Robinson was born in 1790 and came to Texas around 1828. He was a skillful lawyer and a man with a very large ego, but little is known about his personal life otherwise. He signed the Texas Declaration of Independence in 1836 and, after the creation of the *ad interim* government of the Republic, he joined the army as a private. Serving with Mosely Baker's company, he fought at the Battle of San Jacinto.

After independence was achieved and a new government created under Sam Houston, Robinson became a judge. In 1840, when Gen. Adrian Woll captured San Antonio, Judge Robinson was among those taken prisoner and marched off to Mexico. While in captivity there, he persuaded Santa Anna to consider a plan for peace between Mexico and Texas, and the dictator set him free to carry it to President Houston. Although nothing came of this effort, it led to further negotiations and a genuine truce between the two nations in the summer of 1842.

James W. Robinson

Apparently, Robinson and Henry Smith eventually reconciled their differences because in 1849 they set out for California together. Robinson, who settled at San Diego and prospered, fared much better than his old adversary. From 1852 to 1855, he was district attorney and tried his hand at railroad promotion, and when he died in 1857, he left a large estate. He is buried in San Diego.

Note

1. James T. DeShields, *They Sat in High Places: The Presidents and Governors of Texas* (San Antonio: The Naylor Company, 1940), 24.

Sources and Further Reading

Binkley, William C. *The Texas Revolution*. Baton Rouge: Louisiana State University Press, 1952.

Brown, John Henry. *Life and Times of Henry Smith, the First American Governor of Texas*. Dallas: A. B. Aldridge & Co., 1887.

Clarke, Mary W. *David G. Burnet*. Austin: Pemberton, 1969.

DeShields, James T. *They Sat in High Places: The Presidents and Governors of Texas*. San Antonio: The Naylor Company, 1940.

Greer, J. K. "The Committee of the Texas Declaration of Independence." *Southwestern Historical Quarterly* 30 (1927): 239–51.

McDonald, Archie P. *Travis*. Austin: University of Texas Press, 1976.

Phares, Ross. *The Governors of Texas*. Gretna, La.: Pelican Publishing Company, 1976.

Richardson, Rupert N. "Framing the Constitution of the Republic of Texas." *Southwestern Historical Quarterly* 31 (1928): 191–220.

Steen, Ralph. "Analysis of the Work of the General Council, Provisional Government of Texas." *Southwestern Historical Quarterly* 40 (April, 1937): 309–33; 41 (January, 1938): 225–40; 41 (April, 1938), 324–48; 41 (July, 1938): 23–54.

Chapter three

THE REPUBLIC
1836–46

Four men served as president during the nearly nine years of the Republic: David G. Burnet, Sam Houston (who served twice), Mirabeau B. Lamar, and Anson Jones. The main issues they faced included finance, frontier defense, immigration, land policy, foreign policy, and the question of annexation to the United States. There were no political parties, but personal factions evolved (particularly around Houston and Lamar, whose policies differed on most of the issues). Houston tended to pursue financial economy, peace with the Native Americans, peace with Mexico, and annexation to the United States. Almost invariably, Lamar took the opposite view in each case.

Conditions in Texas during this period were not attractive to prospective settlers. The Republic was broke; constantly threatened with violence by Native Americans on the frontier and by Mexico to the south; involved in various foreign intrigues; unable to persuade the

United States to proceed with annexation; and beset with unending internal bickering among politicians. Yet somehow the Republic survived and, under the leadership of two of its four presidents, Houston and Jones, proceeded eventually toward the ultimate goal of annexation and statehood.

DAVID G. BURNET ☆ 1836

David G. Burnet, born in New Jersey in 1788, was descended on his mother's side from two families, the Gouvernours and the Morrises. Most of his male ancestors had been merchants, lawyers, and doctors, and David was educated and trained for a career in business. Having no real taste for business, however, he became an adventurer.

Early in the nineteenth century, Burnet joined the forces of Gen. Francisco Miranda and fought bravely with him in Chile (1806) and Venezuela (1808). After Miranda's break with Simón Bolivar, Burnet escaped to North America, where he soon drifted to the Southwest and lived for three years among the Comanches. While roaming the plains with these noble warriors, Burnet passed through portions of Texas on several occasions and, in 1826, finally decided to set up a law practice in San Felipe de Austin. He was soon appointed judge of the Department of the Brazos and served in this position until the outbreak of the Revolution. From the beginning of the crisis, Burnet was among the most vocal patriots and well-known for his speeches and broadsides, the most famous of which read, in part: "The hope of peace has departed. . . . The contest is for liberty or slavery, for life or death. It admits no neutrals. Those who are not for us are against us. . . . Texas is at war, and every citizen who shall be found in practices inimical to her highest interests will be dealt with according to the utmost rigors of the law."[1]

March 17, 1836, Burnet was elected president *ad interim* of the Republic – probably because of his legal and personal qualifications and his family connections in the United States. These connections, it was thought, would engender sympathy for the revolutionary cause in the people of the North, and his family ties did indeed lead to some tangible aid. His brother, Isaac, then mayor of Cincinnati, Ohio, arranged for two cannon (the famous "Twin Sisters") to be delivered to the Texans, who used these weapons effectively at San Jacinto.

Soon after his election, Burnet moved the government from Wash-

David G. Burnet

ington-on-the-Brazos to Harrisburg. When Col. Juan Almonté threatened the new capital, everyone fled to Galveston Island, and, according to legend, Almonté almost caught Burnet and his family as they were boarding a small boat at New Washington. As the craft pulled away from shore, Burnet and his wife stood in the stern defiantly facing the enemy, and it was this incredible act of bravery, Colonel Almonté said later, that persuaded him to order his men not to fire. Perhaps the fact that the president and his wife each held a child also affected Almonté's judgment.

After Houston's victory at San Jacinto, Burnet traveled there to meet Santa Anna face to face. They signed treaties at Velasco in which the two nations made peace and Santa Anna promised to use his influence to secure recognition of Texas' independence; these agreements, however, were later repudiated by Mexico. Since he also worked to spare Santa Anna's life, Burnet was accused of treachery by some of the more ruthless and hot-blooded Texas leaders and targeted for assassination. Though the plot was never carried out, practically no one followed orders, and the government struggled to direct the state effectively.

The fledgling Republic of Texas also had trouble with its neighbor to the north, as the United States remained reluctant to grant recognition. Even though the commissioners dispatched by the Consultation were still active, Burnet sent his own representatives to lobby the North, but they achieved little. The United States failed to act favorably on annexation and did not even grant diplomatic recognition to Texas until March of 1837.

Acting upon proclamations adopted by the convention at Washington-on-the-Brazos, Burnet issued a call for national elections on July 23, 1836. The date set for the balloting was the first Monday in September, and after Sam Houston was duly elected, Burnet resigned on October 22. He seemed glad to be rid of the burdens of office, although he was not pleased with the election's outcome. He had always hated Houston, who never followed Burnet's orders, and believed that Austin deserved to be president. In disgust he wrote to Memucan Hunt: "Houston is beyond all question president elect. He has beat my worthy friend, Austin, the pioneer of pioneers in Texas in as much as the splendor of military fame (no matter how acquired) excels the mild luster of meditative and intellectual worth."[2]

Burnet's career in politics was not quite over, however, as he was elected vice president to serve with Lamar in 1838. He served in this capacity as one of the commissioners who attempted to negotiate the removal of the Cherokees from East Texas. Burnet and Lamar generally worked well together, and Burnet undoubtedly expected to be nominated for president by the Lamar faction. When Lamar was incapacitated by illness, Burnet became acting president and, flushed with his newfound power, removed several of the president's appointees. This led to a break between the two men and initially cost Burnet the support he needed for the presidential nomination. Lamar's friends attempted to induce first Albert Sidney Johnston and then Thomas J. Rusk to run, but both refused. Reluctantly, the Lamar faction then lent Burnet its support.

During the campaign of 1841, the Houston party blamed Burnet for all the shortcomings of the Lamar regime. Burnet countered by arguing that he was an independent guided only by his principles, but this strategy failed, and Houston won the election easily. Of the contest, James Morgan wrote: "Old Sam Houston with all his faults appears to be the only man for Texas – He is still unsteady, intemperate, but drunk in a ditch he is worth a thousand of Lamar and Burnet."[3]

After leaving office in 1841, Burnet returned to Galveston, where he practiced law for many years. In 1866, immediately after the Civil War, he was elected to the U.S. Congress, but, along with other Southerners, he was denied his seat by the Radical Republicans. Winning that congressional seat was the final act in Burnet's political career, and he died on December 5, 1870. He was buried at Galveston.

SAM HOUSTON ☆ 1836–38, 1841–44, 1859–61

Sam Houston, the fifth child of Samuel and Elizabeth Houston, was born on March 2, 1793, in Rockbridge County, Virginia, not far from Lexington. While Sam was a young teenager, his father experienced severe financial difficulties and was forced to sell the family farm. Samuel planned to move his family to Tennessee but died unexpectedly, and the family had to make the trek without him. They arrived at Maryville, just south of Knoxville, in the spring of 1807 and began the arduous task of developing a new plantation.

Hating farm work, bored with school, and unwilling to clerk in a

Sam Houston

store newly acquired by the family, young Sam left home at age sixteen to live with the Cherokees. He was soon adopted by Chief Oo-loo-te-ka, who gave him the name Colonneh (the Raven), and set about learning the language and ways of the Native Americans. Through his experiences with the Cherokees, Houston developed a love and appreciation for Native American culture that lasted throughout his life and set him apart from practically all the other political leaders of his time.

Though he seemed to hate formal education, Houston opened a school, hoping to raise enough money to pay his debts. He raised the money but did not remain long in the education business, and in March, 1813, at age twenty, he entered the U.S. Army to fight against the British in the War of 1812. His career as a warrior had begun. Having entered the service as a private, Houston rose quickly through the ranks and achieved the rank of lieutenant by December. The following year he saw his only action of the war at the bloody Battle of Horseshoe Bend, where he fought against the Creek Indians under the command of Andrew Jackson. Gravely wounded, he distinguished himself by his bravery and attracted the attention of Jackson, who became his lifelong friend. Houston remained in the army after peace was restored, but his wounds continued to trouble him for several years. He was assigned mostly light duties and eventually served as a subagent to the Native Americans. Ironically, his job was to persuade the Cherokees to give up their lands and move west.

In March, 1818, Houston resigned his commission, and late in the spring he returned to Nashville to study law. He passed the bar after only six months of study and opened his first office in the little town of Lebanon, some thirty miles east of Nashville. He became successful and popular almost overnight and, with Jackson's backing, was soon elected attorney general of Tennessee and appointed to the rank of colonel in the state militia. By this stage of his life, he had developed the most famous attributes of his character – courage, intelligence, and highly proficient oratorical skills – that were to make him a great leader. Unfortunately, his weakness for alcohol was also evident, and it was to be the root cause of many of his problems.

In 1823, Houston was elected to the U.S. House of Representatives, and while in Congress he did all he could to support General Jackson's presidential aspirations. After two successful (if undistinguished) terms, he returned to Tennessee to run for governor. Elected, he took office in October, 1827, his thirty-fourth year. As governor Houston was both popular and effective, and he took the lead in promoting Jackson for president, helping to carry Old Hickory to victory in 1828. As soon as Jackson was safely installed in the White House, Houston had plans to run for reelection and get married.

Houston and Eliza Allen exchanged wedding vows on January 22, 1829, and after a brief wedding trip, Houston began his campaign for reelection against the former governor, William Carroll. Houston appeared to be at the pinnacle of success in both his public and private life, when suddenly his world collapsed. For reasons that have never been fully explained, Eliza left him in April, and although he tried to persuade her to return, all entreaties failed. Brokenhearted, Houston resigned the governorship and fled Tennessee.

Between 1829 and 1830, Houston lived once more among the Cherokees and served as Oo-loo-te-ka's ambassador to Washington, where he ably represented Native-American interests. During this period Houston operated a trading post and married the beautiful Tiana Rogers, who, although she was of mixed ancestry, had lived most of her life among the Native Americans. Life was good for a while.

In April, 1832, there occurred another incident that was to alter Houston's life. Member of Congress William Stanberry of Ohio accused Houston and Secy. of War John Eaton of improper behavior in the negotiation of a contract to provide supplies for the Native Americans. Houston replied to these charges by physically attacking Stanberry on the streets of Washington. As a result Houston was tried for "contempt of Congress" before the House, found guilty, and sentenced to be reprimanded by the speaker and to pay a fine of $500. Jackson later remitted the fine, but more importantly, as Houston himself noted, the affair prompted him to reevaluate himself and rescued him from "obscurity and drunken exile among the Indians."[4]

Later in 1832, Sam Houston made his fateful trip to Texas. Officially he went there as a representative of the Jackson administration to negotiate with the Comanches, but he may also have had a personal agenda involving land speculation and, perhaps, even revolution against the Mexican government. Houston's motives for the trip have long been the subject of speculation, and whatever was the case, he went alone. Tiana had refused to accompany him, and they had divorced; thus, he faced the beginning of a new era in his life without any personal ties to his past. Once in Texas, Houston completed his mission to the Native Americans, applied for a land grant, and agreed to serve as a delegate to the San Felipe Convention of 1832, where he helped draft the constitution for the proposed Mexican State of Texas. Over the next several months, he established a law practice in Nacogdoches and did some more traveling, including undertaking a journey to Washington to visit President Jackson.

Meanwhile, the attitude toward Texas in Mexico was mixed. There were some reforms, including a lifting of the ban on immigration to the state, but the petition for separate statehood was rejected and Stephen F. Austin imprisoned. It was at this time that Santa Anna came to power, and though the Texans believed him to be a federalist (and, therefore, a supporter of separate statehood), he was, in fact, a centralist and sent his brother-in-law, Gen. Martín Perfecto de Cós, to Texas to enforce his will.

The Revolution began shortly after Austin returned to Texas in September, 1835, declaring that war was necessary. Although originally conceived as an armed struggle for statehood under the Constitution of 1824, the conflict soon took on the nature of a war for independence. Houston was a moderate at first, although he accepted a commission in early October to raise an armed force in Nacogdoches. Shortly thereafter, he attended the Consultation in Columbia and participated in its deliberations after a quorum was achieved on November 1. The Consultation set up a provisional state government and named Henry Smith as governor. Also, in the midst of great controversy, Houston was chosen commander in chief of all the Texas armies.

While Houston established his headquarters in San Felipe and attempted to raise an army, chaos reigned elsewhere. Small forces under autonomous commanders pursued their own agendas, and the General Council did nothing to establish a coordinated governmental and military structure. In December, a force under Edward Burleson and Ben Milam took San Antonio from General Cós, and he retired south of the Rio Grande. Many Texans believed this event signaled the end of the war, but Houston knew better, urging that an army of at least five thousand troops be raised. In the mean time, Santa Anna was preparing for an all out invasion.

The disorderly preparations continued in Texas into the early weeks of 1836. Smith was deposed as governor by his enemies on the General Council, hotheads planned an invasion of Mexico that could not possibly succeed, and Houston had practically no luck recruiting men for the regular army. Nevertheless, he participated in the convention at

Washington-on-the-Brazos that declared Texas' independence on March 2. On March 6, while the Texans attempted to organize their army, Santa Anna attacked, defeated, and massacred the small force under William B. Travis defending the Alamo at San Antonio. Following this tragedy Houston was finally able to begin assembling an army for the showdown he knew would come with Santa Anna. Fearing to engage the Mexicans until conditions were right, Houston began a retreat eastward. At last, on April 21, 1836, Houston launched a surprise attack on Santa Anna at the Battle of San Jacinto, and his victory brought the Revolution to a successful conclusion.

Amid the chaos immediately following the Revolution, interim president David Burnet called for elections on September 5. Henry Smith and Stephen F. Austin announced their candidacies, but Houston refrained from doing so – at first. Finally, however, he yielded to the entreaties of his many friends and admirers and agreed to run. Houston easily defeated Austin and Smith, and in the same election Mirabeau B. Lamar was elected vice president, and the voters approved both the March Constitution and the movement for annexation to the United States.

Houston was inaugurated on October 22, and he immediately called for vigilance toward Mexico, peace with the Native Americans, constitutional government, and annexation. He appointed Austin secretary of state, Smith secretary of the treasury, and James Pinckney Henderson attorney general. The president found the issue of annexation to be a nettlesome problem. Although his friend Jackson favored it in principle, he faced opposition from antislavery leaders, like John Quincy Adams, who believed that the annexation of Texas was part of a great conspiracy to expand the empire of slavery. Jackson also feared retribution from the Mexicans, who had yet to recognize Texas' independence.

Houston sought to minimize problems with Mexico by releasing Santa Anna from captivity. The dictator visited Jackson in Washington, where he spoke of amity between the two countries before returning to Mexico and repudiating all the promises he had earlier made. Jackson continued to vacillate on the issue of annexation, finally announcing that such action on the part of the United States would be impolitic (though the United States did grant Texas diplomatic recognition in the last days of Jackson's tenure). In 1837, Houston dispatched James Pinckney Henderson to Europe to establish diplomatic relations with England and France, and though Henderson was received cordially enough, neither England nor France were inclined to grant recognition. Back home Houston faced even greater difficulties. Hotheads in the army clamored to invade Mexico, an adventure that Houston knew could only end in disaster. The president was able to defuse this situation by inviting the commander of the Texas Army, Gen. Felix Huston, to confer with him while sending most of the army on furlough during Huston's absence.

Although Mexico continued to be a potential problem, the Comanches and Kiowas on the frontier proved a much more serious threat. In East Texas, citizens faced problems with the Cherokees. Cherokee lands had been guaranteed by treaty in February, 1836, but the pact was never ratified, and as a result the Cherokees threatened trouble. Lacking sufficient funds or troops, however, there was little Houston could do about them. In 1838, Vincente Córdova, a Mexican citizen living in Nacogdoches, led an uprising of Mexicans and Kickapoos, and, though the Cherokees were not involved, the affair generated a considerable amount of anti-Native-American feeling and made harder the already difficult job of keeping the peace.

Houston also faced a problem with respect to land policy. Land was practically the only source of wealth the nation possessed, and Texas used this potential to attract settlers by offering land grants on very attractive terms. This policy, however, was administered in such a haphazard manner that the stage was set during this early period for conflicting land claims and litigation that would last for many years to come.

Finally, Houston faced insurmountable financial difficulties. Texas was saddled with a $1.25 million debt and had no way to raise the money to pay for it. Taxation was not a valid option because the people were generally too poor to afford it, so Houston and the Texas Congress had to resort to the expedient of printing paper money. This currency ultimately depreciated and led to even greater problems later on.

Since he was unable under the terms of the Texas Constitution to succeed himself, Houston did not run for reelection. Instead, the second administration in the history of the Republic was headed by Mirabeau B. Lamar and David G. Burnet, both of whom disliked Houston and his policies. Lamar adopted a policy of hostility toward Native Americans, including the Cherokees (an attitude which particularly outraged Houston), permitted the printing of so much paper money that the debt soared to more than seven million dollars, and favored making war on Mexico. From Houston's point of view, Lamar's only success came with the achievement of diplomatic recognition from Britain, France, and Holland.

After leaving office, Houston traveled in Tennessee, Louisiana, and Alabama. While visiting with friends on an estate near Mobile, he met Margaret Lea, a twenty-year-old beauty who would soon become his wife. Upon his return to Texas, Houston was elected to the Texas Congress that met in December, 1839, in Austin, the new capital. During the session Houston spent practically all his time opposing Lamar's policies. On some issues, such as the money question, he had much support, but with respect to Native-American policy, he essentially stood alone, and even those who agreed with him could not match the vehemence of his outrage. By this time his views and actions had divided Texans into two factions – pro-Houston and anti-Houston – that were to define Texas politics until the Civil War.

In 1841, Houston ran for reelection to the presidency against Burnet, and in a campaign notable for the intensity of its mudslinging and its lack of attention to the issues, the old warrior prevailed. His second term as president was to be marked by considerable violence and chaos. At the outset Houston reminded the Congress that the Republic was broke. He called for suspension of all payments on the debt and limited the use of paper money, and the Congress endorsed these recommendations with enthusiasm. He called for peace with the Native Americans, and Congress endorsed that as well – but when he called for peace with Mexico, the opposition exploded.

Houston believed that Texas could not conduct a successful offensive war against Mexico because the Republic lacked the necessary means and resources to do so. He believed, rather, that Texas should prepare itself in the event of another Mexican invasion. Few agreed, however. At the end of his term, Lamar had sent an expedition to occupy Santa Fe only to have its men captured by the Mexicans and marched off to Mexico City as prisoners. Rather than curing the war fever, this disaster simply intensified demands for action against Mexico. The actions of the Texas Navy also contributed to Houston's problems. Under the command of Adm. Edwin W. Moore, the navy intervened in the Mexican struggle between the federalists and the centralists. The federalists were paying Moore eight thousand dollars a month for his assistance, and this situation outraged both Houston and the centralist leader, Santa Anna.

In response to the Santa Fe expedition and the adventures of the Texas Navy, Santa Anna invaded Texas in March, 1842, sending an expedition under Gen. Rafael Vásquez to capture San Antonio. Soon thereafter, Vice President Edward Burleson organized a volunteer force and marched against Vásquez. At the same time, Houston issued a call to arms and placed all Texas troops under the command of Alexander Somervell. Many of Burleson's men would not accept Somervell as their commander, and because of the momentary hesitation and confusion on the part of the Texans, Vásquez and his army had a chance to retreat across the Rio Grande.

Houston's situation was now extremely difficult: he had to prepare for the possibility of another attack while at the same time defusing the militants who were calling for all-out war. Declaring that Austin was too dangerous, he called Congress into session in Houston and advised the lawmakers to prepare for a defensive – not an offensive – war. They ignored him and passed a bill that declared war on Mexico and authorized the president to both organize a large army and sell ten million acres of land to raise funds. Houston, who considered this proposition to be madness, vetoed the bill, and Congress adjourned without overriding the veto.

The emergency was abated for the moment, but Houston had no time to relax; he was also embroiled in a dispute over the location of the capital. Few were interested in returning to the City of Houston and the Hero of San Jacinto hated Austin, so he proposed the compromise of establishing the capital at Washington-on-the-Brazos. This plan excited opposition from the Austinites, some of whom went so far as to threaten Houston's life should he attempt to remove the government archives from the village. Late in 1842, he dispatched a small force to Austin to effect removal, but they were thwarted and the documents remained in the city. Houston, however, refused to go there as long as he was president.

While this capital controversy raged on, a Mexican force under Gen. Adrian Woll invaded the Republic once more and captured San Antonio. Woll held the town for only a short time before he was driven out by volunteers under Capt. John C. Hays. He retreated toward Mexico, and Houston ordered a force under Alexander Somervell to pursue him. Somervell decided not to continue once he reached the Rio Grande, but some of his men, led by Col. William S. Fisher, insisted on pursuing Woll. Fisher proceeded down the river and crossed into Mexico at the town of Mier where, on December 25 and 26, 1842, he was defeated by a superior force of Mexicans. Fisher surrendered, but while being marched toward Mexico City his men attempted an escape that resulted in the deaths of five Mexican soldiers. After the Texans were recaptured, Santa Anna ordered that 10 percent of the Texans – seventeen men – be shot in retribution. This outrage led to further demands for war from his constituents, but Houston resisted them, always arguing that all-out war with Mexico could only lead to disaster for Texas.

It is possible, however, that Houston's attitude toward Mexico was more belligerent than he was willing to admit. In the spring of 1843, Col. Jacob Snively set out with a force of 180 men to capture a wagon train en route to Santa Fe from St. Louis. Snively attacked the Mexican troops who were accompanying the caravan and killed several of them, and after plundering the wagons, a portion of Snively's men returned to Texas. On June 20, Capt. Phillip St. George Cooke of the U.S. Army captured Snively's remaining force and sent fifty of them to St. Louis as prisoners. The rest were disarmed and sent back to Texas. It was believed at the time that this unlawful "filibustering expedition" had Houston's support, and there is some evidence to suggest that this was the case. Nevertheless, an armistice between Texas and Mexico was signed in June, 1843, and late in the following year, the survivors of the Mier expedition were released. This helped a little, but with the continuation of financial woes, the future of the Republic appeared very shaky as Houston's second term ended in 1844.

Despite all the other problems, perhaps the most important issue Houston faced during his second term was annexation, and he maneuvered effectively to achieve it. In early 1843, he told the British charge d'affaires that both Texas and the United States favored annexation and that, to prevent it, England would have to induce Mexico to recognize Texas' independence. Houston knew that there was still considerable opposition to annexation in the United States, and he hoped that some overt action by the British would stimulate a more favorable attitude. His ploy succeeded. John Tyler, the defrocked Whig who succeeded William Henry Harrison in the presidency in 1841, was a Virginian who favored annexation, not only because of his Southern sympathies, but also because it might provide him with an opportunity to recoup his political fortunes among Democrats and Southern Whigs. Tyler's second secretary of state, Abel P. Upshur, also a Virginian, was equally responsive to the idea, and in the fall of 1843, they began serious discussions with Isaac Van Zandt, Texas' representative in Washington.

Houston realized that negotiation on this subject was a dangerous game. Pursuing annexation created the possibility of a retaliatory attack by Mexico, and failure to achieve it could yield disaster as well; thus, he proceeded cautiously. Steadily, the process went forward, and in April, 1844, Van Zandt and his colleague, James Pinckney Henderson, reached an agreement with Secy. of State John C. Calhoun that called for Texas to enter the Union as a territory. The United States would acquire the public lands and property of the Republic and assume its debt. Although Houston had high hopes for the treaty, they were dashed when annexation became an issue in the American presidential campaign of 1844. With abolitionists voicing bitter opposition, both the leading candidates, Henry Clay and Martin Van Buren, came out against the treaty, saying its passage would cause a war with Mexico. His stance lost Van Buren the Democratic nomination to expansionist James K. Polk, and, with most Southern Whigs voting against it, the treaty was defeated in the Senate.

The defeat of the treaty, which occurred in June, 1844, caused bitterness in Texas, but Houston was by no means ready to give up. He pushed his ally, Anson Jones, for the Texas presidency and he rejoiced when Polk was elected in the United States over Henry Clay. Before Polk took office, Tyler recommended annexation by joint resolution, and in early 1845, Congress acted. The new proposal called for Texas to enter the Union as a state and to retain its public land and debt. The United States would settle all boundary disputes and new states, as many as four, could be created from Texas with its approval. Houston was not entirely happy with these terms and was accused by his enemies of attempting to obstruct the will of the people. He explained, however, that he simply wanted Texas to join the United States on the best possible terms (as the result of negotiation, not dictation), and this explanation seemed to satisfy the public. A convention meeting in Austin in July, 1845, approved annexation, wrote a constitution, and submitted the question to the people. In October, they approved overwhelmingly and, in December, Polk signed the Texas Admission Act.

Also in December, 1845, the Texans elected James Pinckney Henderson as their first governor and chose a legislature. The latter, in turn, chose Houston and Thomas Jefferson Rusk as Texas' first U.S. senators. They drew lots to determine the length of their terms, and Houston drew the short one that would end in March, 1847. While in the Senate, Houston supported Polk's policies loyally, speaking forcefully on both the Oregon Agreement and the Mexican War. In December, 1847, he was reelected to a six-year term.

In the aftermath of the Mexican War, Houston favored the seizure of territory from Mexico, but he disliked the Treaty of Guadalupe Hidalgo because he thought it did not take enough; thus, when the Senate approved it by a vote of 38 to 14 on March 10, 1848, he cast no vote. Subsequently, he sought to prevent the question of the expansion of slavery into the new territories from becoming a disruptive issue. In this regard Houston favored Henry Clay's proposed compromise and worked especially hard in favor of the section calling for Texas to give up all claim to New Mexico in exchange for a ten million dollar payment from the federal government.

Houston was reelected to the Senate in 1853, and shortly thereafter, the sectional calm that had been produced by the Compromise of 1850 was shattered by the introduction of the Kansas-Nebraska Act. Originally, Stephen A. Douglas, the sponsor of the bill, had merely desired to organize the northern and western portion of the Louisiana Purchase in order to encourage railroad construction from the Northern terminus of Chicago. In exchange for Southern support, however, he gave in to demands that two territories be created, that the Missouri Compromise be repealed, and that the voters be allowed to decide the fate of slavery in each new territory. Senator Houston opposed the Kansas-Nebraska Act, believing correctly that it would stir up sectional antagonism. He favored maintaining the Missouri Compromise and argued that its repeal would simply invite political retaliation from the more powerful North. Houston predicted that the forces unleashed by the Kansas-Nebraska Act would eventually produce the election of a free-soil president, secession, civil war, and the destruction of the South. For this prophetically courageous stand, he was condemned as a traitor throughout Texas and the South.

During the period immediately following the passage of the Kansas-Nebraska Act, Houston flirted with the Know-Nothing party, claiming it was more Unionist than the Democrats. After the Texas Know-Nothings were defeated in the state election of 1855, Houston's enemies had yet another weapon, his affiliation with the losing party, to use against him. In November, the Texas legislature passed a resolution censuring him for his vote on the Kansas-Nebraska Act. His term in the Senate still had three years to run, but Houston seemed to be rapidly losing his base of support, and the congressional session to which he returned in 1856 was consumed by the events unfolding in Kansas. Houston took no part in the debate, but he was concerned by the emergence of the Republican party. Though he believed that a sectional party was extremely dangerous, he openly declared that, even if a Republican were elected president, Houston would lend his support.

In 1857, Houston ran for governor as an independent against Hardin R. Runnels but was defeated. Considering the fact that he was now essentially a man without a party – the Democratic party organization, such as it was, and much of the press opposed him vigorously – it was amazing that he polled 47 percent of the total vote, losing by less than four thousand. After the election he returned to Washington, where he attempted to represent the interests of his state as best he could despite ever mounting pressure against him. He continued to speak out against the Kansas-Nebraska Act with his familiar argument that it threatened sectional peace. He was concerned by events in "Bleeding Kansas," but he voted for the Lecompton Constitution, probably hoping it would bring an end to the bloodshed.

Returning to Texas in March, 1859, Houston seemed ready to retire. His many friends urged him to run for governor, however, and when his old nemesis Hardin Runnels was renominated by the Democrats, Houston allowed his name to be offered in opposition. His friends, calling themselves the National Democrats, did most of the campaigning, with Houston making only one major speech at Nacogdoches that expressed his devotion to the Constitution and the Union. He also declared his support for a Southern route for the transcontinental railroad, said the Native Americans should be put on reservations, and called for the creation of a public school system for the state. In August, 1859, Houston defeated Runnels by about six thousand votes, a result attributable to Houston's residual popularity and the fact that people were unhappy with Runnels over his failure to protect the frontier and the relative extravagance of his administration. Proslavery elements were profoundly disturbed by the election and prepared to do battle with Houston for the next two years.

When Houston was inaugurated in December, 1859, he became the first and only politician in U.S. history to serve as governor of two different states. In his first speech he promised to support internal improvements and frontier defense and called upon the people to support the Union. During the next several months he dealt mostly with local matters, but he kept a close watch on national politics. As the presidential campaign of 1860 approached there was some talk of Houston as the Democratic candidate, but the governor chose not to pursue the nomination. He was also considered as a possible candidate for the newly formed Constitutional Union party, but that effort to recruit him also fizzled.

The election of Abraham Lincoln in November meant that Houston's worst fears would be realized. The secession movement began immediately as town meetings all across the state passed resolutions calling for disunion. The governor counseled delay, arguing that nothing should be done until Lincoln violated the Constitution; yet the secessionists would not be deterred. They called for a convention to meet in January, 1861. Houston responded by calling the legislature into special session at the same time, apparently in the vain hope that somehow the legislature could head off a calamitous decision. The governor was to be sorely disappointed, for the legislature supported secession, and the convention met as scheduled. It passed a secession resolution almost immediately, and Houston called for a referendum. When, on February 23, 1861, Texans endorsed secession by a margin of 46,153 to 14,744 votes, Houston knew all was lost.

On March 14, 1861, the secession convention voted to require all state officials to take an oath of loyalty to the Confederacy. Houston refused, and on March 18, the convention declared the office of governor vacant. Houston responded that all the actions of the convention were a usurpation of power, but he also announced that he would not attempt to hold his office by force. Though President Lincoln offered to send federal troops to support him, Houston refused, saying that he would never be the cause of bloodshed in Texas. Vacating the governor's mansion on March 20, Houston and his family headed south and eventually arrived in Houston. They remained there until late 1862, but the approach of U.S. troops forced them to flee to Huntsville, where Houston procured the famous "steamboat" house that would be his last home. By the summer of 1863, Houston was gravely ill with pneumonia. On July 26, as his wife read to him from the Bible, he said his last words – "Texas, Margaret, Texas" – and died. He is buried at Huntsville.

The Lamar family came originally from France and settled in the Maryland Colony in the seventeenth century. Eventually, some of them drifted into Georgia, and it was there, on August 16, 1798, that Mirabeau was born. He grew up loving the outdoors and receiving only a rudimentary formal education. He developed a passion for reading however, and like Houston became addicted to the classics. He did not attend college, even though he was admitted to Princeton, but instead tried his hand as a merchant. Failing at this, Lamar tried the newspaper business, a venture that also failed.

Mirabeau's life was changed in 1823 when, thanks to family connections, he was named private secretary to Gov. George M. Troup of Georgia. Lamar's duties involved issuing press releases and speaking on behalf of the governor. On one of his trips around the state, he met the beautiful Tabatha Jordan, whom he married in 1826. In 1828, after Troup was defeated, Lamar once more tried the newspaper business, establishing the Columbus *Enquirer,* and this time was a little more successful.

Lamar considered running for the state senate in 1829, but the death of his young wife left him brokenhearted, and he withdrew. He found solace in his work and travel, and he began to study law. In 1833, after his admission to the bar, he ran for Congress but was defeated. The following year his brother Lucius committed suicide, and Lamar, again nearly overcome with grief, resorted to travel; but when the summer of 1835 found him in Texas, he resolved to make it his home.

After a brief return to Georgia, Lamar came back to Texas in the spring of 1836 and went directly into the field to join Houston's army. His bravery at San Jacinto brought him considerable notice and led directly to a career in politics. He was named secretary of war in the *ad interim* government, and later in 1836, he was elected vice president. In 1838, he was the unanimous choice for president to succeed Sam Houston.

Lamar was inaugurated in Houston on December 1, 1838. Upon this occasion the retiring president gave a three-hour "Farewell Address," which so unnerved Lamar that he was unable to read his own inaugural speech. Instead, it was delivered by his aide, Algernon P. Thompson. Three weeks later, however, Lamar made his first formal address to the Texas Congress, and here he outlined his plans. The first

Mirabeau B. Lamar

issue he addressed was the question of the Native Americans, urging that the Cherokees, the Comanches, and other tribes be driven from the lands they occupied, even destroyed if necessary. In the realm of finance he proposed the creation of a national bank and an effort to secure a loan from either the United States or Europe. With respect to foreign policy, he pledged to prosecute the war with Mexico, seek recognition abroad, and oppose annexation.

The president began to translate his proposals into action early in 1839, when he sent a military expedition against the Cherokees and drove them from the Republic in a bloody campaign. Houston's old friend Chief Bowl was killed, and the Hero of San Jacinto vented his rage against Lamar. The expulsion policy was a "success," however, one of the few that Lamar would savor during his troubled administration. The president also conducted military operations against the Comanches, which were even more bloody if not quite so successful.

Lamar next turned to the problem of selecting a permanent site for the capital. He appointed a commission to study the question, and after a two month investigation, it recommended a site on the Colorado River about thirty-five miles north of Bastrop: a small village known as Waterloo. The name was changed to Austin, a few buildings were thrown up, and the transfer of records from Houston was completed in October, 1839. By effecting this move, Lamar substantially increased his support in the western and central areas of the Republic. Among Lamar's other achievements must be mentioned the passage of the Texas Homestead Act in 1840, the founding of the Texas State Library in 1839, and the passage of legislation creating the basis for a system of public education. For this last, the Texas Congress passed resolutions in 1839 granting three leagues of land to each county for equipping schools and fifty leagues for the support of two universities. Although practically nothing was done to implement these resolutions, they nevertheless provided a foundation for the later development of education in Texas.

Unfortunately, Lamar's failures and mistakes far outweighed his achievements, and one of the worst blunders was in the area of finance. Lamar had promised to seek a loan in order to ease the country's monetary burdens, but everywhere he went – the United States, England, France – the request was turned down. Finally, in frustration, he authorized the issue of large quantities of paper money, increasing the amount in circulation from $800,000 to nearly $3 million. This currency, which was practically worthless, only exacerbated the problem, and to make matters worse, Lamar did not cut expenses. Compared with Houston's era, appropriations nearly doubled during the Lamar administration, and by the time he left office, the Republic's financial structure was a wreck.

In foreign affairs the results of Lamar's policies were mixed. His representatives succeeded in gaining diplomatic recognition from England, France, and Belgium, and this led to the growth of trade and commerce. Lamar was consistent in his opposition regarding annexation to the United States. He argued that Texas had been insulted earlier in its efforts to join the Union, and only humiliation would result from further action. Texas should remain independent, he declared, and would prosper through its commercial relations with other nations. This belief proved to be in error, but even if he had favored annexation, Lamar probably could not have achieved it because of the intensity of feeling about the slavery issue.

If Lamar's annexation policy was shortsighted, his Mexican policy was downright catastrophic. During his two years in office, he sent three agents to Mexico with orders to effect a peace settlement, and all of them failed. Meanwhile, Lamar, who believed in the notion that the Rio Grande was the western boundary of Texas, became obsessed with the idea of sending an expedition to Santa Fe. He wanted to open up trade with New Mexico, and he hoped that the people of the northern province would desire to cast their lot with Texas. He was sorely mistaken.

Lamar first proposed an expedition to Santa Fe in 1839, but it was rejected by Congress. He proposed it again the following year and again it was rejected, but Lamar was so taken with the idea that he decided to act on his own. He took $89,000 from the treasury to finance the expedition, and in June, 1841, sent word to the people of New Mexico that the Texans were coming in peace to establish trade and better relations. This effort did not produce the desired result, and when the men finally arrived in the Santa Fe vicinity after an arduous journey, they were summarily arrested. Told they would shortly be released, they were instead marched to Mexico City and treated brutally, many dying on the way.

The Santa Fe expedition was a total failure, for not only were the members humiliated, many of them lost their lives. Moreover, the residents of West Texas lost confidence in the government, and the government, in turn, lost a fortune while failing to develop any trade at all. The fiasco was the culmination of Lamar's nightmare. He had come into office hoping to improve upon the administrative record of Sam Houston; instead, he had fared worse in almost every area. As his term came to a close, peace with Mexico was no closer than it had been two years earlier, and the financial condition of the country had worsened. As a final stroke of misfortune, Lamar's health, always marginal, was ruined by the constant stress.

The public career of Mirabeau B. Lamar was not yet over when he relinquished control of the government to Sam Houston in late 1841. During the Mexican War, Lamar saw action, exhibiting his old gallantry at Monterey. In 1847, he was appointed post commander at Laredo, but he disliked the job (blaming Houston for conspiring to have him assigned to a secondary role) and clamored for more action.

Lamar married again in 1851. His new wife was Henrietta Maffitt, sister of Comdr. John Newland Maffitt (who would gain fame later for his exploits in the Confederate Navy). Henrietta was reputed to be the most beautiful woman in Texas, and Lamar wrote of her and their child:

> Like yon declining sun
> My Life is going down
> All calm and mild
> Illumed by an angel wife
> And sweetened by a cherub child.[5]

After the war Lamar represented the Laredo area for a time in the state legislature, and then, in 1857, President Buchanan appointed him minister to Nicaragua. He liked this job, but after twenty months in Managua his health forced him to resign, and he returned to Texas in October, 1859. As Lamar and his family prepared to celebrate the Christmas season that year, he was suddenly stricken with a heart attack and died on December 19. He is buried in Richmond.

ANSON JONES ☆ 1844–46

Born in Great Barrington, Massachusetts, on January 20, 1789, Anson Jones was descended on his mother's side from Oliver Cromwell. His first American ancestor was William Jones, son of Sir John Jones and Catherine Cromwell, a sister of the Protector. Anson's father, Solomon Jones, was a native of Connecticut who fought in both the American Revolution and the War of 1812. Most of the other men in the Jones family were also soldiers, but military service did not translate into wealth for them. Anson was one of fourteen children, and, during most of his youth, the family lived in poverty. Yet, somehow he managed to acquire an education, and by age twenty-two he was licensed to practice medicine.

The young physician did not settle down to practice his art. Between 1811 and 1823, he wandered about in North and South America, eventually settling in New Orleans where he attempted a business venture that failed. Soon after, he drifted into Texas, landing at Brazoria with nothing save the clothes on his back, a few dollars in his pocket, and a small box containing various drugs and remedies. He turned immediately to the practice of medicine and prospered during his first year. He also became involved in the cause of the Texas patriots, coming under the influence of the Wharton brothers, who also made their home in Brazoria. Jones was chair of the resolutions committee at the convention of March, 1836, which drafted the Texas Declaration of Independence and framed the first Texas Constitution. During the war he temporarily closed his medical practice, joined the army, and fought at San Jacinto.

After independence was achieved, Jones entered the Texas Congress and served from September 25, 1837, to May 25, 1838. In Congress he was one of Houston's most dedicated lieutenants and worked hard to discredit Lamar. During Houston's second term as president, Jones was secretary of state and contributed substantially to both the restoration of a sound financial policy and the complex preparations for annexation. By the end of Houston's presidency, Jones was regarded by many as his logical successor; but he faced significant opposition. There were those who favored Thomas J. Rusk, although he declined to run. Among those candidates who did declare were John Hemphill, chief justice of the Supreme Court, and Vice President Ed Burleson, who had the support of the Lamar faction.

When the campaign finally got underway, it proved to be a battle between Burleson and Jones, and the contest degenerated into one of personal abuse. The Jones group linked Burleson to all the mistakes and scandals of the Lamar era and ridiculed him for his lack of education. Jones, on the other hand, was portrayed as a simple tool of Houston with no will of his own, but his enemies found it impossible

Anson Jones

in the long run to turn his association with the Hero of San Jacinto into a disadvantage. On election day Jones won a decisive victory, beating Burleson by approximately fifteen hundred votes, and Kenneth L. Anderson was elected vice president. During Jones's administration, Congress met for only one brief regular session, from December, 1844, to February 3, 1845, during which time it considered very little legislation. The question of annexation was the only real issue of the day.

Realizing that his administration would probably be short, Jones retained most of Houston's men as members of his own cabinet. At the time of Jones's inauguration it was not yet known whether Texas would choose annexation, soon to be offered by the Tyler Administration, or continued independence. Both the British and the French were hard at work in an effort to promote the latter, but Jones tried to keep all options open. When the American offer finally came, however, he gave in to popular pressure calling for a convention to consider the issue. Mexico finally offered to recognize Texas' independence if the Republic would reject the American offer, and Jones called a special session of Congress to meet on June 28, 1845. The lawmakers considered both the American and Mexican proposals and accepted the former unanimously. On July 4, the convention assembled in Austin and approved annexation with only one dissenting vote. This same body then formulated a state constitution and soon both the annexation proposal and the Texas Constitution were ratified by the people. James K. Polk signed the bill admitting Texas to the Union on December 29, 1845, and James P. Henderson was sworn in as the state's first governor on February 16, 1846.

Upon leaving the presidency, Jones had hoped to be chosen U.S. senator, but Houston and Rusk won out. Jones brooded over this slight and, in fact, never recovered emotionally from it. Meanwhile, he practiced medicine and accumulated a sizable fortune. In 1857, he let it be known again that he would like to be a senator, but he received no support in the legislature. This was the final blow to his ego and on January 9, 1858, he shot himself in Houston, where he is buried.

Notes

1. James T. DeShields, *They Sat in High Places: The Presidents and Governors of Texas* (San Antonio: The Naylor Company, 1940), 39.

2. Stanley Siegel, *A Political History of the Republic of Texas, 1836–1845* (Austin: University of Texas Press, 1956), 54.

3. Ibid., 182.

4. Randolph Campbell, *Sam Houston and the American Southwest* (New York: HarperCollins, 1993), 32.

5. DeShields, *They Sat in High Places*, 137.

Sources and Further Reading

Campbell, Randolph B. *Sam Houston and the American Southwest.* New York: Harpers, 1993.

DeBruhl, Marshall. *Sword of San Jacinto: A Life of Sam Houston.* New York: Random House, 1993.

DeShields, James T. *They Sat in High Places: The Presidents and Governors of Texas.* San Antonio: The Naylor Company, 1940.

Friend, Llerena B. *Sam Houston: The Great Designer.* Austin: University of Texas Press, 1954.

Gambrell, Herbert P. *Mirabeau Bonaparte Lamar: Troubador and Crusader.* Dallas: Southwest, 1934.

———. *Anson Jones: The Last President of Texas.* Garden City, New York: Doubleday, 1948.

James, Marquis. *The Raven: A Biography of Sam Houston.* Indianapolis: Bobbs-Merrill, 1929.

Oates, Stephen B., ed. *The Republic of Texas.* Palo Alto: American West Publishing Co., 1968.

Phares, Ross. *The Governors of Texas.* Gretna, La.: Pelican Publishing Company, 1976.

Ramsey, Jack C., Jr. *Thunder Beyond the Brazos.* Austin: Eakin Press, 1985.

Siegel, Stanley. *Political History of the Texas Republic, 1836–1845.* Austin: University of Texas Press, 1956.

Chapter four

EARLY STATEHOOD
1846–61

During the period between the achievement of annexation and the outbreak of the Civil War, Texas experienced phenomenal growth: the population increased by 400 percent and property values ballooned by 800 percent. On the other hand, there was little cultural progress, and frontier conditions generally prevailed throughout the state. Among the more significant developments of this period were the establishment of constitutional government, the defeat of Mexico, the great Texas boundary dispute (finally settled by the Compromise of 1850), increased pressure to expand into the Native-American frontier caused by the growing population, and the emergence of political parties. Slavery, states' rights, and secession became major issues for the state during this time.

The governors of the period were James Pinckney Henderson, 1846–47; George T. Wood, 1847–49; Peter Hansborough Bell, 1849–53;

James W. Henderson, November 23–December, 1853; Elisha M. Pease, 1853–57; Hardin R. Runnels, 1857–59; and Sam Houston, 1859–61. For a discussion of the Houston administration, see Chapter 3, The Republic, 1836–46.

JAMES PINCKNEY HENDERSON ☆ 1846–47

The first elected governor of Texas was James Pinckney Henderson, who assumed office on February 19, 1846. Born at Lincolnton on March 31, 1808, Henderson was a native of North Carolina. His paternal ancestors were, for the most part, men of distinction with careers in law, business, politics, and the military. Richard Henderson, who played a leading role in the early exploration and settlement of Kentucky, was James's paternal grandfather. It was he who employed Daniel Boone and negotiated the Watauga Treaty with the Native Americans that led to the establishment of the "State of Transylvania." James Pinckney Henderson's father, Lawson, was a prominent political leader in North Carolina.

Henderson received his education at Chapel Hill College (later the University of North Carolina), and he chose the law as his life's work, a profession for which he appeared to be well-suited. He was quick of wit, highly intelligent, and endowed with good looks, speaking ability, charm, and above all, tact. He seemed to know instinctively what to say or do in any circumstance.

Searching for a climate that would be more soothing to his health, Henderson moved to Mississippi in 1835, and he learned there of the events in Texas that were leading to the Revolution. He seems to have become obsessed with the Texas cause, for he raised a company of Mississippians to join the fight against Mexico. They arrived just after the Battle of San Jacinto, thus missing their chance for glory there, but Henderson had already decided to make Texas his new home. He settled in Nacogdoches and at once immersed himself in politics and the practice of law. Along with his business partners, Kenneth L. Anderson and Thomas J. Rusk, he became one of the founding fathers of the Republic.

Gifted with his legal acumen and stunning oratorical skills, Henderson began his career of service to the Lone Star State in 1836. He served short terms as attorney general and secretary of state, and then, in 1837, was appointed minister to England and France. President

James Pinckney Henderson

Houston selected him for this post, not only for his abilities, but also because he was rich enough to pay a portion of his own expenses. Serving abroad until 1839, he secured diplomatic recognition and treaties providing trade and financial assistance from the two great European powers. His task was not easy, since both England and France were skeptical about slavery and were loath to antagonize Mexico, but the breakthrough finally came in 1838, when relations between France and Mexico went sour over unpaid claims.

It was in England that Henderson met Frances Cox. This young lady, barely nineteen years of age when they met, came from a prominent Philadelphia family. She had been educated in Paris and had spent most of her life in Europe. They fell instantly in love, were married in London in October, 1839, and soon returned to Texas. After a round of parties and receptions celebrating the success of Henderson's mission, they settled in San Augustine, where Henderson resumed his law practice, dabbled in business, and continued his interest in politics. In 1844, President Houston once again called upon Henderson to represent the Republic in Washington during the delicate negotiations concerning annexation. Along with Isaac Van Zandt, Henderson signed a treaty of annexation with John C. Calhoun on April 12, 1844, but, owing to the high emotions and suspicions generated by the slavery issue, the treaty was rejected by the U.S. Senate. Some months later, however, annexation was approved by a joint resolution of Congress.

Henderson did not intend to become Texas' first governor. He intended to support his close friend and former law partner Kenneth L. Anderson for the post. Anderson died unexpectedly on July 3, 1845, however, and soon afterward Henderson announced his candidacy. At first he was unopposed, but on November 8, Dr. James B. Miller entered the contest. There followed a short but spirited campaign, which Henderson won easily by a vote of 7,853 to 1,673. Albert C. Horton, a wealthy Matagorda planter, was elected lieutenant governor.

The inauguration of the new state government elicited powerful emotions among most of those who were present in Austin on February 19, 1846. As one reporter described it, "There was a smothering sensation which all felt, yet few desired to display it in public. Broad chests heaved – strong hands were clenched, and tears flowed down cheeks where they had been strangers for long years." Henderson's inaugural was short, dealt largely with the achievement of annexation, and he concluded it with, "We have this day fully entered the Union of the North American states. Let us give our friends who so boldly and nobly advocated our cause, and the friends of American liberty, no reason to regret their efforts on our behalf."[1]

The new administration was made up largely of experienced individuals who had already been serving the Republic. In addition to Henderson and Horton, these included: David G. Burnet, secretary of state; James H. Raymond, treasurer; Thomas W. Ward, commissioner of the general land office; and William Cooke, adjutant general. Also, the senate chose three able lawyers to sit as justices of the first state supreme court. They were John Hemphill, chief justice, with Abner S. Lipscomb and Royal T. Wheeler, both associate justices. Sam Houston and Tom Rusk, widely regarded as Texas' most distinguished citizens, took their places in the U.S. Senate.

In connection with the election of two representatives to sit in the lower house of Congress, the first truly organized party system was born in the state. The election, held on March 30, 1846, sent Timothy Pillsbury and David Kaufman to the House of Representatives. One of Kaufman's opponents had been William B. Ochiltree, a Whig. His candidacy caused great concern among Democrats who, until that time, had given very little thought to party organization. During the entire history of the Republic, practically everyone belonged to either the pro-Houston or anti-Houston factions, but now the voters saw the need for a more formalized system. Hence, on April 21, 1846, most of the leading Democrats assembled in Austin to organize a kind of primitive state committee. This was the beginning of a recognizable party structure in Texas, but it was only a preliminary step at best toward such a system. The committee did not coalesce, took no action, and by 1848, had ceased to exist.

Governor Henderson delivered his first message to the legislature on February 24, 1846. He reminded the members of the need for a school system, adequate public buildings, and a state militia, but more importantly he urged them to recognize the state's most serious problem: finance. Not only was Texas in debt – as it would be more often than not throughout its history – the Lone Star State was broke.

Although the legislature passed a number of measures dealing with the creation of new counties, the organization of state courts, the regulation of slavery, the creation of a state penitentiary, and the collection of taxes, it failed to deal effectively with three vital issues. On the matter of the public debt, debate bogged down over the question of its exact size, and until the precise magnitude of the claims against the state could somehow be measured, it was decided that nothing could be done. The problems remaining unresolved included the need for a public school system and internal improvements. The committees appointed to recommend action could only agree that anything the legislature might do would be "premature." Hence, nothing was done regarding either issue.

War broke out between the United States and Mexico in the spring of 1846, and on May 9, Governor Henderson took a leave of absence to lead Texas troops in the conflict. In the six months that followed, Lieutenant Governor Horton presided over the state government but accomplished practically nothing. The legislature adjourned on May 13, and most of its members either joined the military or returned home to their businesses. Henderson returned to Texas in the fall to resume his duties.

During the last year of the Henderson administration, there were no further legislative achievements of note. A major issue arose, however, that was to plague the relationship between Texas and the federal government for the next four years: the complex question of the state boundary. Texas had always claimed the Rio Grande as its western and southern boundary, and Mexico had always disputed the claim. With the defeat of Mexico and occupation of the Santa Fe area, the Texans thought their claims would be recognized. Instead, Stephen W. Kearney, then military governor of Santa Fe, began to organize a separate territorial government. When Henderson complained, he was told by Secy. of State James Buchanan that the new setup was temporary and would be terminated once the war was over. Assuming this meant their claims would be honored at a later date, the Texans were quiet; but as subsequent events would demonstrate, their original suspicions were justified.

The term of James Pinckney Henderson, Texas' first governor, ended on December 21, 1847, and he returned to his law practice. Ten years later, when his old friend Tom Rusk committed suicide, Henderson was asked to succeed him in the U.S. Senate. Even though his health was poor, Henderson accepted and traveled to Washington, where he died on June 4, 1858, at the age of fifty. He was buried in the nation's capital, but in 1930, his body was exhumed for reinterment in Austin.

George Tyler Wood was born near the town of Cuthbert in Randolph County, Georgia, on March 12, 1795. Little is known about his early life or education except that, when he was nineteen years old, he organized a company of volunteers for the Creek War and participated in the Battle of Horseshoe Bend. According to legend, he met Sam Houston and Edward Burleson during this campaign, and his meeting these men may have contributed to his later interest in Texas.

Wood was a man of native ability, and he prospered in the dry goods business. While on a buying trip in 1837, he stopped off in Millidgeville, where he met an attractive young widow named Martha Gindrat. They were married on September 18 of the same year, and for a time they continued to reside in Cuthbert. In 1839, they decided to move to Texas. Arriving at Galveston, Wood explored the lower reaches of the Brazos, Colorado, and Trinity Rivers and at length chose a site for his home on the lower Trinity in what is now San Jacinto (then Liberty) County. Soon he developed a flourishing plantation.

Wood was a striking figure in appearance, standing six feet tall and weighing two hundred pounds. With straight black hair, a prominent nose, wide set eyes, thin lips, and a powerful jaw, he was a handsome individual who conveyed an impression of great strength. He was careless of his dress and personal appearance and, according to legend, never wore socks.

When Gov. James Pinckney Henderson decided not to run for reelection in 1847, the field lay open for several aspiring candidates. Among these were Jesse J. Robinson, a member of the legislature from Sabine County; Dr. James B. Miller, who was defeated by Henderson in 1846; Nicholas H. Darnell, an unsuccessful candidate for lieutenant governor in the first election; Isaac Van Zandt, who came from Harrison County and was Henderson's personal choice to be his successor; and George T. Wood, whom Henderson liked least of all the contenders. Wood was generally regarded as the choice of the Houston faction; Henderson, not then in favor with the Hero of San Jacinto, disliked Wood intensely, referring to him in his correspondence as a "dog." Whatever Henderson's opinion of him, Wood was the most formidable and, perhaps, the most able of all the candidates.

Although most of the campaign in 1847 focused on personalities, there were vital issues to be discussed, the most pressing of them being

George Tyler Wood

the public debt. All the candidates agreed that the debt question must be settled as soon as possible, but they disagreed on the method to do so. Van Zandt, for example, favored the immediate sale of public land (while Wood counseled patience on that score), and Miller called for a delay until the exact amount of the debt could be determined, the very same demand that had blocked settlement of the issue during the previous administration. The course of the election was altered when Van Zandt died of yellow fever in October. It is possible that many voters who had favored him, especially in East Texas, now gave their support to Wood. In any case, Wood won an impressive victory, receiving 7,154 votes to 5,106 for Miller and 1,276 for Darnell. Together with John A. Greer, who was elected lieutenant governor, Wood took office on December 21, 1847.

The first order of business faced by the legislature was the election of a U.S. senator, and Sam Houston was returned to that post with only light opposition. Then the new governor and legislature turned to more pressing matters of state business, particularly the public debt. Wood had now adopted Van Zandt's position, declaring that the best course of action was to sell state land to the federal government, but he reminded the legislature that the final decision was theirs. After considerable wrangling, the legislators passed a bill calling for the auditor and the comptroller to determine the precise magnitude of the debt, after which they would consider a method of payment. This left things no nearer resolution than before, though one thing was clear from the debate: the legislators intended to scale down the debt before payment on the grounds that very few of the bonds remained in the hands of their original purchasers.

Early in Wood's administration, the dispute between Texas and the federal government over the status of New Mexico intensified. It now seemed clear that Washington did not intend to recognize Texas' claim to the territory, since the territorial government formed earlier had not been disbanded. Wood called upon the legislature to protest federal action and at the same time do what was necessary to exert Texas' control over the Santa Fe Country. It responded by creating Santa Fe County and establishing the eleventh judicial district with Spruce M. Baird as its judge. Then Wood and his colleagues waited to see what would happen. Baird no sooner arrived in New Mexico than he was told that the army intended to sustain the new government whatever the cost. Impressed with the sincerity of Col. John M. Washington, commanding the federal forces in Santa Fe, Baird soon lost interest in his assignment and departed for Missouri in July, 1849.

Having dealt temporarily, if not successfully, with the New Mexico question, the Wood administration now addressed other matters, including a request that Congress establish a string of forts in West Texas to defend the frontier and several proposals to convert numerous state offices from appointive to elective positions. The most controversial issue among those considered was reapportionment. Favored by the northeastern part of the state because it would increase that area's representation and opposed by the central and coastal areas for the same reason, the reapportionment bill sparked bitter debate; but eventually it became law near the end of the session.

As the presidential election of 1848 drew near, Texas Democrats once more attempted to form a statewide organization. As a result, the first true political party convention convened at Austin on February 21, with Governor Wood presiding. The delegates produced a platform calling for the defense of slavery and reiterated Texas' claim to New Mexico.

The Whigs were less well-organized than the Democrats but no less active. There were pro-Taylor clubs in many towns, and numerous Whig speakers campaigned throughout the state. They attempted to show that Gen. Zachary Taylor's support for slavery was unequivocal, a dubious assertion at best, while that of Democratic candidate Lewis Cass was somewhat shaky since he supported the notion of popular sovereignty. In the end, Taylor won the election, but Cass carried Texas by a wide margin, and the state Democrats congratulated themselves on a job well done.

In 1849, Governor Wood ran for reelection against the perennial candidate, Dr. John T. Miller, and Peter H. Bell. Bell was by far the most formidable of the opponents, taking strong stands on both the New Mexico question and the issue of frontier defense. He wanted the state to send a military force to Santa Fe and allocate much more of its resources to the eradication of Native Americans. Wood answered each criticism with a stout defense of his policies, saying he had done everything he could reasonably do regarding both issues, and he felt confident of victory as the campaign reached its conclusion. He had sadly miscalculated, however, and Bell defeated him by a vote of 10,319 to 8,754, with Miller a distant third.

After he left office, Wood returned to his plantation and entered the mercantile business in Galveston. He also remained interested in politics, running unsuccessfully for governor in 1853 and again in 1855. He died at home on September 3, 1858, and is buried there.

PETER HANSBOROUGH BELL ☆ 1849–53

Peter H. Bell was a compelling figure. He was tall and slender with a lithe and sinewy body that bespoke strength and vigor; his hair was long and black and his face usually bearded; and his countenance was supple, easily transforming from seriousness to merriment and projecting the image of a polished, cultured gentleman. He was a superb horseman and a crack shot with both pistol and rifle. During his Ranger days, he usually wore two pistols and a Bowie knife in his belt, boots and spurs, a broad sombrero, a hunting shirt of flannel or buckskin, and trousers or leggings of heavy cloth – he looked every inch the rugged frontiersman. In civilian clothes he was always modestly yet stylishly attired, portraying an image of subtle dignity, and the contrast of this image with that of the frontiersman demonstrated the breadth of his lifestyle.

Bell was born in Culpepper County, Virginia, on March 11, 1810. Practically nothing is known about his youth, but he appeared in Texas in March, 1836, and joined Sam Houston's army before the showdown at San Jacinto. There he distinguished himself, and Houston rewarded him with an appointment to his personal staff as adjutant general. Later, in 1839, he served as inspector general of the army, and in 1844, Bell was named commander of the troops in the Corpus Christi district.

The region lying between the Nueces and the Rio Grande was a dangerous and inhospitable place in the 1840s and would remain so for many years. Yet, across this apparently trackless wilderness, there were many trade routes connecting Texas with Mexico. Corpus Christi and Aransas Pass were the entrepôts for most of the goods destined for Mexico; transport across the wilderness from these ports had to be guarded, and this job became the task of the Rangers under Peter H. Bell. His instructions were to expel or exterminate all the outlaws in the region, whether they were Anglos or Mexicans, and he performed his mission with relish and success. When the Mexican War began, Bell's troop joined Wood's regiment and distinguished itself. Bell returned from Mexico in 1847 and resumed his place with the Rangers,

Peter Hansborough Bell

this time on the western frontier. He continued in that capacity until he entered the race for governor.

During the campaign Bell called for a more aggressive policy with respect to the New Mexico question. In December, 1848, shortly after he assumed office, the legislature designated new boundaries for Santa Fe County and created three new counties to the south. Robert S. Neighbors was dispatched to organize these counties, but he encountered substantial hostility; and when his report to Governor Bell was made public in June, 1850, the people demanded action. Bell then called a special session of the legislature to deal with the problem. Meanwhile, the New Mexicans adopted a constitution, President Taylor died, and his successor, Millard Fillmore, made it clear that he favored a peaceful settlement of the issue. Thus, the New Mexico question was linked to several other issues before Congress and was eventually resolved as a part of the Compromise of 1850.

Several plans were considered, including one devised by a congressional committee headed by Henry Clay. With respect to the Texas boundary, Clay's plan provided that Texas would receive ten million dollars in exchange for giving up all claims to land west of a line beginning at the Rio Grande twenty miles above El Paso and ending at the intersection of the one-hundredth meridian and the Red River. This plan failed, but an alternative was soon found that called for the establishment of the Texas boundary as it now stands: Texas was to give up all claims to land beyond this boundary in exchange for ten million dollars, and New Mexico was to become a territory, not a state. At first there was considerable opposition to this proposal in Texas, but it soon withered, and the voters gave their approval in a special election. Governor Bell signed the act of acceptance on November 25, 1850.

This solution to the boundary question still left the issue of the public debt unresolved. By this time the debt had been specifically defined to include claims (by participants in the Revolution and suppliers to the army) designated as ordinary, or nonrevenue debts, and the principal and interest owed to holders of Texas bonds, designated as revenue debt. Texas soon paid the ordinary debt out of funds delivered by the federal government pursuant to the boundary settlement; but the revenue debt proved more difficult to resolve because the federal government insisted on being involved and the state insisted upon scaling it down. Eventually, through agreements made between the state and federal government in 1855 and 1856, the debt was paid off at about seventy-seven cents on the dollar. Meanwhile, the state made good use of the funds remaining from the boundary settlement. Two million dollars, most of which was subsequently loaned to railroad companies for construction, was set aside for the support of the public schools. From 1852 to 1856, the state also remitted 90 percent of its tax revenues to the counties, which used the tax remission funds for the construction of public buildings, and set aside the other 10 percent for the development of the schools. Hence, Texas was able to develop its public schools, promote internal improvements, and construct public facilities, while at the same time maintaining a low tax rate. Unfortunately, this precedent, set long before the allegedly corrupt Reconstruction era, has carried over into modern times. Texans have always believed that somehow public obligations can and should be met without adequate taxation.

In 1851, Bell was elected to a second term over John A. Greer, Mat T. Johnson, Thomas J. Chambers, and Whig candidate B. H. Epperson. Bell won largely because he was the most pro-Southern of all the candidates and because many Texans applauded his aggressive policies, even if those policies were not always completely successful. The second term was highlighted by the reduction and retirement of the public debt, the settlement of several land claims put forth by former empresarios and their colonists, and frontier defense. Shortly before his term expired, Bell resigned to take the seat in Congress that had been vacated by the death of David S. Kaufman.

Reelected to Congress in 1855, Bell was a favorite of the Pierce administration and a close friend of Secy. of War Jefferson Davis. While serving in Washington, Bell met and married Ella Rives Eaton, the daughter of a wealthy North Carolina planter. When his term expired they settled in North Carolina, and Bell never returned to Texas. During the Civil War and its aftermath, Bell and his wife lost everything and were left impoverished. For years thereafter, their only income was his minuscule pension as a veteran of the Mexican War.

Late in his life, the Texas legislature awarded Bell 1,280 acres of land and an annual pension of $150.00. This was not a princely sum by any means, but it was an important symbolic gesture recognizing his gallant services to the state so many years before. It did not induce him to come home, however, for he remained in North Carolina until his death on March 8, 1898. In 1929, his body was exhumed and reburied in Austin with appropriate honors.

When Governor Bell resigned to take his seat in Congress in 1853, he was replaced by Lieut. Gov. James W. "Smokey" Henderson, who served for one month. Henderson was neither related to nor resembled James Pinckney Henderson in any way. Whereas the latter was a man of education and refinement, "Smokey" was much more earthy and apparently had little formal education. He was born in Summers County, Virginia, on August 14, 1814, and very little is known about his youth, except that, fired by dreams of glory, he came to Texas in 1836 at the head of a small group of volunteers determined to fight the Mexicans. Arriving too late to participate in the Battle of San Jacinto, he soon returned to the United States to raise additional troops, but this mission was cut short when the Texas Army disbanded in 1837. Back in Texas he made his living as a surveyor, began studying law, and was admitted to the bar in 1840.

Henderson served for a time in the early 1840s with Jack Hays and the Texas Rangers before entering politics. Beginning in 1843, he served two terms in the Congress of the Republic and for a time was chair of the Committee on the State of the Republic, which dealt with the annexation question. After annexation he was elected to the state legislature and served as speaker of the Texas house until his election to the post of lieutenant governor.

Little of note occurred during Henderson's brief term as governor. After leaving office he practiced law for a time and then was reelected to the legislature in 1855. He was a member of the secession convention, and during the war he served in the home guard under Gen. John B. Magruder. After the war he practiced law in Houston until illness forced his retirement. He died on August 30, 1880, and is buried in Houston.

ELISHA MARSHALL PEASE ☆ 1853–57, 1867–69

For his contributions during his first administration and courage during his second, Elisha M. Pease must be ranked as one of the finest governors in Texas history. Born at Enfield, Connecticut, on January 3, 1812, the son of Loran T. and Sarah Marshall, Pease received his formal education at the Enfield Academy and the Westfield Academy in Massachusetts, and at the age of fourteen he took a job as a clerk in a

James Wilson Henderson

country store, where he gained much of his practical experience and training in business. From 1829 to 1834, he worked as a post office clerk in Hartford before beginning his journey to the West.

In 1834, Pease and his father visited New Orleans, where they heard glowing accounts of the opportunities awaiting beyond the Sabine; they traveled to Brazoria in January, 1835. The senior Pease soon decided to return to the East, but later in the same year a younger brother, Loran T. Pease, Jr., joined Elisha. While fighting in the Revolution, Loran Jr. was badly wounded at Goliad and died of his injuries on August 31, 1836.

Pease favored the peace party during his early days in Texas but soon changed his views, and, in October, 1835, joined the volunteer regiment of Capt. Robert Coleman. Illness prevented Pease from seeing much action, but upon his recovery he returned to civil service. When the provisional government was established later in 1835, Pease was named secretary of the Council. In the spring he served as clerk of the Constitutional Convention, and following that he served in rapid succession as chief clerk of the Navy Department, clerk of the Treasury, and acting secretary of the Treasury. When the first Congress of the Republic convened in October, 1836, Pease was named secretary of the House Committee on the Judiciary. Following adjournment he left government service for a time to study law with John A. Wharton. This led eventually to the creation of a partnership with Wharton and John W. Harris that produced one of the most successful law firms in Texas prior to the Civil War. As statehood approached, Pease once more entered public life, first as district attorney of Brazoria County and then as a member of the legislature. He served two terms in the house and was then elected to the state senate in 1850. When Governor Bell convened a special session of the legislature while he was absent from the state, Pease resigned in protest. He did not reenter politics actively until his campaign for governor in 1853.

In reaction to the growing strength of the Whigs, Texas Democrats tried twice unsuccessfully, in February and June, 1853, to assemble a state convention to select candidates. This failure left the field wide open for a free-for-all among seven Democrats, including, in addition to Pease, George T. Wood, Thomas J. Chambers, Lemuel D. Evans, Mat T. Johnson, John W. Dancy, and James W. "Smokey" Henderson. The Whig candidate was William B. Ochiltree, and victory for him seemed a real possibility until Johnson withdrew, shifting his support

Elisha Marshall Pease

to Pease. The result was a triumph for Pease, who received 13,091 votes to 9,178 for Ochiltree and 13,883 for the other Democrats combined. David C. Dickson was elected lieutenant governor. Other state officials were Edward Clark, secretary of state, Thomas J. Jennings, followed by James Wiley, attorneys general, James B. Shaw, comptroller, James H. Raymond, treasurer, and Steve R. Cosby, land commissioner.

The Pease era in Texas witnessed significant prosperity and the beginnings of progress. For the first time, the state had some money in the bank, and Pease, who exhibited excellent business sense, sought to make good use of it. His first priority was public education, and in his inaugural address he called upon the legislature to create and support a workable system. The result of his call became the Common School Law of 1854, which envisioned the creation of a perpetual school fund using two million dollars of the federal boundary payment as seed money. Income from the fund was distributed each year on a *per capita* basis. At first this was accomplished through school districts provided for in the law, but after these were abolished in 1854, any community, group, or individual could start a school and receive the money. The amount of money available per child was very small, however, and few public schools were actually established. Pease also urged the creation of a public university, but that was not accomplished until several years later.

A second priority for Pease focused on internal improvements, and, thus, was born the General Railroad Law of 1854. This statute provided for generous grants of land to any company that would build twenty-five miles or more of track within two years after the passage of the act. The governor at first supported this approach, which came to be known as the "corporate plan," but it did not produce satisfactory results. Hence, Pease shifted to support of the "state plan" calling for Texas to build railroads using its own credit. This plan generated significant debate and was finally defeated in the legislature on the grounds that it was too costly. However, it led to a compromise measure that permitted railroads to borrow six thousand dollars from the school fund for every mile of track completed. Passage of this law generated optimism for a time, but drought and recession during the next few years temporarily quieted the ardor of Texans for internal improvements.

Pease's third priority was the revision of the civil and criminal codes. He pointed out that the legal system of the state was a hodgepodge of conflicts and inconsistencies. He urged the appointment of a special three-member committee to prepare new codes for the consideration of the legislators. He also called for the enlargement of the supreme court and the expansion of the penitentiary. To finance these reforms, Pease recommended the leasing of convict labor, but his recommendations did not lead to significant reforms until some time later.

The "Indian question" had long been a controversial issue in Texas, and Pease sought to end the debate once and for all by confining the Native Americans to reservations. Under the terms of a law passed on February 6, 1854, three reservations totaling 53,000 acres were to be established. The Brazos Reserve was to be located on the Brazos River near Fort Belknap and would be the home of the Anadarkos, Caddos, and Wacos. Some forty miles to the southwest would be the Clear Fork Reserve, home to the Comanches, and due south of the Brazos would be the Ionie-Anadark-Waco Reserve for the Mescalero Apaches and the Lipans. The daunting task of directing the Native Americans to their new homes was assigned to Maj. Robert S. Neighbors, and though he fulfilled his mandate remarkably, confining the Native Americans did not end violence on the frontier. Pease called out the Rangers, who were much more effective than the federal troops in defending the frontier, but the state was reluctant to use them because defense against the Native Americans was the responsibility of the federal government. Whenever the Rangers were employed, Texas sought reimbursement for the expense from Washington but with little success. As depredations continued and Texans became convinced that the Native Americans from the reservations were involved, most of the "offenders" were forced to migrate to the Indian territory in 1859.

Pease also used the Rangers in the infamous "cart war" of 1854. In the area between San Antonio and Gonzales, Mexican freighters using large, clumsy carts drawn by oxen hauled large quantities of goods at very low rates. Anglo teamsters hated them for their competition and subjected them to murderous harassment. Pease sent in a Ranger company under Capt. G. H. Nelson, and soon the trouble subsided. Many credited the Rangers, but there has always been some question as to whether it was actually the Rangers or the local vigilantes who solved the problem.

Pease's quest for reelection in 1855 was one of the most important campaigns in the early history of the state. He faced powerful opposition from the rapidly growing American, or Know-Nothing party, a peculiar group made even more dangerous by the presence of Sam Houston among its supporters. The Democratic efforts to organize statewide had never been entirely successful, and the party machinery that year remained, at best, in an embryonic state. Though the state convention of 1855 drew delegations from only twelve counties, the Democrats' attention soon came to be more focused by the Know-Nothing threat.

Formed in the East, the American party was characterized primarily by xenophobia and pro-Unionism. It first appeared in Texas in 1854 and soon gained complete, if temporary, control of city government in San Antonio. It also elected a mayor in Galveston and gained the support of several newspapers. In June, 1855, the Know-Nothings held a state convention at Washington-on-the-Brazos and named a slate of candidates for the forthcoming election, including Lieut. Gov. David C. Dickson as their gubernatorial candidate.

Meanwhile, Houston and Pease were having difficulties. The old warrior differed with the governor on the issue of internal improvements. Houston did not approve the state plan for railroad construction, claiming that it would require a constitutional amendment. He did not want anyone, even a body of elected delegates, meddling with the state's basic law. Though in the spring of 1855 Houston continued to assert his support of Pease for reelection, as the months passed he changed his position and finally announced in November, "I adopt and admire the principles of the American party. It is the only party . . . whose principles will maintain . . . our free institutions. I am for Americans ruling America."[2] This marked a very low point in the relationship between Houston and Pease, although the rancor between the two was only temporary; later they reconciled out of their common devotion to the Union.

The election produced a decisive victory for Governor Pease. He defeated Dickson by a vote of 26,336 to 17,968, while Hardin R. Runnels was elected lieutenant governor over W. G. W. Jowers. This victory established Pease as the savior and leader of the Democratic party, at least for a time. The American party declined precipitously and practically collapsed after the election of 1856.

During Pease's second term his policies were similar to those of his first. His primary concern, however, was the rapid deterioration of the Union, which accompanied the rise of secessionist sentiment among the Southern democrats, and he watched in dismay as the Democratic party disintegrated. Until the final breakup of the Democratic party early in 1860, Pease supported the Douglas-Johnson ticket, but after the breakup, his sympathies moved in favor of the Constitutional Union party. He had hoped Sam Houston would receive the party's presidential nomination, but it went to James H. Bell instead. After secession, Pease remained outwardly neutral. Privately, he believed secession to be illegal, but he made no public comment, and, in fact, even went so far as to retire from his law practice to remain in seclusion, seldom leaving his Austin home.

With the end of hostilities, Pease resumed his public career. After President Johnson named Andrew Jackson Hamilton provisional governor on June 17, 1865, Hamilton, in turn, appointed Pease and Swante Palm to investigate state finances. They discovered that during the war Texas had accrued more than eight million dollars in debt; the question now was whether or not the state should attempt to pay off these obligations, and I address this issue below. Pease also became a "pardon broker" during this period. For those who did not qualify for general amnesty, lawyers like Pease would carry their request for a personal pardon to the White House – for a fee. Some of these pardon brokers charged their clients exorbitant sums and were obviously corrupt, but there is no evidence that Pease and his colleagues ever charged more than $150 to $250 for their services.

Pease sought to be a delegate to the Constitutional Convention of 1866 that would devise a new framework of government under the presidential plan of Reconstruction. He was not elected but attended the convention anyway as an observer. He found that the secessionist-conservatives controlled the proceedings and, hence, the outcome was not entirely satisfactory to him and other loyalists. The convention granted some civil rights, but not suffrage, to the newly freed slaves, declined to ratify the thirteenth amendment, repealed but did not denounce the ordinance of secession by a close vote, repudiated the war debt, passed legislation protecting secessionists from the consequences of their acts, and set a date for state elections.

Two factions emerged out of the convention: the Conservative Union party, made up of states' rights advocates of various stripes, and the Union party, made up of loyalists. In the election for governor, Pease, representing the latter, faced J. W. Throckmorton, representing the Conservative Unionists. Pease ran for governor on this occasion, more out of a sense of duty to the loyalist cause than any desire for office, and, in fact, he harbored no illusions about his chances for victory. In his campaign he criticized the conservatives for their views and actions, which, he said, had hurt the state, and he called for reorganization of state government, tax revision, improvement in the transportation and education systems, and more effective control of the frontier. As he expected, he was defeated by Throckmorton by the lopsided vote of 49,277 to 12,168. After the legislature convened, Pease ran for the U.S. Senate, but he was defeated again and subsequently moved north to Philadelphia.

While living in self-imposed exile, Pease lost confidence in President Johnson and soon slipped into the orbit of the Congressional Radicals. He returned to Texas in the late spring of 1867, now an advocate of Congressional Reconstruction. On July 4, 1867, he presided over the first Republican party convention in the history of the state, where loyalists gave their support to the Radicals in Congress and the program of Military Reconstruction. Shortly thereafter, Throckmorton and his colleagues were removed from office by the military governor, Gen. Charles Griffin, and on August 7, Pease was named provisional governor. Again he accepted reluctantly, more from a sense of duty than a desire for office. It was obvious to him that his administration would not be popular.

On June 1, 1868, a new constitutional convention assembled. This time only a few conservative delegates were on hand; the loyalists, although divided into two factions, predominated. On the one hand were the moderates led by Andrew Jackson Hamilton, and on the other were the extremists led by Edmund J. Davis. Among the delegates were nine African Americans. Though provisional governor, Pease could not control the convention; instead, he sought to influence the proceedings by calling upon the delegates to be temperate and intelligent in their deliberations. He also submitted a list of suggestions for their consideration, including a proposal for the nullification of the Ordinance of Secession and all discriminatory laws passed during the Confederate period. Pease urged, however, that they not attempt to abolish all the acts of the Confederate government *ab initio,* as demanded by the extremists. He proposed that debts existing before the war should be paid and those incurred during the war repudiated; that civil rights be guaranteed to all except those who had forfeited them during the rebellion; and that those who had participated in the rebellion should be temporarily disfranchised until such time as political power in the state was firmly in the hands of the loyalists. He also proposed tax revision in order to provide sufficient revenues for the schools, a homestead law, support for internal improvements, and the encouragement of immigration. Finally, Pease urged the convention to reject the proposal supported by some extremists that the state be divided. With all these issues on the table, the convention was divided into two sessions.

During the first session (June 1 to August 31), there was bitter wrangling between the moderates and the extremists over the issues of division, disfranchisement, and the *ab initio* principle. Among the extremists, *ab initio* was a litmus test of Republicanism: to them it meant that the secessionists had knowingly committed treason and should be dealt with as traitors. Anything less than this was, to the extremists, an unacceptable compromise; yet, they did not have their way. Under the astute leadership of A. J. Hamilton, the moderates successfully blocked all the radical proposals on the major issues. On the other hand, the delegates agreed that there should be more effort against lawlessness, that the party should support General Grant for president, and that the state should lease convict labor as a means of producing revenue. A brief recess of a little over three months followed, during which funds were gathered to pay for the continuation of the convention.

The money was raised, and during the second session (December 7, 1868, to February 8, 1869), the issues of disfranchisement and division received the most attention from the two contending Republican factions. On the matter of suffrage, the extremists wanted to exclude everyone who had ever been previously disqualified and could not take an ironclad oath of allegiance, while the moderates opposed doing anything further. On a close vote the moderates prevailed, and their position became a part of the Texas Constitution. As for division, the extremists were successful in persuading the convention to adopt a prodivision resolution, but then two committees, one for and one against, went to Washington to lobby Congress and the president. At the capital the proposition was dismissed as ridiculous.

As the time for the gubernatorial election of 1869 approached, some moderates urged Pease to run. However, he had no interest in opposing his old friend, A. J. Hamilton, whom he considered the most qualified for the job. In fact, Pease was tiring of his current position. He was a mere figurehead – all power resided in the hands of the military commander, Gen. Joseph J. Reynolds. As the year 1869 wore on, Reynolds became even more dictatorial so that in June, Pease tendered his resignation. Reynolds persuaded Pease to stay on, but when the governor discovered that Reynolds was planning to manipulate the election so that Hamilton could not win, he quit, and between September, 1869 and January, 1870, Texas had no governor.

Pease's last role in politics was to chair the Texas delegation to the National Liberal Republican Convention in May, 1872. This group, appalled by the corruption of the Grant administration, nominated Horace Greeley of New York for president. In Texas, as well as in the rest of the nation, the moderate Democrats united with the Liberal Republicans, but the effort fell short, and Grant was reelected. The victory of the Greeley forces in Texas did nothing to influence the outcome of the election.

By this time Pease was thoroughly disillusioned with politics. He felt that the rebels had regained control of the Democratic party in Texas and the Republicans were utterly corrupt; thus, he retired from the field. In 1874, he was offered the post of collector of the Port of Galveston by Secy. of the Interior Bristow, but Pease declined. During the next five years, he devoted himself to his banking interests in Austin and his plantation on the lower Brazos. In 1879, he accepted the collectorship when it was tendered by President Hayes, and this proved to be his last public service. He died in Lampasas on August 26, 1883, and is buried in Oakwood Cemetery at Austin.

HARDIN RICHARD RUNNELS ☆ 1857-59

By the time the Know-Nothing party held its state convention in 1856, it had already entered a period of decline, and soon it disintegrated altogether. It left behind a two-fold legacy and controversy: the more formal organization of the Democratic party and a more distinct schism between the pro-Houston and anti-Houston factions within that party. The result was a hard fought and bitter campaign in 1857. Waco was the site of the first major Democratic state convention, and delegates from ninety-one counties assembled there on May 14, 1857. The anti-Houston forces controlled the convention, and they nominated Lieut. Gov. Hardin R. Runnels, a wealthy planter from Bowie County, for governor.

Runnels, a native of Mississippi, was born on August 30, 1820. His

Hardin Richard Runnels

grandfather, John F. Runnels, was from Virginia and had fought in the American Revolution. Later, John settled in Mississippi, where he established a farm in the vicinity of Madison. One of his sons, Hardin G. Runnels, moved to Texas in 1842, settled in the lower Brazos country, and served several terms in the state legislature during the 1840s and 1850s. Another son, Hardin D. Runnels, died in 1842, and his widow moved to Texas with her three sons, one of whom was Hardin R. Runnels, that same year. Hardin R. entered public service in 1847 upon his election to the state legislature. He was speaker of the house between 1853 and 1854, lieutenant governor in 1855, and a delegate to the Waco convention in 1857, where he was nominated for governor.

Believing that he could not be reelected to the U.S. Senate and wanting to test his political strength at home, Sam Houston entered the race for governor as an independent on May 12, 1857. The campaign that followed emphasized states' rights more than any other issue, but, more importantly, became a war of personalities. Houston attempted to marshal all of his resources and residual support on behalf of a pro-Union position, while the Democrats, led by Runnels, attacked the old warrior for having sold out the interests of the state. They criticized Houston for his free-soil stance in 1848, his opposition on the Kansas-Nebraska Act in 1854, and his affiliation with the Know-Nothings in 1855. This strategy proved successful, and Runnels won an impressive victory of 36,552 to 28,678 votes.

During the Runnels administration the major issues were frontier defense and the slavery controversy. Like his predecessor, Runnels called out the Rangers to quell frontier violence, and on January 27, 1858, he commissioned Col. John S. "Rip" Ford as senior captain of the Rangers with instructions to augment his forces and move against the marauders as soon as possible. In May, Ford set out upon his mission, and in subsequent weeks he engaged the Comanches at Antelope Hills and in the battles of the Wichita and Pease Rivers. Also, in 1858, he engaged Juan Cortina, the infamous Mexican bandit, in the Rio Grande Valley, but the outcome was inconclusive. These efforts did not bring peace, however, and frontier depredations continued, causing public dissatisfaction with the Runnels administration which, in turn, contributed to his defeat in the election of 1859. By that year, Sam Houston was back in the hunt for office. Now there was considerably more support for his pro-Union position than two years previously, and this change, coupled with mounting criticism of Runnels for his failure to subdue the Native

Americans and his alleged financial extravagance, aided Houston's campaign against the governor. Houston won by a vote of 33,375 to 27,500.

When his term as governor ended, Runnels returned to his home and never again sought elective office. He remained active in politics, however, serving in the Secession Convention of 1861 and the Constitutional Convention of 1866. He died on December 25, 1873, and was buried in the family cemetery in Bowie County. His remains were exhumed in 1929 for reinterment in the state cemetery at Austin.

Notes

1. James T. DeShields, *They Sat in High Places: The Presidents and Governors of Texas* (San Antonio: The Naylor Company, 1940), 170.

2. Ibid., 198.

Sources and Further Reading

Campbell, Randolph B. *An Empire for Slavery: The Peculiar Institution in Texas, 1821–1865.* Baton Rouge: Louisiana State University Press, 1989.

Coyner, C. Luther. "Peter Hansborough Bell." *Quarterly of the Texas State Historical Association* 3 (July, 1899): 49–53.

DeShields, James T. *They Sat in High Places: The Presidents and Governors of Texas.* San Antonio: The Naylor Company, 1940.

Griffen, Roger Allen. "Connecticut Yankee in Texas, A Biography of Elisha M. Pease." Ph.D. diss., University of Texas, 1973.

Jordan, Terry G. "The Imprint of the Upper and Lower South on Mid-Nineteenth Century Texas." *Association of American Geographers, Annals* 57 (1967): 667–90.

Phares, Ross. *The Governors of Texas.* Gretna, La.: Pelican Publishing Company, 1976.

Richardson, Rupert N. *The Comanche Barrier to South Plains Settlement: A Century and a Half of Savage Resistance to the Advancing White Frontier.* Glendale, Calif.: A. Clarke, 1933.

Sherman, S. H. "Governor George T. Woods." *Southern Historical Quarterly* 20 (January, 1917): 260–68.

Winchester, Robert G. *James Pinckney Henderson: Texas's First Governor.* San Antonio: Naylor, 1917.

Wooster, Ralph A. "Early Texas Politics: The Henderson Administration." *Southern Historical Quarterly* 83 (October, 1969): 176–92.

———. "Early Texas Politics: The Wood Administration." *Texana* 8 (Summer, 1970): 183–99.

Chapter five

SECESSION AND THE CIVIL WAR
1861–65

The vast majority of those who migrated to Texas between 1846 and 1860 came from the South, bringing with them their attitudes and their politics. It was not until 1857, however, that states' rights advocates gained control of the Democratic party, after which they became even more aggressive. Elected governor in 1859, Sam Houston attempted to keep Texas in the Union but failed, and soon the state was embroiled in the Civil War.

There was relatively little fighting in Texas during the war, but the state nevertheless sacrificed thousands of men to the Confederate cause. The economy suffered, the financial structure of the state nearly collapsed, and there were constant shortages of supplies throughout the war. Politically, the Texas government proclaimed its loyalty to the Confederacy throughout the crisis, but there were strains on the relationship. Confederate military commanders occasionally behaved unreasonably, and at times there were complaints that the government in Richmond ignored the plight of its Western constituents. By the end of the war in April, 1865, Texas' society and political system were in disarray.

The governors during this period were Edward Clark, March 16–November 7, 1861; Francis R. Lubbock, 1861–63; and Pendleton Murrah, 1863–65. Fletcher Stockdale, 1865, served as provisional governor.

EDWARD CLARK ☆ 1861

Edward Clark was born in New Orleans on April 1, 1818. While he was still quite young the family moved to Alabama, and Clark received a university education, worked, studied law, and was eventually admitted to the bar in that state. He came to Texas in 1842, settled in Marshall, and soon entered politics, serving on the constitutional committee of 1845, in the first state legislature, as secretary of state (under Governor Pease) from 1853 to 1857, and as commissioner of claims in 1858. In 1859, he was elected lieutenant governor in the administration of Sam Houston.

When Houston refused to take the oath of allegiance to the Confederacy required by the Ordinance of Secession, Lieutenant Governor Clark ascended to the governorship; but not everyone was thrilled by his gesture of Southern patriotism. A witness to the event, Amelia E. Barr later wrote, "the Lieutenant Governor, a certain Edward Clark, was eager to subscribe to the oath. He was an insignificant creature whose airy concept was a direct insult to Houston's sad countenance and dignified manner; and I remember how contemptible he appeared as, spry and pert, he stepped up to the bar of the House to take the oath."[1]

Although Clark was certainly no Sam Houston, Barr's indictment was probably a bit harsh, for Clark proved to be a resolute governor with an unqualified commitment to his state and the Confederacy. His nine months in office were devoted almost exclusively to the preparation for war. After the attack on Fort Sumter in April, 1861, the governor moved quickly to raise and equip volunteer companies from every county. He confiscated all available ammunition and located 400,000 weapons in private hands for the war effort. He appointed thirty-two brigadier generals to organize the assembly of the troops, and he ordered all federal troops to leave the state. As a result of his efforts, more than eight thousand men were made available to the Confederacy before the end of 1861.

Edward Clark

Governor Clark ran for reelection in June, 1861, but Francis R. Lubbock defeated him by the scant majority of 124 votes. Immediately after leaving office, Clark raised a regiment of his own and joined Walker's division, serving bravely until he was severely wounded in the bloody Battle of Pleasant Hill, Louisiana, on April 9, 1864. Clark demonstrated that he was brave, if not downright foolhardy, by leading a frontal assault against an entrenched enemy position. His men took the position and inflicted heavy losses on the federal troops while suffering their own losses of only three men killed and ten wounded (including Colonel Clark).

After Appomattox, Clark, like many Confederate leaders, feared the vengeance of the Radical Republicans and fled to Mexico. He soon returned, however, and settled down in Marshall, where he practiced law and dabbled in various business pursuits until his death on May 4, 1880. He is buried in the city cemetery at Marshall.

FRANCIS R. LUBBOCK ☆ 1861–63

Born at Beaufort, South Carolina, on October 16, 1815, Francis R. Lubbock was descended on both sides from families of English merchants and mariners. His father, Dr. H. T. W. Lubbock, was a well-known physician. Francis was preceded in coming to Texas by his brother Tom (who participated in the capture of Bexar with Ben Milam in December, 1835) and arrived himself in Texas on April 24, 1836, just three days too late to help out at the Battle of San Jacinto.

Lubbock entered Texas at Galveston and proceeded to Houston by way of Columbia. Upon arriving in Houston he was elected clerk of the Texas Congress in November, 1837, and a little later was appointed comptroller of the Republic by President Houston. From the very beginning of his public career, Lubbock developed a reputation for honesty, bravery, chivalry, and an unbreakable devotion to duty and principle. He was also a great campaigner and orator, and it was said that few could surpass him in the quality of his speech making; but he was also quick-tempered and capable of violence. On one occasion in 1838, Lubbock attempted to shoot his adversary, Land Commissioner Thomas W. Ward, and missed him only because a bystander deflected Lubbock's weapon.

In the fall of 1838, Lubbock joined George W. Bennett's Ranger Company and campaigned along the Brazos, San Gabriel, and Little Rivers against marauding Native Americans. Returning to civilian life,

Francis R. Lubbock

he was elected district clerk in Harrison County and held that position until he became lieutenant governor in 1857.

Because of the war, there were no party nominations in 1861, thus making the race for the governorship a free-for-all pitting Governor Clark against Lubbock and Thomas J. Chambers. Lubbock won by only 124 votes in what proved to be the closest gubernatorial contest in the history of the state. Upon entering office Lubbock resolved to devote his time and energy to the war effort. He was not only a committed states' rights advocate and fervent secessionist, he was also possessed of the dominant and forceful type of personality seemingly so necessary during periods of dislocation and conflict.

Lubbock, the "Texas War Governor" fulfilled his obligations all too well. Foreseeing that the need for soldiers of the Confederacy would far outstrip the numbers provided by volunteers, he imposed a rigid system of conscription proposing that all males between the ages of sixteen and sixty capable of bearing arms be inducted into the armed forces. He was accused by some of harsh, arbitrary, and tyrannical behavior in carrying out his policies, but under the circumstances, there was no doubt some justification for his acts. Nevertheless, his popularity suffered, and he chose not to run for reelection in 1863.

After leaving office Lubbock set out for Richmond, Virginia, where he became aide-de-camp to Jefferson Davis. He served in that capacity until the end of the war and was captured along with Davis, as they attempted to flee the country. After his release he returned to Texas and reentered public life in 1878, when he was elected state treasurer. He held this post with distinction for twelve years, developing a reputation for skill, economy, and above all, honesty. So well did he perform that by 1883, there were actually several million dollars in the state treasury, whereupon a member of legislature proposed that the bond of the state treasurer be increased. Asked what he would do if such an act were passed, Lubbock replied, "I would resign the damned office in fifteen minutes."[2]

During his final years, Lubbock spent most of his time writing his memoirs, *Six Decades in Texas*. Published in 1900, they remain an indispensable source for Texas history in the late nineteenth century. Lubbock died on June 22, 1905, just shy of his ninetieth birthday. He is buried in the state cemetery at Austin.

Pendleton Murrah was born in South Carolina, but little otherwise is known of his heritage, except that he may have been illegitimate. He was educated by a charitable society of the Baptist Church and eventually sent to Rhode Island, where he graduated from Brown University in 1848. Afterward he studied law and was admitted to the bar in Alabama, but Murrah soon decided to migrate to East Texas and settled in the town of Marshall. There he practiced law with considerable success and gained a statewide reputation for his honesty, knowledge, and skill. He married Sue Taylor, daughter of a wealthy planter, and soon amassed a fortune of his own from his successful law practice. He first entered politics in 1855 as a candidate for the U.S. Congress but was defeated by Lemual Dawes of the Know-Nothing party; still, by the late 1850s, Murrah had become one of the most influential members of the State Democratic Executive Committee. He suffered from ill health throughout most of his adult life – probably tuberculosis – but never considered retiring from public life.

Though times were dreadfully difficult in 1863, he consented when friends urged him to run for governor. Murrah's opponent in the election was Thomas J. Chambers, who had run twice previously. Because of the war there was little interest in the campaign, and Murrah was elected on August 3, along with his lieutenant governor, Fletcher S. Stockdale, after a light turnout. The inauguration in November was the simplest on record: the state dinner consisted only of cornmeal cakes and there was no inaugural ball at all.

Conditions in Texas in 1863 were deplorable. Public confidence in the Confederacy was rapidly eroding, social order was breaking down, and in fact, the state had become a Confederate military camp. The military authorities generally ignored the civil government so that the laws and the courts were of little or no significance. In addition, the system of universal conscription, relentlessly pursued by Murrah's predecessor, Francis Lubbock, had contributed even more dramatically to the decline of public morale. Thus, Murrah faced extraordinarily difficult problems, and he encouraged the legislature to challenge the conduct of the military authorities. This it did by the passage of laws preventing the arbitrary seizure of private property and limiting the power of conscription. When challenged, these laws were ultimately sustained by the state supreme court.

Pendleton Murrah

Although there was little fighting in Texas during the Civil War, the effect of the struggle on the state was catastrophic. Murrah noted in 1864 that many thousands of family members and dependents of soldiers were practically destitute and that little could be done for them. Even more significant was the breakdown of law and order. Addressing the legislature on May 11, 1864, the governor lamented:

> In some sections society is almost disorganized; the voice of the law is hushed and its authority seldom asserted. It is a dead letter. . . . Murder, robbery, theft, outrages of every kind against property, against life, against everything sacred to civilized people, are frequent and general. Whole communities are under siege of terror. . . . The rule of mob, the bandit of unbridled passions, ride[s] over the solemn ordinances of government. Foul crime is committed and the criminal steeped in guilt . . . goes unwhipped of Justice.[3]

There were no reforms for or recovery from these conditions as the war raged on, but vigilantism became ever more common, ironically contributing to rather than controlling the level of violence.

As the Confederacy neared collapse in the spring of 1865, Governor Murrah did his best to provide for an orderly surrender and transfer of power. He appointed Ashbel Smith and W. P. Ballinger to negotiate with General Canby, commander of the occupying Union Army, over matters of reorganization. He issued proclamations looking to the protection of public property, called a special session of the legislature to deal with vital matters, and issued a call for the election of delegates to a constitutional convention; yet, his heart and spirit were broken. An ardent states' rights advocate, he had seen his beloved cause go down in fire and fury. Feeling helpless, dispirited, physically and mentally exhausted, and fatally ill, he resigned and fled the state on June 11, 1865. He died in Mexico shortly thereafter.

FLETCHER STOCKDALE ☆ 1865

Between the date of Murrah's resignation and July 25, 1865, the date when A. J. Hamilton was appointed provisional governor by Pres. Andrew Johnson, Fletcher Stockdale served as acting governor. He accomplished little by way of enforcing the functions of civil government, but he was a member of the citizens committee who escorted

Fletcher Stockdale

Governor Hamilton to the capitol and turned the reins of authority over to him. Born in 1826, he came to Texas in 1850 and settled in Indianola, where he practiced law. He was in the state senate in 1860 and also served in the secession convention. During Radical rule he was a leading member of the Redeemer faction, and after the fall of Governor Davis, he was a member of the Constitutional Convention of 1875. He died on February 5, 1890, and is buried at Russellville, Kentucky.

Notes

1. James T. DeShields, *They Sat in High Places: The Presidents and Governors of Texas* (San Antonio: The Naylor Company, 1940), 223.
2. Ibid., 236.
3. Ibid., 243.

Sources and Further Reading

Ashcraft, Allan C. *Texas in the Civil War: A Résumé History.* Austin: Texas Civil War Centennial Commission, 1962.

Bowen, Nancy H. "A Political Labyrinth: Texas in the Civil War – Questing Continuity." Ph.D dissertation. Rice University, 1974.

Buenger, Walter L. *Secession and Union in Texas.* Austin: University of Texas Press, 1984.

DeShields, James T. *They Sat in High Places: The Presidents and Governors of Texas.* San Antonio: The Naylor Company, 1940.

Elliott, C. "Union Sentiment in Texas, 1861–1865." *Southwestern Historical Quarterly* 50 (1947): 449–77.

Lubbock, Francis R. *Six Decades in Texas or Memoirs of Francis Richard Lubbock, Governor of Texas in War Time, 1861–1863: A Personal Experience.* Edited by C. W. Raines. Austin: Ben C. Jones and Company, 1900.

Meiners, Frederica Ann. "The Texas Governorship, 1861–1865: Biography of an Office." Ph.D. diss., Rice University, 1975.

Phares, Ross. *The Governors of Texas.* Gretna, La.: Pelican Publishing Company, 1976.

Wooster, Ralph A. "Analysis of the Membership of the Texas Secession Convention." *Southwestern Historical Quarterly* 62 (1959): 322–35.

———. "Texas." In *The Confederate Governors.* Edited by W. B. Yearns. Athens: University of Georgia Press, 1985.

Chapter six

RECONSTRUCTION

1865-74

The era of Reconstruction varied in length from one Southern state to another. In Texas the ordeal lasted slightly less than nine years and can be divided into three periods. First was Presidential Reconstruction, which included Andrew Johnson's provisional government from June 19, 1865, to August 20, 1866, and the new state government from August 20, 1866, to March 2, 1867, established under the Constitution of 1866. The second was the period of Congressional Reconstruction from March, 1867, to April, 1870, when all civil authority was restored to the state. The third period was that of Radical Republican rule under the Reconstruction Constitution, which lasted from April 16, 1870, to January 17, 1874, at which time Richard Coke succeeded E. J. Davis as governor. During the latter two periods, the Radical Republicans and their allies exerted substantial control over the affairs of the state and generated increasing animosity from the Democrats. Governor Davis was especially unpopular both because of his patronage policies and the harsh measures he employed to maintain order. In 1872, the Democrats (or Redeemers as they were sometimes called) finally regained control of the legislature, and in 1873, the people elected a Democratic governor.

The effects of Reconstruction in Texas were profound. The economy had collapsed during the war, and recovery was slow but steady. By 1870, the sharecropping system had become common in agriculture, and cotton production was on the rise. The development of the long drive in the range cattle industry contributed somewhat to the recovery of the economy, and there was substantial railroad building – more than one thousand miles of track were laid between 1860 and 1874. The political system, of course, was greatly affected by Reconstruction, but with the collapse of the Davis administration, the Republican party all but died and Texas became effectively a one-party state, with all the evils attendant to that system. Most significant was the effect of Reconstruction on African Americans. They exercised their civil rights as long as the Republicans were in power, and many Anglos came to blame them for all the ills of Reconstruction. Once the Democrats were back in power, there began a gradual process of reversing earlier gains, and by the turn of the century, a fully developed system of segregation, disfranchisement, and discrimination was in place.

The governors during this period were Andrew Jackson Hamilton, 1865–66; James W. Throckmorton, 1866–67; Elisha M. Pease, 1867–69; Edmund J. Davis, 1870–74; and Richard Coke, 1874–76. For a discussion of the Pease administration, consult Chapter 4, Early Statehood, 1846–61.

ANDREW JACKSON HAMILTON ☆ 1865–66

The year 1865 saw a number of momentous events that ushered in a new destiny for Texas. Robert E. Lee surrendered the Army of Northern Virginia to General Grant on April 9, 1865, and on June 2, on a federal warship anchored in Galveston Bay, Gen. E. Kirby Smith surrendered the trans-Mississippi Department to the federal government. With that the last vestige of Confederate military authority in Texas vanished and for a temporary period, in the absence of civil government, chaos reigned. Within weeks, however, a large Union force under the command of Gen. Gordon Granger occupied the state, and on June 19, Granger declared all actions of the state government since secession null and void and all the slaves to be free. On April 14, 1865, Abraham Lincoln was shot and killed by John Wilkes Booth, and Andrew Johnson, who was thrust into the presidency, appointed Andrew Jackson Hamilton (widely known as "Colossal Jack") as provisional governor on June 17.

Hamilton, a descendant of Alexander Hamilton, was born in Alabama on January, 28, 1815. Trained in the law, he arrived in Texas in 1846, and in 1849, he was elected attorney general of the state and later served in the legislature. In 1859, running as an independent, he was elected to the U.S. Congress, where he spoke eloquently against secession and supported Governor Houston steadfastly until Texas seceded in 1861. Returning home after secession and finding his life endangered by his former friends, Hamilton fled to New Orleans. He later moved on to Washington, where he was commissioned a brigadier general of volunteers and given the title military governor of Texas. He then returned to Louisiana and established his headquarters at New Orleans.

Hamilton assumed office as provisional governor on July 25, 1865. Although he issued a proclamation stating his authority and purpose, there was little he could do in reality, since actual power remained in the hands of the army. His primary concerns were the violence and disorder that paralyzed the state and the problems of the freed slaves immediately following the war. He feared for their future should they pin their hopes too heavily upon assistance, particularly in the form of land grants, from the government and encouraged them to go to work and acquire property on their own. He believed the freed slaves should be accorded all the rights of citizenship as soon as possible, but at the same time, he did not believe they should be allowed to vote until they had received some form of training. In fact, he advocated educational qualifications for both Anglo- and African-American voters. In addition to the issue of the freed slaves, Hamilton also desired to reconcile the citizens of the state to the defeat of the Confederacy and restore Texas to its normal place in the Union as soon as possible.

Pursuant to President Johnson's plan for Reconstruction, Hamilton and the military authorities set up voter registration offices in various locations and called for a constitutional convention to meet in Austin on February 7, 1866. Under the leadership of James W. Throckmorton, the convention adopted necessary modifications to the Constitution of 1845, and its work was ratified by popular vote in June. The conven-

Andrew Jackson Hamilton

tion also selected candidates for governor, and James W. Throckmorton and Elisha M. Pease were, respectively, the choices of the Democrats and the Radical Republicans. Throckmorton won by a large majority, and on August 9, 1866, he was inaugurated along with the members of a newly elected legislature; thus began the new and short-lived state government under the presidential plan of Reconstruction.

When Congress returned to session in December, 1866, it declared the Reconstruction program as it then existed null and void. In March, 1867, it passed the Military Reconstruction Act, under which Southern states were required to disband their existing governments and call new constitutional conventions. After the military registered all eligible voters and delegates were elected, the Texas convention met on June 1, 1868, with the membership generally divided between moderates led by Hamilton and Radicals led by Edmund J. Davis. For the next several months, excluding a pause from September 1 to December 7, 1868, this raucous assemblage debated the future of Texas. The Radicals had a majority and they attempted to permanently disfranchise everyone who had supported the Confederacy; but Hamilton, in a heroic effort, was able to push through a substitute agreement that limited disfranchisement to those who had violated a constitutional oath.

In November, 1869, both the new constitution and new state officials were selected. E. J. Davis was the Radical candidate for governor, and Hamilton represented the moderates. The constitution was ratified, and in a very close race, thought by many to have been manipulated by the Radicals, Davis beat Hamilton by 39,901 to 39,092 votes. After his defeat Hamilton remained in Austin, where he devoted himself to practicing law and fighting what many regarded as the corruption and extravagance of the Radical government. He died on April 11, 1875, and was buried in the state cemetery at Austin.

JAMES W. THROCKMORTON ☆ 1866–67

Born in Sparta, Tennessee on February 2, 1825, James Webb Throckmorton was descended from a notable English line. One of his ancestors, Sir Nicholas Throckmorton, was a prominent leader in the days of the Tudors. Albion Throckmorton, his grandfather, served as an officer in the Continental Army during the American Revolution, and his father, Dr. W. E. Throckmorton, was a prominent physician in

Virginia before moving to Tennessee. James Webb Throckmorton was also trained in medicine but later shifted to the law. In politics he was at first a Whig, but when the party collapsed in the 1850s, he affiliated with the Democrats and served ten years in the state legislature. He was a leading advocate of internal improvements, especially railroads, advocated the Southern route for the transcontinental line, and was one of the founders of the Texas-Pacific.

As the secession crisis approached, Throckmorton believed that everything possible should be done to keep Texas in the Union. He did not believe that Republican success in the election of 1860 would be adequate cause for secession unless Lincoln should attempt to abolish slavery. He believed in the constitutional right of secession, but at the same time he was convinced that the federal government would use force to prevent it. Also, he was convinced that the abolitionists wanted war and that the South could not prevail in an extended conflict. At the Secession Convention of 1861, he was one of the Immortal Seven who voted "No" on the Ordinance of Secession. In casting his vote Throckmorton declared, "in the presence of God and my country – and unawed by the wild spirit of revolution, I note 'No'."[1]

Even though he opposed secession, Throckmorton remained loyal to Texas during the war. He raised a company of volunteers and served with distinction throughout the conflict, and afterward he returned home and was immediately caught up in Reconstruction politics. Governor Hamilton issued his proclamation calling for a constitutional convention on November 15, 1865, and the election occurred on January 8, 1866. The delegates assembled in Austin on February 7, where Throckmorton was elected president of the convention and the Democratic candidate for governor. He won by a large majority, took office on August 6, and on August 20, President Johnson formally declared the insurrection in Texas to be over.

Along with Throckmorton, Oran M. Roberts and David G. Burnet were elected to the U.S. Senate, while George W. Chilton, B. H. Epperson, A. M. Branch, and C. C. Herbert were elected to the House. These men were all secessionists and as such would not take the iron-clad oath as proposed by the Wade-Davis Bill and later required by the Reconstruction laws; hence, they were denied their seats in Congress. This action clearly reflected the intent of the Radicals to override Johnson's program, but for his part, Throckmorton regarded the proclamation of August 20 as legally binding, and he devoted himself to

James W. Throckmorton

establishing the supremacy of civil over military authority, though he knew he was doomed to failure. He wrote: "I know I shall have the consolation of serving my country faithfully, and I do not doubt the approbation of my people. But I am harassed by the thought and cares of a heart lacerated with a knowledge of wrongs imposed upon an outraged and suffering people which I . . . have no power to avert."[2]

On March 16, 1867, Gen. Philip Sheridan was installed as Commander of the Fifth Military District headquartered at New Orleans, with Gen. Charles Griffin in immediate control of Texas. On July 30, declaring him to be "an impediment to Reconstruction," Griffin removed Governor Throckmorton from office and replaced him with Elisha M. Pease.

From 1867 to 1873, Throckmorton was disfranchised, but afterward he secured a pardon and was elected to the U.S. Congress. After serving two terms in the House, he attempted to secure the gubernatorial nomination, but was defeated by Oran M. Roberts. Later, in 1892, he tried once more but was defeated by James Stephen Hogg. Between his forays into political life, he had continued to practice law and was to do so until his death on April 21, 1894. He is buried in Pecan Grove Cemetery at McKinney.

EDMUND J. DAVIS ☆ 1870–74

Edmund J. Davis was born in Saint Augustine, Florida, on October 2, 1827, and at the age of twenty-one came to Texas along with his widowed mother and three siblings. At first the family settled in Galveston, but Edmund eventually moved to South Texas, where he lived successively in Laredo, Corpus Christi, and Brownsville. At some point he studied law and was admitted to the bar, but the precise date and circumstances are unknown.

From 1850 to 1852 and while living in Laredo, Davis was deputy customs collector of the Rio Grande. In 1853, he was elected district attorney in Laredo, and in 1854 he became a district judge in Brownsville, remaining in that position until 1861. When the secession crisis erupted, Davis sought election to the Texas secession convention, but he was defeated because of his uncompromising Unionist position. He believed that the preservation of the Union was paramount to all other considerations and spoke openly of his conviction. As a result, once

Edmund J. Davis

the state left the Union and war broke out, he found himself in danger and was forced to flee for his life to Mexico.

In 1862, Davis raised a regiment of pro-Unionist cavalry from among the expatriate Texans in Mexico, and in March of 1863, Colonel Davis and several of his men were captured by a Confederate detachment, returned to Texas, and threatened with execution for treason. Davis narrowly escaped from this predicament, after which he returned to Mexico and then moved on to Louisiana. From there he launched an unsuccessful attempt to capture Laredo in 1864, an escapade which proved to be the highlight of his military career. At the end of the hostilities he returned to Texas and was discharged from his service to the Union in August, 1865, at San Antonio.

By 1866, Davis had emerged as one of the leaders of the Republican Radicals in Texas. At the Constitutional Convention of 1866 he called for unrestricted Negro suffrage, permanent disfranchisement of all Confederates, and the nullification of all acts of the Texas legislature since 1861. He and his cohorts did not prevail because, at this stage of Reconstruction, the Redeemers were still in power; by 1868, however, things changed dramatically as the Radical Republicans in Congress repealed Presidential Reconstruction and replaced it with their own form.

During the election of 1868, many registered voters stayed away from the polls, hoping to defeat the call for a new convention by a small turnout. They failed; however, the Radical-controlled convention gathered in Austin on June 1, 1868, and it soon developed that the Radicals were divided into two factions. The extremists were led by Davis and Morgan C. Hamilton, while the moderates were led by Governor Pease and ex-governor Andrew Jackson Hamilton. As they had in 1866, the extremists demanded that all legislation passed since 1861 be nullified and that everyone who had participated in the "rebellion" should be disfranchised. After weeks of wrangling, the moderates succeeded in adopting a constitution that met all the requirements of the Radicals in Congress while at the same time avoiding the more objectionable demands of the Texas extremists. Then each faction named a slate of candidates for office and prepared to do battle in 1869, with Davis as the extremist candidate for governor and A. J. Hamilton representing the moderates.

In the 1869 campaign, the extremists received assistance from the Grant administration because the president was told that the Hamilton faction had sold out to the rebels. Gen. J. J. Reynolds, the military commander of Texas, made sure the Davis supporters controlled the polling places and that the election was supervised by the army. Under these conditions and amid considerable fraudulent voting, Davis won the contest, and Reynolds declared him duly elected on January 11, 1870. The moderates demanded a federal investigation, but the government ignored their pleas, and Davis was formally inaugurated on April 28, 1870. This occasioned a later controversy over the question of when Davis's administration actually began, on January 11 or April 28. In fact, for the next three-and-a-half years Texas was wracked by political turmoil and violence. The moderate Republicans and Democrats heaped all the blame on the Radicals, and the latter responded in kind. Hence, there has been controversy ever since over the real nature of the Davis regime, and only one thing about it is certain: Edmund J. Davis was the most unpopular governor the Lone Star State has ever had.

Controlling the twelfth legislature that convened in the spring of 1870, the Radicals proceeded to pass several laws, which their enraged opponents called the "Obnoxious Acts": these included the Militia Act, the State Police Act, the Enabling Act, and the Public Printing Act. The legislature also passed more than fifty bills providing cash subsidies and land grants for railroad companies (and in doing so, according to their enemies, practically drove the state into bankruptcy).

Moderates and conservatives found the Militia and State Police acts particularly loathsome. The former provided that all able-bodied men were liable for military duty and that the governor was commander in chief of the state's military forces. The law also gave the governor broad discretionary powers to declare martial law, and Davis used these powers extensively. In 1871, for example, he declared martial law on three occasions and then assessed the costs to the residents of the affected counties. In spite of Davis's protestations that these efforts were necessary to prevent the spread of violence, the incidents served mostly to enrage the opposition.

During the debate over the Militia Bill, the Radicals in the state senate arrested several conservatives and charged them with violations of their oath of office. During a period of three weeks, while the conservatives were held illegally, the legislature passed several measures, including the State Police Act. This law, enacted on July 1, 1870, provided for the creation of a state police force of 250 men under the control of the governor. This body existed for three years and played an important role in the Davis administration. Its official purpose was to prevent crime, but the conservatives viewed it as an institution for violence and oppression. The real truth may never be known because while some abuses certainly existed, the state police effectively quelled much of the random violence that characterized this period of Texas history.

Most of the incidents that gave the state police their odious reputation occurred in 1871, but the events of the following year also contributed to the problem. The incident of the chief, James Davidson, absconding with $35,000 from the state treasury practically destroyed what little credibility the force had left; and, when the police undertook to monitor the state elections, their fate was sealed. The Radicals failed, despite their best efforts, to rig the election of 1873, and the conservatives won a majority in the state legislature. Shortly thereafter, the State Police Act was repealed.

During the summer of 1871, a number of leading moderates and conservatives called for a taxpayer's convention in Austin to protest the abusive practices of the Davis administration. Accordingly, ninety-four counties elected delegates and dispatched them to the capital, where for several days they discussed taxation and demanded that state expenditures be reduced. These efforts had no immediate effect, but in the Congressional elections that followed, four Democratic candidates were elected. In one case, however (the contest between Republican W. T. Clark and Democrat D. C. Giddings), Governor Davis issued a fraudulent certificate of election to Clark. Subsequently, Davis was indicted for fraud and tried on this charge, but since the prosecution failed to present any evidence, he was acquitted.

While the thirteenth legislature, dominated by the Democrats, repealed many of Davis's programs and otherwise harassed him, the governor clung doggedly to his position and sought reelection in 1873. His opponent was Richard Coke, one of his most ardent foes. There was fraud on both sides in the December election, but the outcome was an overwhelming victory for the conservatives, with Davis receiving only 42,663 votes to 85,549 for Coke. Moreover, the Democrats won a majority in the legislature.

Davis was not prepared to accept the outcome of the election, and he attempted to declare it null and void on the grounds that the voting had not continued for four consecutive days as required by law. The conservatives appealed Davis's actions to the state supreme court, but the court, in the infamous "semi-colon decision," sided with the governor in declaring the election unconstitutional. The decision of the court was generally ignored throughout the state, however, and the newly elected officials began their service on the appointed day. Simultaneously, Davis and his supporters refused to give up their offices, and two governments occupied the capitol in January, 1874. Davis appealed to President Grant for support, but when the president declined and advised him to abide by the outcome of the vote, Davis was left in an untenable position: his only alternatives were to fight or give up. He chose the latter course, although, upon handing over the reins of authority to Governor Coke, he condemned the election as an illegal usurpation of power; thus ended the Reconstruction era in Texas.

After leaving office, Davis resumed the practice of law in Austin. He died on February 27, 1883, and is buried in the state cemetery. Years later he was remembered by C. E. McLaughlin, one of his political foes, in the following way: "I was always opposed to him politically. As a Republican politician he was ranked 'pizen.' He would go to great lengths in fighting his battles but personally and socially he was a clever and upright southern gentleman, and as a business-man he was irreproachable. I had many dealings with him, and in business matters the word of Governor Davis was as good as the bond of any Democrat in Texas."[3]

RICHARD COKE ☆ 1874–76

The first post-Reconstruction Democratic governor of the state, Richard Coke, was born in Virginia on March 13, 1829. He was of English ancestry, tracing his family tree back as far as Richard Coke of Trusley, who lived in the fourteenth century. Our Richard graduated from William and Mary College, read law under Beverly Tucker, and set out for Texas in 1850. He passed through Galveston and settled in Waco, which became his permanent home. Coke was a states' rights advocate who supported the secessionist movement and the Confederacy during the Civil War. In 1865, Governor Hamilton appointed him to a judgeship under the provisional government, and in 1866, he was elected to the state supreme court. However, he was removed from office in 1868.

The beginning of the end of Radical rule in Texas may be traced to the Non-Partisan Taxpayers Convention of 1871 that enlightened people to the alleged abuses of the Davis regime. Presided over by ex-Gov.

Richard Coke

Elisha Pease, this group of Democrats and conservative Republicans aired all their grievances against the Radical government. Partly as a result of the rancor generated by this convention, the Democrats won the election of 1872, thereby regaining control of the legislature. This set the stage for the gubernatorial election of 1873. The Democratic candidates were Coke for governor and Richard B. Hubbard for lieutenant governor. For the Republicans, Gov. E. J. Davis ran for reelection. The campaign was bitter, and there was violence and almost certainly voter fraud on both sides, but in the end Coke and Hubbard won by a margin of nearly two to one. Davis, however, was not prepared to give up his power so easily.

As the fourteenth legislature gathered on January 13, numerous armed men also gathered around the capitol determined to make certain that Davis retired. Davis was also backed up by an armed force, which gathered in the basement of the capitol building. During the night just before the session was to begin, Coke's forces scaled ladders, entered the two-story white limestone capitol building, and occupied the second floor. When the morning of the thirteenth dawned, two governors, both claiming legitimacy and both surrounded by swarms of warriors, claimed control of the government. In this bizarre setting, Coke had two advantages. In the first place the legislative hall was on the second floor, where he was located; thus, he and his supporters were able to convene the legislature as scheduled. Secondly, Davis found that he had lost the support of the federal government when President Grant refused him military assistance. He probably could have attempted to hold on with what forces he had, but he chose to avoid bloodshed and retire quietly. According to one story, as Davis left the capitol building, John Ireland, later to be governor, kicked him in the seat of the pants.

Coke was sworn in at midnight on the thirteenth amid great rejoicing. In his inaugural address, a classic example of the florid oratory common in that day, he declared: "Let the hearts of the people throb with joy, for the old land-marks of constitutional representative government, so long lost, are this day restored, and the ancient liberties of the people of Texas reestablished."[4]

Now political power passed into the hands of the Redeemers. Only the judiciary was still controlled by the Republicans, and that branch of government was soon to be reclaimed by the Democrats as well. Coke replaced hostile district judges with his friends, and a constitutional amendment allowed him to name a new supreme court manned by five Democrats.

One of the most important events of Coke's administration was the Constitutional Convention of 1875. Completely dominated by the Redeemers, this body created a new framework of government that was an obvious overreaction to the excesses, both alleged and proven, of Radical rule. The powers of both the governor and the legislature were curtailed, tax rates were lowered, and the state was forbidden to incur a debt in excess of $200,000. The number of courts was reduced, and judgeships were made elective offices. With respect to education, an issue needing vital attention, the provisions were utterly inadequate. There was some opposition to ratification, but Coke, the Grange, and much of the press supported the document, and it was easily adopted by a vote of 136,606 to 56,652.

When Coke came into office, the state was badly in debt. Although he did what he could to decrease expenditures, one of his efforts caused him to be severely criticized and even threatened. In response to pressure from the citizens of West Texas, the legislature passed a bill granting substantial financial assistance to the International and Great Northern Railroad to build a line from Austin through San Antonio to the Rio Grande. Coke vetoed the measure, declaring it foolishly extravagant. So serious were the threats to the safety of the governor and his family that followed, a group of his friends came to the mansion to protect him; however, Coke was anything but frightened and sent them away saying, "This is for the time being my home, my wife and children are here and I can protect them. The howling mob can, so far I am concerned, hang me in effigy from every tree in the city, but if any man mounts these steps or enters that gate with the purpose of insult or assault upon me, I'll be damned if he ever goes out until he is carried out on a board."[5]

Another problem that Coke, like his predecessors, could not solve was frontier defense. His administration made an effort by reinstituting the Texas Rangers, but the Native Americans and the Mexicans on the border continued their depredations and were not to be thoroughly pacified for several years.

When the state Democratic convention assembled in Galveston in January, 1876, Coke, Hubbard, and all the Redeemer state officers who had been elected in 1873 were renominated and later reelected. One month later, the legislature elected Governor Coke to the U.S. Senate, where he would remain until his voluntary retirement on March 4, 1895. He died in Waco on May 14, 1896, and is buried there.

Notes

1. Claude Elliott, *Leathercoat: The Life of James W. Throckmorton* (San Antonio: Privately published, 1938), 54.

2. James T. DeShields, *They Sat in High Places: The Presidents and Governors of Texas* (San Antonio: The Naylor Company, 1940), 267.

3. Ibid., 281.

4. Ibid., 288.

5. Ibid., 290.

Sources and Further Reading

Ashcraft, Allan C. "Texas in Defeat: The Early Phase of A. J. Hamilton's Provisional Governorship in Texas, June 17, 1865 to February 7, 1866." *Texas Military History* 7 (1970): 199–219.

DeShields, James T. *They Sat in High Places: The Presidents and Governors of Texas.* San Antonio: The Naylor Company, 1940.

Elliott, Claude. *Leathercoat: The Life of James W. Throckmorton.* San Antonio: Privately published, 1938.

Gray, Ronald N. "Edmund J. Davis: Radical Republican and Reconstruction Governor of Texas." Ph.D. diss., Texas Tech University, 1976.

Moneyhon, Carl H. *Republicanism in Reconstruction Texas.* Austin: University of Texas Press, 1980.

Moore, Richard R. "Radical Reconstruction: The Texas Choice." *East Texas Historical Journal* 16 (1978): 15–23.

Nunn, William C. *Texas Under the Carpetbaggers.* Austin: University of Texas Press, 1962.

Owens, Nora E. "Presidential Reconstruction in Texas: A Case Study." Ph.D. diss., Auburn University, 1983.

Phares, Ross. *The Governors of Texas.* Gretna, La.: Pelican Publishing Company, 1976.

Ramsdell, C. W. *Reconstruction in Texas.* New York: Columbia, 1920.

Richter, William L. *The Army in Texas During Reconstruction, 1865–1870.* College Station: Texas A&M University Press, 1987.

Shook, Robert W. "The Federal Military in Texas." *Texas Military History* (1967): 3–53.

Waller, John L. *Colossal Hamilton of Texas: A Biography of Reconstruction Governor.* El Paso: Texas Western Press, 1968.

Chapter seven

THE GILDED AGE IN TEXAS
1876–91

Under the Constitution of 1876, the Democrats controlled state politics, and conservative governors were regularly elected until 1890. Even though incipient reform movements, like the Greenback party and the Farmers' Alliance, emerged amid economic and social problems, the Democrats dominated because of their willingness to co-opt some of the reformers' programs and the weakened state of the Republican party. The state's finances were in a shambles at the end of Reconstruction and improved only slightly during the following decade as a result of land sales. Public land administration, in fact, became one of the main issues debated by Democratic politicians during this period.

Two other developments during this period were important as well. Threats from Native Americans on the frontier and crime were both brought under control by the efforts of the Texas Rangers, local vigilantes, and the courts; and the state finally began to develop a nascent educational system. Thus, the stage was set for Texas to enter the modern age.

The governors of this period were Richard B. Hubbard, 1876–79; Oran M. Roberts, 1879–83; John Ireland, 1883–87; and Lawrence Sullivan Ross, 1887–91.

RICHARD B. HUBBARD ☆ 1876–79

Taking residence in the governor's mansion when Richard Coke resigned to go to the U.S. Senate on December 1, 1876, Hubbard began an administration that was generally pleasing to Texas Redeemers, even if only partially successful in dealing with issues. As lieutenant governor he had demonstrated considerable skill in presiding over the legislature in 1873 and 1875. During his tenure as governor, however, the legislature did not meet; thus, Hubbard was forced to deal with several major problems on his own.

Born in 1832, Richard Bennett Hubbard was a native of Georgia. His father, who was Welsh, had come to the Colonies before the American Revolution and fought bravely for independence. Later, he prospered and was able to provide his family with a comfortable life and a first class education. Richard attended Mercer College and graduated from Harvard Law School in 1852. He came to Texas in 1853, settled in Tyler, and began to practice law. Soon he became involved in politics and was prominent among those who fought the rise of the Know-Nothings during the mid-1850s.

In 1856, at the age of twenty-four, Hubbard was appointed U.S. attorney by President Buchanan. Later, he attended the disastrous Democratic party convention in Charleston in 1860, where he was among those who bolted from the party in support of John C. Breckenridge's candidacy. Hubbard was a secessionist, and when the Civil War broke out in 1861, he raised an infantry regiment for the Confederacy and led them until the end of the conflict. At the close of the war he returned to Tyler, where he resumed his law practice with a special interest in railroads. He also joined in the anti-Republican movement and was elected lieutenant governor on the ticket with Richard B. Coke in 1873.

When Hubbard became governor in 1876, it was a time of turmoil and transition in Texas. The end of Reconstruction had left the state exhausted, uneasy, and deeply in debt, and the waves of violence that

Richard B. Hubbard

swept the state during the 1870s reflected these problems. As Hubbard settled into the governor's mansion in Austin, the bloody Pidcock-Lee feud in northeast Texas was just dying out, the Morris County war had just ended, and the notorious outlaw Cullen Bates had just been killed. But the bloodshed was not over: the Sutton-Taylor feud in southwest Texas had yet to be quelled; the Horrell-Higgins feud in Central Texas soon reached alarming levels of violence; and the "Salt War" of 1877 in the El Paso area portended the threat of renewed war with Mexico. Ben Thompson and King Fisher, both notorious gunmen, terrorized Austin and San Antonio respectively, while Bill Longley, John W. Hardin, and Sam Bass ran wild elsewhere. This was also the age of the infamous Juan Cortina and his frontier escapades. Viewed as a hero in Mexico, but as a worthless bandit, rustler, and horsethief in Texas, Cortina posed the most serious threat of all to civil peace. Hubbard sought to put down the crime wave that terrorized the state, but he was only partially successful. Longley, Hardin, and Bass were all brought to justice between 1877 and 1878, while the Texas Rangers, led by Capt. Lee Hall, ended the Sutton-Taylor feud in December, 1877. The problems posed by many other badmen, however, were not solved until later.

Unrest was also reflected in the rise of the Patrons of Husbandry, or the Grange as it was more commonly known, in Texas in the 1870s. Economic and living conditions for farmers, already desperate as the decade opened, declined further with the onset of depression in 1873. This economic downturn, which lasted until 1879, featured plummeting cotton prices, relatively high living costs, and ruinous interest rates. Especially hard hit were the tenant farmers and sharecroppers, who represented more than one-third of all Texas farmers. Coke and Hubbard had the support of the Grange in their successful campaign of 1876, but during the next two years there were only nine Grangers in the legislature, and they accomplished relatively little.

Under these conditions Hubbard found himself facing mounting criticism. Despite his efforts to suppress violence, he was under constant pressure to do more. There were those who claimed that he was meek in the face of danger, and some leveled charges of cowardice at his Civil War service. He was also accused of financial irregularities, appropriating public funds to his own use, and accepting bribes for penitentiary leases. From other quarters came allegations of patronage abuse and criticism of his support for certain railroad companies, especially the International Railway. Most of these allegations were based upon technicalities, however. Hubbard had done nothing illegal and was never accused of any crime.

Governor Hubbard actually worked to promote frontier defense, railroad construction, debt reduction, and tax reform, but in the absence of legislative support, he accomplished little on any of these issues. Moreover, by the time for the election of 1878, the political scene in Texas had deteriorated into competition between personality cults. Issues had relatively little to do with the process of nominating candidates in that year.

With most of his strength concentrated in East Texas (especially around Tyler) and in West Texas (where his support of railroad building was most popular), Hubbard sought renomination in 1878. His primary opponent was former Gov. James W. Throckmorton who had run for the U.S. Senate in 1876, and he faced a second important opponent in the person of William W. Lang, leader of the Grange. The views of the two primary candidates on most of the issues were remarkably similar, but they were surrounded by dedicated supporters who followed them for personal reasons and showed little willingness to compromise.

At the Democratic party convention in Austin in July, 1878, the factions finally agreed to the selection of a joint committee of thirty-two men empowered to name a candidate by a majority vote. Hubbard led the voting, but could never achieve the necessary majority of the votes. At length all the factions reluctantly agreed upon a compromise candidate, and Oran M. Roberts was nominated. Hubbard was sorely disappointed, but he accepted the outcome with grace.

The Democratic platform in 1878 called for the repeal of the Resumption Act, the free coinage of silver, the replacement of national bank notes with U.S. currency, and debt reduction – all aimed at restoring the state's economy through inflation. The Democrats also called for regulation of the railroads, the exemption of farm products from taxation, the prohibition of convict labor outside of penitentiaries, and the avoidance of state expenditures in excess of revenue.

After leaving office, Hubbard returned to Tyler to practice law, but he remained active in Democratic party politics. He was a delegate to the national conventions of 1880 and 1884 and served as temporary chair of the latter meeting. He campaigned extensively outside Texas for Grover Cleveland, and after the New Yorker was elected president, he appointed Hubbard minister to Japan, in which capacity the former governor served from 1888 through 1889. During that period Hubbard negotiated the first extradition treaty between the United States and Japan, as well as a treaty of amity and commerce. After his return he lectured frequently on his experience and wrote a book entitled *Japan and the Far East.*

Richard B. Hubbard holds the distinction of having been the largest governor Texas ever had. Tipping the scales at more than 400 pounds, he was known to his friends as "Jumbo," and at that weight was even more rotund than James S. Hogg. He was also known as a master orator. He was well-educated, well-informed on most issues, and demonstrated his qualifications in a melodious voice and with an engaging manner of delivery. Hence, he was able to captivate and influence his audiences. Perhaps his most famous oration occurred in 1876 when, at the Centennial Exposition in Philadelphia, he spoke for Texas in the symposium of famous speakers of the United States. Governor Hubbard died on July 12, 1901, and is buried at Tyler.

ORAN M. ROBERTS ☆ 1879–83

Descended from Scotch-Irish ancestors, Oran M. Roberts was born in the Laurens District of Alabama on July 18, 1815. His father, Obe, was a farmer who died when the boy was ten years of age. For several years thereafter, Oran continued to toil on the family farm while attempting to acquire the rudiments of an education. At age sixteen he went off to attend the University of Alabama, and later he studied law and was admitted to the bar. In 1841, he migrated to Texas and settled in Old San Augustine, where he practiced law. He established a good reputation, and Sam Houston became one of his early clients.

In 1843, Houston, then president of the Republic, appointed Roberts district attorney in the San Augustine area. Following annexation Gov. James Pinckney Henderson made him a district judge, and he served in that capacity for a decade. While a judge Roberts distinguished himself as a states' rights advocate and strict constructionist. As a dedicated advocate of the Southern point of view, he took a leading role in the secessionist movement by serving as president of the secession convention and personally engineering the resignation of Governor Houston.

During the Civil War Roberts resigned from the bench, raised a

Oran M. Roberts

regiment (the 11th Texas Infantry), and served with distinction until 1864, when he relinquished his commission to become chief justice of the Texas supreme court. He assisted in writing the Constitution of 1866 and also in that year, along with David G. Burnet, was elected to the U.S. Senate. He and Burnet, however, were denied their seats by the Radical Republican majority. For six years following his dismissal from the Senate, Roberts operated a private law school in Gilmer; but at the end of Reconstruction he once more entered public service, when he was again appointed chief justice of the supreme court, this time by Governor Coke. He remained in that position until he was elected governor in 1878.

Roberts was nominated for governor under rather unusual circumstances. At the outset of the state Democratic convention, Governor Hubbard was the leading candidate, followed by James Throckmorton and William W. Lang, head of the state Grange. During five days of furious contention, the factions supporting these three battled for the prize, but no one was able to command a majority. After several ballots Roberts, who was not even present at the convention, received eighteen of thirty-two votes and, thus, the nomination. Civil War hero Joe Sayers was picked to run for lieutenant governor. Legend has it that Roberts was at home on his farm near Tyler when news came of his nomination, and so he rode into town on his spotted pony and met his friends at a local saloon. There he borrowed fifty cents to wire the convention that he would accept the nomination.

At the time of Roberts's nomination, the Greenback party was on the rise in Texas. The Greenbackers wanted to increase the amount of currency in circulation in order to promote inflation, raise prices, and bring down interest rates. They charged that both the mainline parties were controlled by foreign financiers, especially "German Jews and English Capitalists." In Texas, they had some support from Republicans, including ex-Gov. E. J. Davis of Austin. Their gubernatorial candidate was W. H. Hamman of Robertson County.

During the summer of 1878, Judge Roberts campaigned aggressively in North and Central Texas. Hoping to neutralize the Greenback threat, he charged that the Republicans favored big business, not the common citizen, and that the Greenback party was actually a creation of the North made up of Republicans, African Americans, and disenchanted Democrats. In this campaign Roberts appealed to farmers not to abandon the party and, primarily as a result of the loyalty and continued support of Lang and the Grange, he was successful, sweeping to victory in November over Hamman and Republican A. B. Norton. Apparently most of the Greenback support in the election had come from counties with large African-American populations, from farming areas in Central and East, and from areas where there had been widespread Republican-Unionist sentiments.

Roberts believed in limited government and rigid economy, and these views defined his administration. Specifically, he sought to reduce government expenditures and taxes while finding necessary revenues elsewhere, especially through the sale of public land. While highly successful in the short run, his politics were shortsighted and cost Texas dearly in the future. On one occasion Roberts reportedly went so far as to declare that the conservation of natural resources for the benefit of the future was nothing but "damn nonsense."

During the first session of the legislature, the governor vetoed the appropriations bill that provided for a maximum public school appropriation (25 percent of *ad valorem* tax revenues) because he believed it would increase the deficit. In a subsequent special session, the legislature cut the school appropriations to one-sixth of the *ad valorem* revenues and Roberts approved it; and, though he favored the concept in theory, he vetoed a proposal to increase revenues by selling public lands at fifty cents an acre in unlimited amounts. This anomaly occurred because most of Roberts's support came from landowning farmers who paid most of the state's taxes. Sale of public land under existing laws, however, went forward apace. Roberts believed that land belonging to public institutions should be sold at the lowest possible price for cash or interest-bearing notes, since it was producing no tax revenues, and this was the policy he followed. Unfortunately, as land values rose later, the state lost vast revenues that might have been realized if sales had been deferred. Still, Roberts's policies succeeded in the short term by reducing the public debt. In fact, when he left office in 1883, there was a cash balance in the treasury of over $300,000.

During his administration Roberts was also devoted to higher education. The University of Texas at Austin was finally established while he was in office, as were the Sam Houston and Prairie View normal schools, and there were efforts to improve the Agricultural and Mechanical College. In addition, Roberts supported the improvement of various humanitarian institutions and the upgrading of the Rangers for frontier defense.

Many people who knew Roberts thought him an eccentric man, but it is probably more accurate to characterize him as "unusual." He was a man of few words – he believed in saying just what was necessary and no more. He had no interest in sartorial splendor, dressing always for comfort in his beloved Prince Albert coat. He was also an habitual smoker, favoring a corncob pipe. He was no genius, but his mind was bright and alert and remained so throughout his long life. His posture was straight and erect, although he was not overly tall. He possessed dark eyes that usually reflected a pleasing or humorous expression, and he also seemed possessed by unlimited energy, exhibiting industry in everything he did.

After he left office in 1883, Roberts joined Judge Robert S. Gould in being the only two members of the law faculty at the University of Texas. After several years of teaching he resigned to write his memoirs, which were later published under the title *Fifty Years of Politics, Legislative and Judicial History of Texas*. Governor Roberts died on May 29, 1898, and is buried in the state cemetery at Austin.

JOHN IRELAND ☆ 1883–87

The son of Irish immigrants, John Ireland was born in Hart County, Kentucky, on June 1, 1826. His family was poor, and the conditions of his upbringing were harsh. He received very little formal education, but he showed promise to those around him, so he was made a deputy sheriff at age eighteen though he lacked the necessary formal qualifications. He also began to study law, was admitted to the bar, and migrated to Texas in 1852, where he settled in Seguin and began to practice law.

Ireland was an ardent states' right advocate and secessionist, and he was a delegate to the Secession Convention of 1861. When hostilities began he joined the army as a private but rapidly rose through the ranks to become a colonel. During the war he remained in Texas, where he served along the Rio Grande border and the Gulf Coast with those units guarding against Union invasion. His greatest military exploits occurred in connection with the defense of Corpus Christi.

A major participant in the Reconstruction Convention of 1866, Ireland was subsequently elected judge of the Seguin district but was removed, along with most of the other state officers, when the Radicals seized power in 1867. For the next five years he was out of politics, but

John Ireland

in 1872 he was elected to the Texas house and chaired the executive committee of the Democratic party. He played a major role in the expulsion of the Radicals led by E. J. Davis and the installation of Richard B. Coke. Subsequently, he participated in the Constitutional Convention of 1875, although his role was controversial because some of his enemies accused him of opposing ratification. Nevertheless, after Coke was safely installed in office, Ireland was appointed to the state supreme court.

In December, 1875, Ireland informed the governor that he intended to run for the U.S. Senate. Coke responded with a letter wishing Ireland well but saying nothing about his own intentions. Soon he also entered the race, thus generating bitter recriminations from Ireland's friends. Ireland, in fact, had substantial support. Most of it came from the area around Seguin and from East Texas, where he was seen as a Bourbon (and where this label was regarded as a compliment, not an insult). But there were those, however, who tried to discredit him: Ireland's enemies accused him of having been a Know-Nothing, of opposing ratification of the new constitution, and of questionable relations with the International Railway Company (it was said that he had supported land grant legislation in exchange for railroad bonds). Coke won in the balloting and resigned his governor's seat to go to Washington. Ireland remained on the court.

In the two years that followed, Ireland's views on various major issues matured. He backed the university bill and low taxes, but he also favored adequate support for the public schools, land sales (only to actual settlers), an end to the practice of repurchasing state bonds at premium prices, currency expansion, the abolition of the national banks, and a revenue tariff. With respect to railroads, he favored regulation and opposed land grants, and this latter position earned him the nickname "Oxcart John." In 1882, he made it clear that he wanted to be governor, and when Roberts declined to run for reelection, Ireland was nominated by acclamation.

G. "Wash" Jones was Ireland's opponent in the election of 1882, and this Greenback candidate, sometimes called the "Sage of Bastrop," was a man of substantial ability with considerable support among the older generation. Ireland opened his campaign against Jones and the Greenbackers in late August in his hometown, defending the Democratic party and claiming that he had never been a Greenbacker despite his support for currency expansion. He admitted that he had flirted with the Know-Nothings but claimed that he had dropped his affiliation when he discovered their xenophobia. Although Jones campaigned strenuously and effectively, Ireland defeated him in November by a vote of 150,809 to 102,501.

Reflecting his commitment to education, one of Ireland's first acts came on behalf of the public schools. In January, 1883, he secured an amendment to the constitution providing for an *ad valorem* tax not to exceed twenty cents per one hundred dollars valuation. He also withdrew the public school lands from sale on the low terms that had been fixed by Roberts and instead sold them on thirty year notes at two dollars per acre. This policy at first increased the state's revenues but eventually led to large accumulations of land in the form of cattle ranches, which in turn led to major social problems as the use of barbed wire spread over the state.

First introduced into Texas in the early 1870s by hardware salesperson John W. Gates, the use of barbed wire became commonplace by the early 1880s, especially in West Texas. Cattle ranchers tended to enclose not only their own holdings, but also public land they were grazing without legal claim. In the process they often cut off farmers or other ranchers from water on their own farmland. This practice produced tensions that became acute especially in times of drought; one such period occured in 1883, when desperate men resorted to wirecutting and trespass in order to reach water. Wirecutting led to violence, and by 1884, the situation was rapidly getting out of hand. Ireland responded by calling a special session of the legislature in February that passed a law authorizing the Rangers to intervene. They were sent into the areas of most violent activity in the western, southwestern, and north-central areas of the state, where they achieved partial success in restoring order. Even so, sporadic difficulties continued on the prairies for a considerable period of time.

At the end of his second term, Ireland decided to run for the U.S. Senate. His opponents included the incumbent, Sam Bell Maxey, Members of Congress John H. Reagan and John Hancock, and state Sen. A. W. Terrell. After an extended battle before the legislature, Reagan was ultimately elected. Ireland then retired from the political arena and returned to his law practice in Seguin. Unfortunately, he soon became involved in land and railroad investments that collapsed during the panic of 1893, and he lost everything. His health shattered by worry, he died on March 15, 1896, and was buried in the state cemetery in

Austin. The inscription on his tombstone includes only his name and the years of his life.

LAWRENCE SULLIVAN ROSS ☆ 1887–91

Lawrence Sullivan Ross was born in Bentensport, Ohio, on September 27, 1838. While he was still an infant, his father, Shapley P. Ross, moved the family to Texas, where they settled at first near the site of the present town of Cameron. Later they moved to Austin and after that to Waco. All these locations were on the frontier, and Ross grew up amid all the dangers and excitement of that environment. On one occasion his father actually outran a band of marauding Comanches on foot while carrying the boy on his back.

The Ross family arrived in Austin in 1845, when "Sul" was seven years of age. There he received his early education, went on to Old Baylor University and then to Wesleyan University in Florence, Alabama. Ross idolized his father, and the love of frontier adventure never left him. Shapley Ross was a Texas Ranger who had fought alongside such heroes as Jack Hays, Ed Burleson, "Big Foot" Wallace, and "Rip" Ford. Despite his education and the excitement of other career possibilities, Sul wanted more than anything to emulate his father, and his first chance to do so came in 1858.

Troubles with the Native Americans broke out while Sul was home for the summer vacation of 1858. He raised a band of volunteers and joined a force led by "Rip" Ford and Maj. Earl Van Dorn to go in pursuit of the Comanches. During this campaign he displayed the courage and coolness under fire that marked him as a natural soldier and foreshadowed his brilliant career in the Civil War. In the fierce fighting at Antelope Hills, in the Wichita Mountains, and along the Pease River, Ross distinguished himself. At the Pease River encounter in December, 1860, Ross killed Nobah, a leader of the Comanche band (although at the time Sul thought his adversary to be the more famous chief, Peta Nocona). Ross also rescued Cynthia Ann Parker, Nocona's wife, from Indian captivity during this fight, although the white woman known as Naduah ("Keeps Warm With Us") was not particularly grateful.

Following these exploits young Ross became famous. Governor Houston appointed him aide-de-camp with the rank of colonel and commander of all Ranger forces on the northwest frontier; simul-

Lawrence Sullivan Ross

taneously, Gen. of the Army Winfield Scott offered him a commission in the regular army. Ross refused both appointments, however, because of secession and the outbreak of the Civil War.

Ross enlisted in the Confederate Army as a private, but his abilities and his incredible bravery soon distinguished him. He experienced a meteoric rise to the rank of brigadier general, and as his brigade engaged in some 135 skirmishes and battles, Ross became one of the most famous of all the Confederate military leaders. After the war he retired to his farm near Waco, but in 1873, he was asked to become sheriff of McLennan County. Again Ross distinguished himself in quelling the violence that characterized life in that area during Reconstruction, and in 1876, after the ratification of the new constitution, Ross was elected to the state senate.

Senator Ross was the only potential candidate for governor who might have opposed the nomination of John Ireland in 1882, but his backers declined to nominate him, hoping for Ireland's support four years later. When Ross's turn finally came in 1886, he faced several opponents in the Democratic party convention. These included A. C. "Clint" Giddings of Brenham, Marvin "Howdy" Martin of Corsicana, San Antonio banker John T. Brackenridge, and former state legislator William J. Swain. That all were concerned about the potential influence of the Knights of Labor and Farmers' Alliance in state politics was evident in the issues they addressed during the campaign for the nomination.

Ross supported the sale of agricultural land to settlers, the short leasing of grazing land to others, and the taxation of alien-owned land. He opposed the creation of a regulatory agency for the railroads, hoping the companies would regulate themselves through competition. He also proposed that labor problems should be controlled without endangering public rights, but he offered no specific formula for action. Giddings, who was a former member of Congress, wanted regulated public land sales and said nothing about railroad regulation. However, he opposed public disruption caused by labor unions, especially strikes. Martin, an ex-lieutenant governor and candidate of many Knights and Alliance men as well as of the Prohibitionists, favored the sale of public land to settlers but opposed leasing. He also supported railroad regulation. Finally, Brackenridge favored land sales in amounts governed by use and called upon the courts to settle labor disputes but took no position on railroad regulation.

In the hot summer of 1886 and before the state convention, the candidates traded barbs and hurled charges back and forth. Ross was charged with pandering to the Knights, the Greenbackers, and the Republicans, while his backers, often speaking through the Waco *Examiner,* accused Brackenridge of being a crypto-Republican, called Giddings a tool of large business interests (particularly the Galveston Wharf Company), and attacked Martin and Swain on a personal level. At the convention in August, Ross's supporters controlled the chair and, with the support of the Alliance men, the Knights, and the East Texas farmers, they secured his nomination on the first ballot. The convention then adopted a platform that generally reflected Ross's views. It called for sale of land to active settlers, leasing to graziers, protection of corporate property from injury or interference, maintenance of offices and records in the state by railroads operating in the state, forfeiture of land grants by railroads failing to meet their obligations, stockholder liability for corporate debts, and state charters for land corporations. Ross faced two opponents in the November election, Republican A. M. Cockran and Prohibitionist E. L. Doheny, but defeated them both, polling 278,776 votes to 65,236 and 19,186 respectively.

Ross was elected to a second term in 1888 on a platform calling for the abolition of the national banking system, the regulation of railroads and monopolies, tariff reduction, and currency inflation. Ross still had the support of the Farmers' Alliance, but farmer discontent was on the rise, especially in East and West Texas. Ross campaigned aggressively in order to overcome it, and his primary opponent was Marvin Martin, now the nominee of the newly organized Union Labor party and the Prohibitionists. Martin accused Ross of failure to reduce taxes, improve education, protect voting rights, and regulate the railroads effectively, but Ross successfully parried this challenge, defeating Martin handily by a vote of 250,388 to 98,447.

As governor, Ross exhibited tendencies that marked him as a Jeffersonian Democrat who believed in the old adage that the "government governs best which governs least." Yet, not all his colleagues in state government agreed with him. Regarding railroad regulation, for example, Ross continued to believe that competition would regulate rates. The legislature considered several regulation bills, however, and one of them, though defeated in the senate, actually passed in the house. Ross would surely have vetoed such a bill had it come to his desk, but the house's efforts represented a demand for action that was finally to come in 1891.

Ross remained consistent while in office on most other issues. The legislature essentially carried out his policies on land sales, permitting sales only to settlers and short leases. When ranchers in the West were tried for illegal enclosures but found innocent, the legislature, with Ross's approval, attempted to pass resolutions of censure but was unable to push these through both houses. Public land law in Texas, in fact, remained substantially unchanged until the mid-1890s.

Prohibition was also a major issue during Ross's administration. Under pressure from the Prohibition party, the legislature adopted a constitutional amendment to prevent the manufacture or sale of liquor in the state. A nonpartisan group with headquarters in Waco soon emerged to fight for passage of the amendment, its leaders including many bankers, lawyers, politicians, farmers, and preachers. They were well-endowed with a war chest of nearly fifteen thousand dollars.

Those who opposed Prohibition also organized a committee chaired by George Clark, who had been Governor Ross's campaign manager. This group argued that the amendment would harm business, destroy a lucrative source of tax revenue, and was undemocratic because it would force the moral and philosophical views of one group upon another. The debate raged throughout the summer of 1887, and when the vote came in August, the amendment lost by a count of 220,627 to 129,270 votes. Ross played no part in the campaign but was pleased by the outcome.

Among Ross's significant contributions to the state were his support of the legislature's desire to purchase the Huddle portrait gallery (a collection of paintings of all the governors that still hangs in the rotunda of the capitol building); his proposal that the legislature establish an "Arbor Day" to encourage the planting of trees; and his proposal for a Confederate soldiers' pension fund. Also during his administration, the new capitol building was completed and dedicated on May 10, 1888.

Soon after his retirement from office, Ross became president of the A&M College, now Texas A&M University. He remained in that position until his death on January 4, 1898. He is buried in Waco.

Sources and Further Reading

Bailey, Leila. "The Life and Career of O. M. Roberts." Ph.D. diss., University of Texas, 1932.

Barr, Alwyn. *Reconstruction to Reform: Texas Politics, 1876–1906.* Austin: University of Texas, 1971.

Brenner, Judith Ann. *Sul Ross: Soldier, Statesman, Educator.* College Station: Texas A&M University Press, 1983.

DeShields, James T. *They Sat in High Places: The Presidents and Governors of Texas.* San Antonio: The Naylor Company, 1940.

Eby, F. *The Development of Education in Texas.* New York: MacMillan, 1925.

Holden, W. C. "Law and Lawlessness on the Texas Frontier, 1875–1890." *Southwestern Historical Quarterly* 44 (1940): 188–203.

McKitrick, R. *The Public Land System of Texas, 1823–1910.* Madison: University of Wisconsin Press, 1918.

Martin, Roscoe C. "The Greenback Party in Texas." *Southwestern Historical Quarterly* 30 (1927): 161–77.

———. "The Grange as a Political Factor in Texas." *Southwestern Political and Social Science Quarterly* 6 (1926): 363–83.

Miller, E. T. *Financial History of Texas.* Austin: University of Texas Press, 1916.

Phares, Ross. *The Governors of Texas.* Gretna, La.: Pelican Publishing Company, 1976.

Smith, Ralph A. "Farmers' Alliance in Texas, 1875–1900." *Southwestern Historical Quarterly* 48 (1945): 346–69.

Chapter eight

EARLY REFORMERS
1891–99

Pressures for reform began producing results by 1890, and for the next two decades numerous changes were effected as Texas' economic and political systems strove to meet the emerging needs of a modern society. Farmers' demands for recognition of their problems had first been championed by the Farmers' Alliance, and now their cries for reform found political expression in the People's (Populist) Party, which for a time seemed destined to become a permanent feature of the political scene. The party collapsed after the mid-1890s, however, when economic and agricultural conditions improved; many of its demands – especially those relating to the regulation of big business and the railroads – were endorsed by the Democrats. These efforts were the foundation for the development in the early twentieth century of a broad-based program of reform that tried to forge a more democratic and competitive system through the political process.

The governors during this period were James S. Hogg, 1891–95, and Charles A. Culberson, 1895–99.

JAMES S. HOGG ☆ 1891–95

The man who would one day be Texas' first native governor was born in Cherokee County on March 24, 1851. His Scotch-Irish ancestors came to Virginia in the early eighteenth century, and one of the second generation immigrants, John Hogg, moved to South Carolina some years later. John Hogg had three sons, one of whom was named Lewis, and settled in Alabama around 1818. Among Lewis's sons was Joseph Lewis Hogg who, with his wife Lucanda, came to Texas in the winter of 1836–37. These were the parents of James Stephen Hogg. Joseph Lewis Hogg was a major general in the Confederate Army who served with distinction but died of disease in 1862. His wife died the following year, leaving James and his two brothers to be raised by an older sister. The family was neither poverty-stricken nor rich; sister Frances did the best she could, but the boys received only a basic education and went to work at an early age.

One of James's first jobs was at the *Rusk Chronicle,* where he worked as a printer's devil for the publisher, a former Confederate officer named Andrew Jackson. One of the pioneer news reporters of Texas, Jackson instilled a love of the business in young Jim, who soon set out on his own. In 1867, he walked from East Texas to Cleburne, where he obtained a job with the Cleburne *Chronicle.* Unfortunately, the building in which the newspaper was published soon burned down and Jim returned to East Texas, where he became a farmhand. During the next several years, he worked and studied, somehow learning enough law to pass the bar. His first business ventures, however, once again involved newspapers. For a time he ran the Longview *News* and a little later founded the Quitman *News.* Then in 1873, he was elected justice of the peace in Quitman, and this was the beginning of his career in public service. In 1878, he became county attorney and was elected district attorney in 1880.

By the time Hogg ran for attorney general in 1886, he had become convinced that the essential question in Texas politics was the regulation of railroads and corporations. He rode the issue into office as an advocate of reform, and four years later it carried him to the governor's mansion in Austin. As attorney general, Hogg first moved against the

James S. Hogg

"wildcat" insurance companies, driving several out of the state and forcing others to operate within the law. Hogg also promoted antitrust legislation, and under his leadership Texas became the second state in the Union to pass a workable antitrust statute. In its original form, it forbade combinations in restraint of trade and price-fixing, but later the law was upgraded and improved on several occasions.

Hogg's major issue in his reform efforts as attorney general was railroad regulation. All the abusive practices found elsewhere – rate discrimination, long haul/short haul discrimination, and monopolization of service – were common in Texas. At the time Hogg entered office in 1887, the state already possessed the power to regulate the transportation industry, but the existing laws were inadequate in some cases and unenforced in others. Hogg moved vigorously to exert more effective state control over the railroads; he forced an end to pooling and, by various legal maneuvers, he reduced the control exerted by out-of-state corporations on railroads operating in Texas by forcing them to set up operating offices in the state.

The pinnacle of Hogg's railroad regulation policy was the drive to establish a railroad commission, but the creation of such an agency required a constitutional amendment. Hogg entered the race for governor in 1890 with the support of the farmers, ranchers, and small merchants, most of whom favored more aggressive action by the state (including the establishment of a commission) to protect their interests against the practices of large corporations. Arrayed against Hogg were many able leaders, such as J. W. Throckmorton and Gustave Cook, who were aligned with various corporate interests. But in 1890, the power of agrarian unrest and the demands of the common citizen proved too powerful for most politicians to resist. Hogg's forces dominated the state convention at San Antonio in August, 1890, and he was easily nominated. In November, he swamped his Republican opponent, Webster Flanagan of Rusk, and saw the commission amendment approved by a substantial margin as well.

In the 1891 session of the legislature, Hogg's foremost goal was the passage of the railroad commission bill, but he also favored support for education, improvement of the penal system, and reform of the criminal code. He would be hampered in his efforts to complete his agenda by the fact that many members of the legislature were first termers and, thus, inexperienced; but he had the support of some highly skilled lawmakers, including Alexander W. Terrell of Austin, Thomas Jefferson Brown of Grayson County, Martin M. Crane of Cleburne, and George Jester of Corsicana. These men were, in large part, responsible for the ultimate success of the governor's program.

Opponents of the commission idea included most of those in the railroad industry, along with their attorneys and lobbyists, and many entrepreneurs. Foremost in the group was George Clark, a railroad lawyer and former associate of the governor who had broken with him on the commission issue. Realistically, Clark and his friends did not believe they could prevent the passage of a commission bill, so they concentrated on an effort to make the commission elective rather than appointive. They failed, however, and on April 3, 1891, a bill authored by Terrell was passed by a vote in the house of ninety-two to five (with nine members abstaining) and in the senate of twenty-six to zero (with five members abstaining).

Governor Hogg persuaded Sen. John H. Reagan, author of the Interstate Commerce Act, to become the first chair of the commission. The other members were L. L. Foster and William P. McLean. Foster was a former member of the legislature who, in 1891, was serving as state commissioner of insurance, statistics, and history. He was very knowledgeable in railroad affairs. McLean was also a former lawmaker and longtime Hogg supporter who, since 1884, had been a district judge.

Initially, as the long-awaited commission began its work, critics included not only the railroad and business communities, but also some of the more radical members of the Farmers' Alliance, who favored the creation of a third party. They were disturbed by the appointment of Reagan, who opposed the third party movement, and they were outraged that the first three commissioners did not include a member of the Alliance. Hogg defended his appointments, arguing that he wanted the best commission possible, but the Alliance was not satisfied.

Over the next two years, a time of political turmoil and economic chaos, Hogg and his friends faced the formidable task of holding the Democratic party together. On the left, the radical Alliance continued its support for the creation of a third party and, indeed, many of its members cast their lot with the People's Party when it came into being in the summer of 1892. On the right, the Democratic reactionaries, led by Clark, continued to fight practically all of Hogg's reformist efforts, and by 1892, they also seemed ready to leave the party if by doing so they could achieve their goals. Thus, Hogg's drive for reelection that year was to be a difficult experience.

The governor opened his campaign on April 21, 1892, with a major address at Wills Point in Van Zandt County. There he reviewed his previous achievements and pledged himself to five major policies: to uphold the constitution; to support the commission; to prohibit the issuance of watered stocks by railroad companies; to regulate the issuance of county and municipal bonds; and to regulate alien land ownership. These policies were to be the bulwark of his administration from this time forward.

George Clark was determined to wrest the Democratic nomination from the governor, and he campaigned energetically on the proposition that Hogg sought to consolidate too much power in the hands of state government. At the party convention, which met at Houston in August, Clark's forces soon discovered that they could not prevail; so they adjourned to an alternative location, declared Clark to be the leader of a new party – the Jeffersonian Democrats – and nominated him for governor. Meanwhile, Governor Hogg was easily renominated by those remaining Democrats, who adopted a platform calling for the enactment of legislation in support of all Hogg's policies. Reaching out to the Alliance, they also endorsed the free and unlimited coinage of silver, support for the working class, and an elective railroad commission (Hogg reluctantly agreeing to this last proposal in the interests of party unity).

The Populist candidate for governor was Thomas L. Nugent of Erath County, a man for whom Hogg had the highest personal regard. Because of his feelings for Nugent and because he hoped to draw as many members of the Alliance as possible back into the fold, Hogg did not focus his attacks upon the Populist candidate. He concentrated instead on Clark, an effort made all the more effective because the Jeffersonian Democrats had accepted the endorsement of the Republicans. The governor, however, had to defend himself from the attacks of both his adversaries, and he did so with considerable skill. In one of his finest speeches, delivered in Dallas (a Clark stronghold), Hogg summarized his position as follows: "Nugent is for government ownership of the railroads: Clark is for turning them loose. I want neither, but advocate their just control and regulation through the commission."[1]

Hogg won by a plurality in the general election, with 190,486 votes to 133,395 for Clark and 108,483 for Nugent. This was the first time in the history of the state that a winning Democratic candidate had not received a majority, but it did not mean that Hogg had lost much popularity. He received only 7,000 fewer votes than in 1890, and his support was fairly evenly distributed. Still, Hogg and his friends could not ignore the fact that Clark and Nugent combined had polled 56 percent of the vote. It would require courage and skill if the governor were to bring his program of progressive-conservative reform to fruition.

When the twenty-third legislature assembled in January, 1893, Hogg set before them an agenda that included the support of the railroad commission, regulation of watered stocks and bonds, regulation of the issuance of county and municipal bonds, prohibition of large-scale land speculation in the state, support for education, a workable mechanics *lien* law, and the prohibition of convict leasing. Hogg also endorsed three constitutional amendments: one to provide for the election of the railroad commissioners, a second for the chartering of state banks, and a third to provide pensions for indigent Confederate veterans. Finally, Hogg's program included a general pledge to oppose communism in any form and to support the just and equitable protection of both capital and labor interests.

The session saw many difficulties, but upon its conclusion in May, Hogg could look back upon a reasonable level of success. Many of his proposals had become law, most importantly perhaps the one enhancing the powers of the railroad commission by granting it the authority to fix rates based upon fair valuation and check many of the practices that railroad companies had commonly used to manipulate stocks. With this law in place in 1894, when the U.S. Supreme Court upheld the constitutionality of the commission in the case of *Reagan* v. *Farmers Loan and Trust*, the stage was set for the commission to fulfill its mandate.

A second major achievement was the county and municipal bond law passed in April, 1893. It required that bond issues be accompanied by provisions to collect sufficient taxes to pay interest and establish a sinking fund. Its purpose was to prevent town boosters and unscrupulous contractors from mortgaging future generations. Hogg received considerable abusive criticism for his support of this measure, but he was proud of it nevertheless and regarded it as one of his foremost accomplishments.

The third important reform passed in 1893 was the Perpetuities and Corporation Land Law, designed to limit speculation in agricultural and grazing lands. It required that private corporations divest themselves of all land held for speculative purposes within fifteen years. This was certainly a noble effort, but the law was full of loopholes and did not work. Few companies complied within the time limit and, in fact, large holdings remain common today.

Others of Hogg's proposals fell short of their goals as well. The amendment to provide adequate pensions for Confederate veterans failed, as did the one to charter state banks. The amendment to make the railroad commission an elective body passed, but the governor was not entirely happy with it. Nevertheless, he had achieved most of his major goals and was content. He saw no need to call a special session and was, in fact, ready to contemplate retirement to private life. As Hogg looked back over his career in public office, he had much to be proud of. He had been scrupulous, honest, and true to his principles. He was responsible for the passage of much beneficial legislation and, perhaps more importantly, Hogg had always been willing to put his ideals into practice, a characteristic he maintained from his youth. Three incidents that occurred in 1894 illustrate this facet of his character.

Hogg's sympathy for labor (and, more specifically, the plight of the working class caused by the depression of 1893) was tested early in the year when a contingent of Coxey's Army passed through Texas on its way from Los Angeles to Washington. Jacob Coxey, an Ohio entrepreneur and reformer, had organized a march on Washington to dramatize the problems of the unemployed and to demand that Congress establish public works projects. This was an extremely radical idea for those days, and Coxey's Grand Army of the Commonweal, as it was called, was regarded with suspicion and even fear by both the upper class and public officials everywhere. The group arrived in El Paso in March, and almost at once the mayor requested that Governor Hogg put the garrison at Fort Bliss into state service in order, as he put it, "to repel the invasion." Hogg, of course, refused. Meanwhile, the Coxeyites, some seven hundred of them, loitered in El Paso for two days and then boarded an eastbound Southern Pacific freight train, which they apparently thought would carry them to the capital. However, seventy miles east of the city, in an extremely isolated area without access to food or water, train operators uncoupled their cars and left them stranded.

Railroad officials defended their actions by claiming they were overrun by tramps and hoboes, but the governor knew perfectly well that most of the Coxeyites were legitimate workers whose livelihood had been lost to hard times. He was outraged at the actions of the Southern Pacific and demanded that the company provide the men with transportation. His argument ran that, since the company had brought them into the state, it was responsible for getting them out. At first the railroad officials refused, saying that no power on earth could compel them to operate the trains if they did not want to. Public opinion tended to support the governor, however, and soon a group of private citizens in El Paso hired a special train to pick up the stranded men and convey them to San Antonio. From there they traveled to Longview and then to Little Rock, Arkansas. Some of the workers actually reached Washington a few weeks later, but by then Jacob Coxey had been arrested for "trespassing" and his movement had disintegrated.

This incident showed Hogg at his best, and he was widely praised for his stand. Even though he did not entirely approve of Coxey's project, he dealt with the marchers in a statesmanlike and civilized manner. He agreed that genuine tramps and hoboes should not be tolerated, but people in trouble who were honestly seeking work should be assisted, not arrested. "Food, not fines, will be the treatment of the law-loving, law-abiding element in this state when men commit no greater crime than travelling as tramps for lack of work," he declared.[2]

In addition to his vigorous pursuit of antitrust legislation, Hogg also demonstrated a willingness to pursue the villains who ran them, no matter how powerful they might be. In 1894, one of his most remarkable efforts occurred in connection with a lawsuit against John D. Rockefeller's Standard Oil Company and its Texas subsidiary, the Waters-Pierce Oil Company of Missouri. After a vigorous investigation, Hogg and Atty. Gen. Charles A. Culberson were able to show that in Texas, the Standard/Waters-Pierce combination was engaged in rebates, price-fixing, consolidation, and other activities that violated the state antitrust act of 1889. In a case styled *The State of Texas v. John D. Rockefeller, et al.,* numerous indictments were handed down. Among those accused were, in addition to Rockefeller, his brother William, his close associate Henry M. Flagler, John D. Archbold, and several officers of the Waters-Pierce Company. After the indictment Sheriff John W. Baker of McLennan County was expected to arrest these people and present them for trial in the fifty-fourth state district court in Waco. When that did not occur (none of the accused men were in Texas), Governor Hogg intervened to request the extradition of Rockefeller from New York and Flagler from Florida. The governors of both states refused, arguing that Rockefeller and Flagler had not "fled" from Texas within the meaning of Article IV of the U.S. Constitution, but both the business titans were unnerved nevertheless. Samuel T. Dodd, Rockefeller's lawyer, attempted to calm him by pointing out that Texas had "one of those crazy, socialist [antitrust] laws which are unconstitutional."[3] Neither Rockefeller nor Flagler ever came to Texas for trial, but over the next few years several Waters-Pierce employees were tried and convicted. In fact, the Waters-Pierce matter was to be a legal cause célèbre in Texas for many years to come. Perhaps it was quaint of Hogg to threaten the great John D. Rockefeller with extradition, but without question the governor was dead serious.

The third remarkable incident in 1894 was Hogg's "liver and lights" speech, which reflected his attitude on labor as well as the relationship between the state and the federal government. In July, Hogg had just returned from a trip to the East, where he saw considerable evidence of the bitterness between labor and management. There were many strikes that summer, often accompanied by violence, and one of the worst was the walkout against the Pullman Sleeping Car Company near Chicago. Eugene V. Debs, president of the American Railway Union, sympathized with the strikers and ordered his workers to refuse to handle Pullman cars. This action threatened mail deliveries, and Pres. Grover Cleveland sent federal troops to Chicago to ensure that the trains would roll even though he had received no request for assistance from Gov. John P. Altgeld of Illinois. This unprecedented act excited considerable comment around the country, and many governors expressed their approval; but Hogg, at first, remained silent. He sympathized both with Altgeld's view that Washington should stay out of state affairs unless requested to intervene and with the right of workers to organize and demand their rights; but he did not condone violence.

On July 18, 1894, while visiting an encampment of the Texas Volunteer Guard, Hogg was asked to comment on the situation in Chicago. He responded with a few off-the-cuff remarks that condemned unrest and civic commotion and warned the men that sometime they might be called out to quell disorder. He hastened to add that problems of this kind in the state should be handled by state authorities and said that he regretted that President Cleveland, the leader of the Democratic party, had sent federal troops into Illinois without the request of the Democratic governor.

A reporter who was present at the event wrote a version of Hogg's speech from memory that substantially exaggerated the governor's remarks, and soon the front pages of "enemy" newspapers all over the state were emblazoned with a story that made Hogg appear to be a radical states' rights enthusiast, the equal of any pre-Civil War fire-eater. According to this account Hogg had declared: "This strike is but the preliminary of terrible times in this country. . . . Unless a change is made, those fourteen story buildings in Chicago will be be-spattered with blood, brains, hair, hides, liver and lights, and the horrors of the French Revolution will be repeated two-fold."⁴ According to the story, he went on to say that he would never tolerate the calling out of federal troops without his consent and he would rather see Texas secede from the Union than put up with it. And he allegedly concluded, "Though the order was given by a Democratic president, who is the chief of the party to which I belong, my spirit revolts at it. My heart sickens at the thought of the consequences."⁵

Hogg's enemies had a field day with this story. Anti-Hogg newspapers like the Dallas *News* and the San Antonio *Express* accused him of "truculence" and "boorishness" and even sedition and treason. The governor was at first taken aback by the virulence of these attacks, but with characteristic vigor he quickly recovered and went on the offensive. On August 1, 1894, in San Antonio, he delivered a major address that clarified his position. Asserting that he had been deliberately misquoted, Hogg described what had actually happened and repeated what he had actually said at the encampment. He continued with an analysis of the federal system, in which he emphasized the Jeffersonian notion of a national government of limited powers and the people's capacity for self-government. He then analyzed Cleveland's actions, repeated his disagreement with them, and pointed out that the president could have set a dangerous precedent. And yet, he concluded, all should know that Texas and its governor, while upholding constitutional liberty, would always stand by and defend the Stars and Stripes. This effort more or less ended the controversy (although, if Hogg had not been near the end of his term, the papers would probably have continued their assaults); in any case, the governor had done well. Upon reading the speech, John P. Altgeld wrote to Hogg to offer his compliments and congratulations. He said, "The country must in the end sustain this position or else free institutions are at an end."⁶

James Stephen Hogg was one of Texas' few truly great governors. Not only was he courageous and skillful in the conduct of political affairs, more importantly he recognized the needs of his times. He saw that the people alone could not effectively defend their interests against the rapidly growing power of corporate wealth; they needed the assistance of the state through the creation of regulatory laws and agencies. Yet, Hogg was no radical. He believed in private enterprise and had no desire to impede legitimate growth and development. In fact, he saw clearly, long before those in the business world did, that they too would benefit from regulation through the elimination of cutthroat competition and other detrimental business practices. Hogg deserves to be remembered as a harbinger of change; one who recognized that rapid economic growth and development would inevitably produce major social and political changes and who attempted to chart a course that would allow government and society to deal with these changes effectively. His administration was significant because it marked a watershed between the conservative elements that had controlled state politics after Reconstruction and the progressives who would dominate after the turn of the century.

Committed though he was to public service, Hogg was also a devoted family man. He and Sarah Ann Stinson were married in 1874, and they had four children: Will (1875–1930), Ima (1882–1975), Mike (1885–1941), and Tom (1887–1949); all of whom were well-loved by both their parents. It has often been suggested that the Hoggs's behavior in naming their only daughter Ima was peculiar; however, their intent was anything but strange. The child was named after the heroine of a novel, *The Fate of Marvin,* written by Hogg's beloved older brother Tom, in 1873. Truly peculiar, even bizarre, is the myth that the Hoggs had a second daughter whom they named Ura. Even though no such person ever existed, there are still many people in Texas who insist that she did.

The death in 1895 of his wife, Sarah, devastated Hogg. In his grief he wrote to his sister Julia: "My feelings overcome me. She never spoke an unkind word to me and I never had to account to others for a word or act of hers. God knows that if all men were so blessed earth would be like heaven. My ambition is to raise my children after her model. If I succeed the world will be much better for it."[7]

He succeeded beyond his fondest dreams. All four of his children grew to adulthood as substantial citizens with highly developed feelings for their civic responsibilities. Hogg had left office a poor man, but through his connections he was able to amass a large fortune, mostly through land deals and oil, during the last ten years of his life.

After his death the children used a substantial portion of the proceeds from his estate to support education and many other humanitarian efforts. Indeed, Ima was for many years, even after World War II, one of the leading philanthropists in the state.

In January, 1905, while on a business trip, Hogg was severely injured in a railroad accident and never fully recovered. He expired in his sleep on the morning of March 3, 1906, at the age of fifty-four, still a comparatively young man. Only the night before he had commented that he wanted no monument or statue. "Let my children plant at the head of my grave a pecan tree and at my feet an old-fashioned walnut tree. And when these trees shall bear, let the pecans and the walnuts be given out to the plain people so that they may plant them and make Texas a land of trees."[8] On March 5, 1906, the governor was buried beside his wife in Oakwood Cemetery in Austin. His final wishes were followed, but later a handsome statue was also erected in his memory.

CHARLES A. CULBERSON ☆ 1895–99

Charles A. Culberson was born at Dadeville, Alabama, on June 10, 1855; but his parents, David and Eugenia, brought their family to Texas in 1856 to settle in Jefferson, near the Louisiana line. David was a distinguished lawyer and politician, and after serving in the Confederate Army during the Civil War, he was elected to the U.S. Congress, where he served for twenty-two years. When he retired, President McKinley appointed him to the commission to codify the statutes of the United States.

"Charley" Culberson, as he was popularly known, grew up in East Texas but attended college at the Virginia Military Institute and law school at the University of Virginia. Shortly after he returned to East Texas, Culberson was elected to the office of county attorney and, thereby, began his political career. In 1887, he married Ellie Harrison, the daughter of a Fort Worth banker, and moved his law practice to "Cowtown" that same year. He succeeded Governor Hogg in the office of attorney general in 1891.

By 1894, the Democratic party in Texas faced a potential split over the silver question, and its leaders were desperately seeking ways to maintain unity and fend off the challenge of the Republicans and Populists. It was at this point that Culberson decided to run for governor. Among his opponents were Speaker of the House John H. Cochran,

Charles A. Culberson

Comptroller John D. McCall, and Member of Congress S. W. T. Lanham. Culberson was the early leader and had a couple of advantages: he stood with Hogg on most major issues, and he had attracted Col. Edward M. House of Houston to be his campaign manager. House, who would later attain international prominence as friend and adviser to Woodrow Wilson, skillfully directed the campaign and gathered most of Hogg's supporters into an efficient statewide organization. Later, John H. Reagan entered the contest and drew some of Hogg's followers away, but when the state convention endorsed President Cleveland and passed a resolution supporting the coinage of silver only at parity with gold, Reagan withdrew. Culberson was then easily nominated.

During the campaign Culberson reacted to the Populist threat by endorsing free and unlimited coinage of silver, a stance which outraged the Gold Democrats; by this time, however, they had little choice but to continue to support him. In the election Culberson polled 216,373 votes, winning with a plurality over Populist Thomas L. Nugent (159,676 votes), "Regular" Republican W. R. McKeneson (57,147 votes), "Reform" Republican John B. Schmitz (5,304 votes), and Prohibitionist J. M. Dunn (21,295 votes).

Because he did not oppose President Cleveland's use of military force to put down the Pullman strike in Chicago, Culberson lost much of his labor support in Texas, which went over to the Populists. On the other hand, his decision to emphasize his pro-silver views saved him many votes that might also have been lost if he had continued his earlier, lukewarm approach. Moreover, Culberson remained consistent on the silver question. In 1896, he served on a strong pro-silver delegation to the Democratic National Convention, which was committed to the candidacy of Richard P. Bland. This delegation voted for the pro-silver national platform and maintained its support for Bland, even though William Jennings Bryan was eventually nominated.

Back at home the Texas Democrats renominated Culberson for governor, and once again his campaign was engineered by Colonel House (even though House secretly favored the gold standard). In the campaign Culberson defended his administration, during which several important laws had been passed, including statutes that regulated primary elections; revised the antitrust laws to include insurance companies and exempt farm and labor organizations; strengthened the railroad commission and the courts; and set aside land for an African-

American college. In a highly publicized but not critically important move, Culberson also succeeded in banning prizefighting in Texas. When it was announced that the fight for the world heavyweight championship between Robert Fitzsimmons and "Gentleman" James J. Corbett would be held in Dallas in 1895, Culberson announced that such a display of barbarism would not be permitted. When the state supreme court ruled that the governor had no power to stop the fight, he called a special session of the legislature and got the law he wanted.

Culberson knew he was in for a serious fight in 1896 because of the fusion of the Populists and Republicans. Luckily, the Gold Democrats remained loyal, or the outcome might have been disastrous for the party. As it was, Culberson won by 298,528 to 238,692 votes over fusion candidate Jerome C. Kearby.

Early in his second term, Culberson, who still had the support of Colonel House and his powerful organization, announced his candidacy for the U.S. Senate to succeed Roger Q. Mills, whose term was to expire in 1899. During the next year and a half, Mills announced that he wanted reelection, and John H. Reagan also entered the contest. Both eventually withdrew, however – Reagan for reasons of age and health and Mills when he learned that he lacked sufficient support. By the time for the election in the state legislature, Culberson was unopposed. Elected, he remained in the Senate, where he built a reputation as a moderate progressive for twenty-four years. He also gave important support to President Wilson during World War I.

During the last several years of his life, Culberson, confined to a wheelchair, was in ill health. Finally, he was forced to retire from the Senate in 1923 and spent his last days arranging his records and writing his memoirs. He grew rapidly weaker, and on March 18, 1925, he died peacefully in his sleep. In accordance with his wishes, his body was brought back to Texas, where he was buried in the family plot in Fort Worth.

Notes

1. Robert C. Cotner, *James Stephen Hogg: A Biography* (Austin: University of Texas Press, 1959), 310.

2. Ibid., 427.

3. Ibid., 438.

4. Ibid., 379.

5. Ibid., 380.

6. Ibid., 391.

7. Ibid., 461.

8. Ibid., 576–77.

Sources and Further Reading

Alvord, Wayne. "T. L. Nugent, Texas Populist." *Southwestern Historical Quarterly* 57 (1953): 65–81.

Barr, Alwyn. *Reconstruction to Reform: Texas Politics, 1876–1906.* Austin: University of Texas Press, 1971.

Cotner, Robert C. *James Stephen Hogg: A Biography.* Austin: University of Texas Press, 1959.

DeShields, James T. *They Sat in High Places: The Presidents and Governors of Texas.* San Antonio: The Naylor Company, 1940.

Finty, Tom, Jr. *Anti-Trust Legislation in Texas.* Galveston: A. H. Belo and Company, 1916.

Gambrell, H. P. "James Stephen Hogg: Statesman or Demagogue?" *Southwest Review* 13 (1928): 338–66.

Hughes, Pollyanna B., and Elizabeth B. Harrison. "Charles A. Culberson: Not a Shadow of Hogg." *East Texas Historical Journal* 11 (1973): 41–52.

Martin, Roscoe C. *The Peoples' Party in Texas: A Study in Third Party Politics.* Austin: University of Texas, 1933.

Norvell, J. R. "The Railroad Commission of Texas: Its Origin and History." *Southwestern Historical Quarterly* 68 (1965): 465–80.

Phares, Ross. *The Governors of Texas.* Gretna, La.: Pelican Publishing Company, 1976.

Richardson, R. N. *Colonel Edward M. House: The Texas Years, 1858–1912.* Abilene: Abilene Printing and Stationery Company, 1964.

Chapter nine

PROGRESSIVISM AND WORLD WAR I
1899–1921

D uring the early twentieth century, the Texas political scene was dominated by debates over both the influence of Sen. Joseph Weldon Bailey and Prohibition. Bailey was a conservative who was thought by many to have been involved in an unethical and perhaps illegal relationship with the Waters-Pierce Oil Company. His apologists argued that he had done nothing wrong and that all the charges against him were politically motivated. Bailey, who was never found guilty of anything, temporarily retired from politics in 1912, but the controversy left Democratic party unity battered for a considerable period of time. Prohibition, even more a divisive issue, was debated extensively in practically every campaign between the turn of the century and World War I, and was only partially settled by the ratification of the Eighteenth Amendment. In the midst of this political turmoil there were substantial gains effected by some progressive reformers, most notably under Gov. Thomas M. Campbell. Even Jim Ferguson made some proposals for reform early in his administration, but his reformist efforts were terminated by his dispute with the University of Texas and subsequent impeachment. After that his influence served largely to hurt causes rather than help them.

World War I had a profound effect on Texas. The declaration of hostilities against Germany in 1917 received overwhelming approval, and people threw themselves into supporting the cause with willful determination. There were noticeable effects on Texas society, as thousands of soldiers trained in four large camps scattered about the state, and nearly 200,000 Texans joined the armed forces. The war impacted the state's economy as well, and inflation forced the cost of living to soar beyond advancing incomes. The demands on the state's purse also increased dramatically, with appropriations soaring from $13 million to $27 million between 1913 and 1919. Thus, many people during the period felt a pinch in spite of general prosperity.

Significant social changes during the period included Prohibition, which finally triumphed as a direct result of the war, women's suffrage, and increased employment opportunities. On the other hand, the state experienced a dramatic rise in racial and ethnic intolerance. African Americans found themselves the objects of harsh discrimination in spite of their patriotic contributions to the war effort, and German Americans were often unjustly accused of disloyalty. In one of the most absurd manifestations of xenophobia, Gov. William P. Hobby actually vetoed the appropriations for the German Department at the University of Texas in 1919.

The governors during this period were Joseph D. Sayers, 1899–1903; Samuel W. T. Lanham, 1903–07; Thomas M. Campbell, 1907–11; Oscar B. Colquitt, 1911–15; James E. Ferguson, 1915–17; and William P. Hobby, 1917–21.

JOSEPH D. SAYERS ☆ 1899–1903

The man who would be Texas' first governor of the twentieth century was born at Grenada, Mississippi, on September 23, 1841. His parents were Dr. David Sayers and Mary T. Sayers, and two years after his birth, William, a brother, was born. Mary Sayers died in 1851, and soon thereafter the doctor and his two sons migrated to Texas, where they settled in Bastrop. The boys received their education there at the Bastrop Military Institute.

In 1861, Joe Sayers joined the 5th Texas Regiment, a cavalry unit led by the famous Tom Green. He saw his first action at the Battle of Val Verde, New Mexico, in February, 1862, where he distinguished himself by his bravery. Colonel Green was so impressed by Sayers's coolness under fire while attacking and capturing an artillery battery that he recommended him for promotion. Sayers and his company returned to Texas in May, 1862, and then were sent to Louisiana. There, during the Battle of Camp Bisland in April, 1863, Sayers was severely wounded. Again commended for his bravery, Sayers was promoted to the rank of major and became Green's chief-of-staff. At the Battle of Mansfield in April, 1864, he was wounded again. After Green was killed at the Battle of Blair's Landing, Sayers, still recovering from his injuries, joined the staff of Gen. Richard Taylor and served as his assistant adjutant until the end of the war.

Soon after his return to Texas, Sayers opened a school and simultaneously studied law. After his admission to the bar, he formed a partnership with G. "Wash" Jones. His entry into politics came near the end of Reconstruction as a senator in the thirteenth legislature (1873), where he participated in the process of reversing most of the legislation passed during the last days of the Davis administration. From 1875 to 1878, Sayers chaired the Texas State Democratic Executive Committee, and in this capacity he presided over the state conventions of 1876 and 1878. At the latter gathering, Sayers was nominated for lieutenant governor on the ticket with Oran M. Roberts. During the Roberts administration, Sayers and the governor differed on land policy. Consistent throughout his public career on this issue, Sayers always believed that the public lands should be saved for homesteaders and the support of schools, not sold cheaply to speculators as an immediate source of revenue.

Sayers was elected to Congress in 1884 and served there until he ran for governor in 1898. As chief executive of the state he was not generally known as a reformer; still, there were a few progressive measures passed during his administration, most notably those involving labor. In 1899, unions were exempted from the antitrust laws, and in 1901, blacklists were outlawed. Also during Sayers's administration the state increased expenditures on education, the prisons, and social service institutions; railroad rebates were outlawed; the antitrust laws were

Joseph D. Sayers

upgraded; and there was legislation passed authorizing the creation of school districts.

There were an unusual number of natural disasters while Sayers was at the helm of the Texas government. In 1899, there came the great Brazos River flood, and in 1900, the most destructive hurricane ever recorded struck Galveston. A severe drought struck many portions of the state, and the boll weevil began to appear, creating widespread destruction in the cotton fields. After the flood and the storm, millions of dollars in assistance poured into the state. Sayers administered the distribution of this relief honestly and fairly, and thereby added substantially to his reputation as a man of integrity by his efforts.

Though he remained in public service after leaving office in 1903, Sayers focused primarily on his law practice. At various times during the next quarter of a century, he served on the University of Texas Board of Regents, the industrial accident board, the state board of legal advisers, and the pardon board. He died on May 15, 1929, and is buried at Bastrop.

SAMUEL W. T. LANHAM ☆ 1903–07

Samuel Willis Tucker Lanham was born in South Carolina on July 4, 1846. He was only fifteen when the Civil War broke out, but he volunteered for the service and fought throughout the conflict, mostly in Virginia. He married immediately after the war, and he and his wife set out for Texas and settled in Weatherford, where Lanham began to work and study law. He was admitted to the bar in 1869 and soon thereafter was appointed district attorney. In this job his most famous case was the prosecution of Big Tree and Satanta, the Kiowa chiefs who led the raid on the Warren wagon train in 1871.

In 1892, Lanham was elected to Congress and served for a decade until his race for governor. Like Culberson and Sayers before him, Lanham had the support of Col. Edward M. House and his friends, which helped Lanham's cause substantially. Established in office in January, 1903, he was the last ex-Confederate to serve as governor of Texas.

Like Sayers, Lanham was a polished, genteel, high-minded gentleman, but he was no reformer. Still, there were some progressive gains during his administration, and he did not oppose them once they passed the legislature. These included a 1903 statute limiting the working hours of railroad employees and improving safety regulations on

Samuel W. T. Lanham

street railways. The same year also saw the passage of a law regulating child labor, a step in the direction of badly needed reform, though it was never adequately enforced. Lanham's term also saw the creation of a state banking system. State banks had been explicitly prohibited by the Constitution of 1876, but in 1904, the voters approved an amendment that changed the law. The following year the legislature created the state insurance and banking commission, and Thomas B. Love was named director. During the ensuing five years, Love and his colleagues supervised the creation of more than five hundred banks.

In 1905, Lanham took the lead in tax revision. For years the general property tax had provided most of the state's income, but by the turn of the century, valuations for tax purposes lagged far behind needs. Hence, in response to the governor's request, the legislature raised taxes on the intangible assets of railroads and other industries and passed laws imposing tax levies on the gross receipts of express companies and pipelines.

In addition, Lanham's term featured the revision of the state's election system. Before 1903, there was no set procedure for nominating candidates for public office. Some counties used primaries, or some type of convention, and there was considerable abuse and fraud: at times unscrupulous officials would fail to advertise the time and place of conventions; in other cases, the dates for primary elections were announced in a confusing fashion; and in all cases, there was considerable ballot-box fraud.

During Lanham's administration, the first serious effort was made to remedy some of these problems. Two laws were passed by the legislature, one in 1903 and another in 1905, designed to regulate both primary and general elections. Both laws were named after Judge Alexander W. Terrell, their author. The first law, which provided simply that political parties could choose to nominate candidates by means of either a convention or a primary election, was not particularly effective. The second law, however, was much more complex. It set forth voter qualifications, required candidates to file itemized statements of expenditures, required primary elections for major parties (in Texas this meant only the Democratic party), and set the date for primaries. Finally, it required that precinct and county candidates could be determined by the results of the first primary, but that a second primary, a runoff, might be called to decide between the two leading candidates. District and state candidates were still to be chosen by convention. The rules laid down in the "Terrell Election Laws" were modified over the next few years. In 1907, a new law required that all candidates receiving the highest number of votes in a primary should be considered the party's nominees. Six years later, a new provision was added that required a runoff election between the two leaders if no one received a majority of the votes in the first primary. In 1918, this provision was extended to all district and state elections.

In some ways, these reforms made the electoral system more democratic, but there were still major problems with it. The poll tax, imposed in 1902, discouraged the poor, especially African Americans, from voting; but worse, as the primary system evolved it was effectively closed to African-American voters who were, thus, denied any voice in the election process. It was not until 1944 that the U.S. Supreme Court outlawed "all-white" primaries, and not until 1966 that it struck down the poll tax.

There was some improvement in the areas of public service and education during the Lanham years. An institute for the prevention of rabies opened in 1903, and the Abilene State Hospital for Epileptics opened in 1904. Public education benefited from the earlier creation of independent school districts, which were taxing entities. By 1904, nearly 90 percent of the school districts in the state were collecting local property taxes, but the positive effects were seen mostly in the towns. Rural schools continued to lag far behind.

Finally, the Bailey controversy exploded during the Lanham administration. This related to an antitrust action initiated in 1897, when state officials brought suit against the Waters-Pierce Oil Company, the Texas subsidiary of Standard Oil. They secured a court ruling that revoked the company's license to do business in Texas and was upheld by the U.S. Supreme Court in 1900. Claiming to have severed all ties with Standard, Waters-Pierce secured a new license, but another suit brought by the state in 1905 revealed that Standard owned most of the stock in the company. The state then secured a court order for ouster, and the corporation was hit with a large fine.

Meanwhile, during the first court battle in 1900, Joseph Weldon Bailey, then a candidate for the U.S. Senate, had urged Governor Sayers to allow Waters-Pierce to return to the state. At the same time he represented the company in certain legal matters and borrowed money from Henry Clay Pierce, the company's manager. When this relationship became known in 1905, it triggered a major controversy in which the state was sharply divided into pro- and anti-Bailey camps. Bailey, declaring that the whole thing was a political conspiracy, was re-elected to the Senate in 1906 and controlled the delegation to the Democratic National Convention in 1908. Yet, the controversy over his alleged ethics violations raged on, and he retired from public life in 1912.

Amid all these developments, Sam Lanham did not enjoy serving as governor and often expressed the wish that he had stayed in Congress. As he put it, "office seekers, pardon seekers, and concession seekers overwhelmed me. They broke my health."[1] After leaving office, Lanham retired to Weatherford, where, broken in health and spirit and devastated over the death of his wife, he died on July 19, 1908. He is buried at Weatherford.

THOMAS M. CAMPBELL ☆ 1907–11

Thomas Mitchell Campbell was born on April 22, 1856, in Cherokee County, near Rusk. His father, Thomas Duncan Campbell, had come to Texas from Alabama in 1855. The family was not wealthy, and Thomas Duncan was barely able to eke out a living by farming and doing various odd jobs. The Civil War affected the Campbell family directly, for Thomas Duncan enlisted to fight for the Confederacy, leaving his wife, Rachel, at home with several small children. Thomas Mitchell thus became the man of the house at the age of five, and when Rachel died in 1864, the children were left practically destitute until Thomas Duncan returned the following year.

During the ensuing five years Thomas Mitchell helped his father on the farm and attended classes sporadically at the Rusk Male and Female Academy. In 1870, Thomas Duncan remarried, and the family moved to Longview seeking greater opportunities. Lumber and agriculture were the principal industries there, but far more important to the economic development of the area were the railroads. Both the Texas and Pacific and the Houston and Great Northern built lines into Longview in the early 1870s, and the town flourished. The elder Campbell entered politics during this period, becoming mayor of Longview in 1871 and being elected to the county court in 1873.

Meanwhile, Thomas Mitchell attempted to secure a better education. He attended the Rusk Masonic Institute in 1873 and began work in law school at Trinity University in 1874. He was admitted to the bar in 1875, and that same year, on Christmas Eve, he married Fannie

Thomas M. Campbell

Brewer of Shreveport. Settling in Longview, young Campbell began his law practice and his family. During the next ten years, he and Fannie had five children, and Campbell developed a respectable practice. He also entered politics, and in February, 1889, he was named master of chancery by his friend, Atty. Gen. James S. Hogg, to oversee the affairs of the financially troubled International and Great Northern Railroad.

Campbell's relationship with the railroad company was to last for several years and would affect his career dramatically. After serving as master of chancery for two years, he became receiver for the company in 1891. Acting in that capacity, he handled the financial affairs of the railroad subject to litigation. He managed or disposed of company property as directed by judicial decree, and he worked feverishly to save the line from bankruptcy. He not only succeeded in this endeavor, he gained a reputation for high moral standards and ethics in the process.

In 1893, the Gould family, owners of the International and Great Northern, asked Campbell to become general manager. He served effectively in that capacity, but made the Goulds unhappy when he openly supported the presidential aspirations of William Jennings Bryan in 1896. The following year he resigned and returned to private law practice in Palestine; in the meantime, he had become increasingly more active in politics as a reform Democrat, and in 1886, he served on the platform and resolutions committee of the party. Four years later he campaigned vigorously on behalf of James Hogg in the latter's successful race for governor. Throughout the 1890s, he gained a reputation as both an effective campaigner and a party loyalist, and he became associated with the party machine directed by Col. Edward M. House. Even though Campbell and House were not always on the best of terms, this association usually worked to Campbell's advantage.

Campbell's first try for public office came in 1902 when, with Hogg's blessing, he sought the Democratic gubernatorial nomination. Unfortunately, he did not seek House's blessing as well and so lost out to S. W. T. Lanham; but Campbell swallowed his pride, campaigned for Lanham, and thereby regained the good graces of the machine. In 1906, his loyalty and determination finally paid off when he became the Democratic nominee for governor. With the support of the machine as well as many old line Populists, Campbell waged a vigorous campaign, calling for democracy, honesty in government, tax revision, better support for education, control of big business (especially the railroads), and support for the farmers and workers. He took a moderate position on the liquor question, favoring local option rather than statewide prohibition.

Campbell's opponents in the primary were Railroad Commissioner Oscar B. Colquitt, former Atty. Gen. Charles K. Bell, and Court of Criminal Appeals Judge M. M. Brooks, all more conservative than the front-runner. Campbell faced an uphill battle, but with a well-organized, loyal campaign staff and the enthusiastic support of such groups as the Farmers' Union, the State Federation of Labor, and the Texas Federation of Women's Clubs, he emerged as the leading contender (though he lacked a clear majority). At the state convention, where he secured the support of Sen. Joseph Weldon Bailey, Campbell was nominated on the first ballot.

The general election in November, 1906, was a mere formality, and Campbell won easily. He was inaugurated on January 15, 1907, and he embarked upon a demanding crusade to effect major social, economic, and political changes and, thereby, to usher Texas into the twentieth century. During the next four years, he would encourage and approve far-reaching legislation that would affect business, the railroads, prisons, natural resources, health, education, and the general welfare of the state.

After a lengthy struggle to curb the abuses of the railroad companies, Governor Hogg had finally succeeded in creating the railroad commission in 1891. This effort, important as it was, was only a first step. By 1907, it was clear to most reformers, including Governor Campbell, that more extensive regulation was needed. Hence, he supported proposals in the legislature to limit the working day of railroad employees and to require full crews on all runs. He also supported additional legislation that required the railroads to furnish sufficient track, switches, yards, depots, and other facilities. The governor and the lawmakers did not agree on all issues, however. Campbell favored the reduction of passenger fares from 3 cents to 2 cents per mile, while the legislative leaders were willing to settle for 2.5 cents. At length a compromise bill on passenger rates was submitted, and though it failed, the legislature did empower the railroad commission to lower freight rates.

A dispute over the merger issue also arose. There was a bill in 1907 that would have allowed the Santa Fe Railroad to purchase other lines. The bill passed after considerable debate, but Campbell, generally opposed to consolidation, vetoed it, saying it fostered monopoly. He found there was not enough support in the legislature to sustain his veto, and, though it was overridden, this was by no means the end of the merger debate. In 1909, still arguing that consolidation went against sound public policy, Campbell vetoed a bill that would have allowed the Wichita Falls Railway Company to buy two neighboring lines, and this time he prevailed. Campbell also supported and signed the Claim Bill of 1910, which provided that anyone purchasing a railroad company was liable for all unsecured debts.

The governor and the legislature devoted considerable attention to railroad safety and passed laws requiring basic safety equipment, such as power brakes, automatic couplers, grab irons, handholds, and foot stirrups on all trains. They also initiated worker's compensation, employer liability, and more rigorous equipment inspection laws, as well as additional laws affecting the working hours of engineers and conductors and the level of safety and comfort in train depots.

To the public, one of the most obnoxious abuses committed by the railroads was the creation of the free pass system. Viewed by the reformers as an obvious form of discrimination and corruption, the practice of giving free passes to public officials had long been a subject for complaint. After considerable debate, in March, 1907, the legislature approved a measure prohibiting free passes and providing for substantial fines or even imprisonment for violations.

Big Business also attracted Campbell's attention. Between 1907 and 1909, he and his legislative allies promoted antitrust legislation, tax revision, and the regulation of insurance companies, banking, and lobbyists. Reformers in Texas were particularly concerned about the tendency toward monopoly in the lumber, beef, oil, and communications industries. Hoping to hand state government more power to regulate these businesses, the reformers passed legislation that permitted the attorney general to examine financial records, forced company officials to appear in court, and provided stiff penalties for failure to cooperate with authorized agents of the state. Armed with these new laws, the state won some impressive legal victories, including judgments against the Waters-Pierce Oil Company, the Fort Worth Live Stock Exchange, International Harvester, the Wichita Mill & Elevator Company, Security Oil, and the Standard Mutual Fire Insurance Company. Antitrust prosecutions between 1907 and 1909 netted the state nearly two million dollars in fines and penalties.

Campbell's views on taxation were far ahead of their time. He believed in adequate public support for state services, such as education, and he thought the graduated income tax should be the primary source of state revenue. Early in his administration, he proposed a new fiscal system to include an income tax and a property tax based on full value. The legislature was not ready to support the income tax idea in 1907 (nor is it in 1995, for that matter), but it did support property tax reform. In the face of substantial conservative opposition, progressives passed a new property tax measure styled the "full rendition law" that revised assessment procedures and created a new tax board empowered to set rates. It also established the franchise fee system and imposed additional levies on communications, transportation, public utilities, and insurance companies. These new procedures excited considerable opposition, but they also increased state revenues.

The behavior of insurance companies in Texas had always been suspect, and the legislature enacted several important insurance reforms under Campbell's leadership. Foremost among them was the creation of the Texas Department of Insurance and Banking with Thomas B. Love as the first insurance commissioner. In an effort to provide for the stability of insurance companies, the legislature also passed the Robertson Law. Proposed by Rep. James H. Robertson, this measure required that all incorporated stock and mutual companies invest 75 percent of their revenues in Texas and that all out-of-state companies post bonds and sureties. In addition to the Robertson Law, the solons provided for the creation of the state fire insurance rating board to ensure that premiums were just and reasonable. Of course, representatives of the insurance industry loudly protested all these reforms, howling that their business would be destroyed, but Campbell and his backers stuck to their guns, and during the next few years, the insurance industry was materially strengthened. By 1914, the amount of capital invested by insurance companies in Texas had increased by more than twenty-four million dollars.

Campbell and his reformers also sought to overhaul the antiquated state banking system. The demand for change was especially acute after the panic of 1907, and even though it required overcoming considerable opposition, the legislature finally passed a deposit guarantee bill in May, 1909. It also created a state banking board and provided for the periodic examination of the state's banks.

Lobbyists provided another target for the reformers. Campbell hated lobbyists, calling them "the hired instruments of selfish schemes," and he badly wanted to curtail their activities. The legislature responded to his wishes by passing several laws between 1907 and 1909. One required that no inducement save "reason" could be utilized when a paid lobbyist negotiated with a state official, and another prohibited corporate donations to political parties and campaigns. A third law prohibited business contributions that might influence the outcome of a vote on an issue submitted to the public.

When Campbell entered office in 1907, the state's prison system was in a catastrophic condition. Living conditions in state facilities were appalling, unspeakable abuses were committed on contract work farms, and there were practically no controls imposed upon the behavior of prison employees. Campbell became the first governor in decades to attempt serious reforms in these areas. He declared that contract labor should not be used to enrich selfish individuals or corporations, and he pledged to do what he could to abolish the contract labor system. The governor initiated a policy that would gradually shift inmates from private to state-owned work projects, and he requested funds from the legislature to overhaul dilapidated prison facilities, such as those at Rusk. Slowly improvements became apparent so that in early 1910, Superintendent J. C. Herring could cautiously report that "improvements as to food and conditions continue, . . . [but] much needs to be done."[2] That year the recently appointed board of prison commissioners released a report stating that cruelty toward prisoners was still the rule, not the exception, and that it had to be stopped. Also, most prison facilities were still primitive at best and required major upgrades; and, although contract labor had been reduced, it nevertheless continued under appalling conditions.

On the basis of this report, Campbell called a special session of the legislature to deal with these issues. Meeting in August, 1910, the legislators set to work, and by September, they had prepared a bill that completely restructured the prison system. It abolished contract labor, placed the system under the control of an appointed commission, made prison officials responsible for the living conditions and safety of their facilities, prohibited unauthorized or excessively cruel punishment, required generally humane treatment of prisoners, and required special facilities and treatment for female prisoners. This law proved to be a watershed, and after it had been in effect for only two years, substantial improvements were noticeable. Still, the prison system was to remain a problem for many years to come because there was no way to monitor "improvements."

Like most progressives, Campbell was interested in the conservation and maintenance of human and natural resources, and he sought both to improve the conditions of workers and farmers and to preserve the bounty of nature. Under his leadership, some gains were made in these areas. The legislature created the bureau of labor statistics and the state mining board, and it enacted numerous safety regulations. It also passed laws protecting the right of workers to strike.

To ease the burdens of Texas' farmers, the progressives created the Texas Department of Agriculture to be headed by a commissioner who would gather and disseminate useful information. This agency began its work in 1907 and was soon providing services to farmers that county agents would later be responsible for. On the economic side, Campbell undertook to regulate the commodities market, and in 1907, he approved the "anti-bucket shop" law, which curtailed the activities of unscrupulous speculators.

With respect to conservation, Campbell was clearly a disciple of Theodore Roosevelt. He appointed delegates to the inland waterways commission and the National Irrigation and Conservation congresses, and he read their reports with interest. At home he was particularly concerned about the problems caused by floods, the depletion of the state's forests, and the endangerment of many species of wildlife. After Campbell's prodding the legislature passed the State Levee and Drainage Act, which stimulated reclamation projects. Other provisions of the law required state officials to cooperate with federal agencies in the regulation of the state's rivers and their basins for future projects. As to the problems of wildlife, Campbell's friends in the legislature amended the game, fish, and oyster law in such a way as to expand the powers of the wildlife commission. They also limited hunting seasons and prohibited certain techniques, such as the poisoning and dynamiting of fish.

Campbell was concerned about the quality of education in Texas, which was very low. He promoted increases in the *ad valorem* taxes and salaries for teachers and lengthened the school term from four to six months. During his administration the state also set up kindergartens, established a new teachers' college at Canyon, and, perhaps most importantly of all, passed the uniform schoolbook law. His concern for children also drove Campbell to seek reform of the juvenile delinquency laws. This resulted in the enactment of measures to provide for the separate treatment of youthful offenders and the establishment of rehabilitation programs. Campbell also induced lawmakers to provide funds for the improvement of the state orphan home at Corsicana and to outline new procedures for the regulation of foster homes.

Likewise, the needs of the mentally ill came under the scrutiny of the reformers. They increased appropriations for the state mental hospitals and began the long process of providing for more humane treatment. Some sick and disabled Texans also benefited from Campbell's leadership as state institutions for the deaf, blind, and those with certain diseases like epilepsy and leprosy were improved. The reformers failed to deal constructively with tuberculosis, however, though this dread malady was spreading at an alarming rate. Yet, Campbell was vitally concerned for the general health needs of the state. He called for measures to deal with the prevention and control of communicable diseases, and he demanded more effective regulation of the medical profession. As a result, the legislature created the state board of medical examiners, the state board of pharmacy, and the state board of nursing examiners. Even more significant was the creation of the state board of health in 1909, for this agency gathered and disseminated information and statistics and studied the prevention of disease.

During the 1907–1909 period, the legislature also passed the Pure Food and Drug Act. This law provided for the implementation of a state food and dairy commission to regulate the purity and quality of all products marketed for human consumption. Feeling that alcohol also constituted a health problem, the reformers under Campbell enacted legislation to restrict the sale and consumption of liquor, but their efforts to implement statewide Prohibition failed.

When Campbell left office in January, 1911, he could point with pride to a remarkable record. He had fostered the passage of scores of laws that met the demands of reformers from practically every walk of life; this governor had been a true progressive. He returned to Palestine, where he intended to live quietly and practice law, but the allure of politics was still too great. For the next several years Campbell participated actively in state affairs as an advocate of Prohibition, and in 1912, he worked hard at the state level to ensure the election of Woodrow Wilson for president. Following that success, he sought to get more Texans appointed to federal offices.

In 1914, Campbell joined with the Prohibitionist forces to prevent the election of James E. "Pa" Ferguson as governor, but their efforts failed. Two years later he sought the Democratic nomination for the

U.S. Senate, but here also he failed. This proved to be his last bid for public office, for soon his health began to decline. He learned that he had leukemia in early 1923, and on April 1 of that year he died at the age of sixty-six. He is buried at Palestine.

OSCAR B. COLQUITT ☆ 1911–15

Oscar Branch Colquitt was born at Camilla, Georgia, on December 16, 1861. His mother's family had been among the original settlers there, and his father's people arrived after the American Revolution. The Colquitts were prominent in Georgia politics: one uncle was a U.S. senator before the Civil War, and another was governor just after the conflict and later a U.S. senator as well. Colquitt's father, who served as an officer in the Confederate Army, was a planter and lawyer in Mitchell County. After the war he invested in land and attempted to farm using freed slaves as laborers, but the weather destroyed his crops and he lost everything.

Attempting to make a new start, the Colquitt family migrated to Texas in 1878 and settled near Dangerfield in Morris County. For three years Colquitt worked as a tenant farmer, after which time he moved into town and worked at various jobs until, in 1881, he became a printer's devil at the Morris County *Banner*. This launched his career in journalism, and within a few months Colquitt's employer opened a new paper at Greenville where Colquitt worked until 1884, when he bought his own small paper, the Pittsburgh *Gazette*. Two years later he purchased two newspapers in Terrell, the *Times* and the *Star*, and consolidated them into one enterprise, the *Times-Star*. He operated this paper until 1890, when he sold it to enter politics.

Colquitt was an outspoken Hogg supporter in 1890 and worked vigorously in favor of the railroad commission proposal. He also ran for the state senate in that year and was elected over William H. H. Murray, who would later be better known as "Alfalfa Bill" when he served as governor of Oklahoma in the 1930s. After four years in the senate, Colquitt served briefly in the office of the state revenue agency and then became a member of the Texas Tax Commission. In 1902, he was elected to the railroad commission and was reelected in 1908. While serving on the commission, he was instrumental in promoting the construction of the Galveston Causeway.

Colquitt's first attempt to run for governor came in 1906, when he

Oscar B. Colquitt

entered the primary race against Thomas M. Campbell, Charles K. Bell, and Judge M. M. Brooks. In this contest Campbell had the support of the Hogg people, while Brooks was known to have had the support of Sen. Joseph Weldon Bailey. All four candidates criticized the trusts and called for tax reduction (while simultaneously demanding more generous support for state institutions), but Colquitt was the only outspoken opponent of Prohibition and, perhaps because of this position, ran third in the field.

The year of 1910 was to be Colquitt's year. His opponents in the primary election were Robert V. Davidson, then state attorney general, Judge William Poindexter of Cleburne, a well-known jurist, and Cone Johnson of Tyler. Both Colquitt and Poindexter sought the support of Senator Bailey's friends, while Johnson and Davidson were anti-Bailey. Poindexter and Johnson were "dry" (or Prohibitionists), while Colquitt and Davidson were "wet" (or anti-Prohibition), and all four candidates campaigned around the entire state, each seemingly confident of victory.

Without a doubt, Prohibition was a major issue in the campaign, and Colquitt found himself severely criticized from some quarters because of his stance on it. One minister, the Rev. George C. Rankin, was particularly harsh in his attacks on Colquitt. Rankin denounced Colquitt for being on good terms with the liquor interests and claimed that he drank beer on Sunday. On the other hand, there were groups who praised Colquitt for his stand, including the Anti-Statewide Prohibition Organization headed by Col. Jacob F. Wolters, the German-American Alliance, and the Texas Staatsverbund, organizations which were to aid Colquitt materially in his ultimate victory. The debate over Prohibition was accentuated by the fact that submission was also a question in the campaign. In 1909, the legislature had refused to submit the Prohibition question to a vote of the people, even though a referendum was called for in the Democratic party platform. Now those favoring Prohibition were demanding that the referendum be called, and they waged a vigorous campaign to have their way through the efforts of the Anti-Saloon League. They hoped to unite behind one of Colquitt's opponents in the governor's race but were unable to agree on whom to support.

The results of the election were unusual. Colquitt won the primary and was elected governor, but the Prohibitionists carried a majority in each house of the legislature. Also, the people voted in favor of submission by a substantial margin, 154,601 to 125,809; but later, when the legislature submitted the Prohibition amendment to the people, it was defeated by about 6,000 votes after a vigorous and particularly bitter campaign.

Colquitt's term in office was a particularly stormy one, with the governor and his "wet" supporters in the legislature pitted against the "dry" majority. The two factions frequently made it unpleasant for each other on issues that had nothing to do with the liquor question, and Colquitt often made things even worse than they might have been by his lack of tact. This carried over into his dealings with the federal government on the question of border defense. Twice he sent Rangers to the Mexican border to maintain order, but they had only partial success and were charged with mistreating peaceful Mexican-American citizens. Eventually, federal troops were required to replace them.

In spite of these problems and the fact that Colquitt was no reformer, some notable progressive measures passed the legislature and were signed into law. The legislature enacted reforms in the penal system; a hospital for tuberculosis patients was built; a school for delinquent girls was established; and some important steps benefiting labor were passed, including a child labor law, a factory safety law, a law limiting women's working hours, and most importantly, a worker's compensation act. On the other hand, Colquitt attempted to block some labor legislation, and he vetoed some public school appropriations. This last action caused him to be soundly criticized in some quarters because he had promised in his campaign never to obstruct the support of education.

Despite his vacillation on fulfilling campaign promises, Colquitt continued to have the support of labor during his first term and benefited from the loyalty of the tenant farmers and organizations like the Farmers' Union. One of his most popular moves on behalf of agriculture involved an effort to stabilize the cotton market in 1912. He called a Southern governors' conference to consider the problem, and meeting in New Orleans, this body recommended the creation of state warehouses and acreage reduction. In Texas, the Farmers' Union promoted this effort, and the result was a reduction of two million acres planted in 1912. Subsequently, cotton prices went up, and Colquitt took the credit, even though it is possible that world conditions, not the acreage program, effected this change.

In the 1912 primary, Colquitt was opposed by the well-known and widely respected Judge William F. Ramsey of Cleburne. Ramsey hoped to unite the Prohibitionist forces, which had split their vote in 1910, and thereby defeat Colquitt's bid for reelection. The judge waged a vigorous campaign in which he denounced Colquitt for his policies, his actions, and his lack of morality, and the governor soon realized that he was in for a serious struggle. Colquitt responded to the challenge with a vigorous campaign of his own in which he defended himself mostly by blaming others for the problems of his administration. In the end the governor won by nearly 40,000 votes, but most observers agreed that it was the tradition of giving a governor two terms to prove himself, not Colquitt's record, that had produced the victory.

From 1914 to 1916, Colquitt was pro-German and shortly after he retired from office, he tried to purchase the New York *Sun,* which he planned to operate as an organ of German propaganda. This scheme failed (no doubt in Colquitt's best interests), and he was sorely disappointed at the time. In 1916, he returned to politics and ran for the U.S. Senate, winning the primary election by a substantial margin but suffering defeat at the hands of Senator Culberson in the runoff. He retired to the business world following the election and became president of a Dallas oil firm. In 1928, he supported Herbert Hoover's bid for the presidency and was rewarded with an appointment to the U.S. Board of Mediation, where he remained until Hoover left office in 1929. In 1935, he became a field representative for the Reconstruction Finance Corporation and served in that position until his death on March 8, 1940. He is buried in Oakwood Cemetery at Austin.

JAMES E. FERGUSON ☆ 1915–17

Except for Sam Houston, James E. Ferguson was Texas' most colorful and controversial governor – though for different reasons than the Hero of San Jacinto. Ferguson, known early in his career as "Farmer Jim" and later simply as "Pa," was born near Salado on August 31, 1871. His father died when he was only five, leaving the family, as Ferguson himself put it, "as poor as Job's turkey."[3] At twelve he entered Salado College, a local prep school, but was expelled in 1887. After that he traveled west to seek his fortune, wandering from Texas to California and back again doing odd jobs. Returning to Texas in 1889, he worked on the railroads for six years before he began to study law and gained admission to the bar in 1897. According to a story told later by his daughter Ouida, James was asked no questions at his bar examination because the chair of the committee had been a close friend of his father. After his marriage to Miriam Wallace in 1899, his rise began in Bell County business and financial affairs. In 1907, he moved his family to Temple, opened a bank, and prospered there. By the time he entered politics in 1913, he was worth close to half a million dollars.

Although Ferguson had flitted around the political game for several years, he did not enter it seriously until 1913, when he announced as a candidate for governor. He had never run for any public office and was virtually unknown outside his home county. In his campaign he appealed to tenants, small farmers, and workers, and effectively adopted a folksy style that was to serve him well. That style was something of a charade, however, for Ferguson was quite well-read and could quote Samuel Johnson, Thomas Jefferson, Alexander Hamilton, and Shakespeare on any appropriate occasion. Ferguson enhanced his popularity early in the campaign by announcing that he would veto all legislation dealing with Prohibition and dedicate his administration to more important matters, such as land tenure.

Ferguson's major opponent in the primary was Thomas H. Ball, a well-known Houston attorney. Ball, who had served in Congress from 1897 to 1903, was a veteran of thirty years in politics, and he had the support of the Prohibitionists as well as all the party leaders, President Wilson, William Jennings Bryan, and the press. He asserted that it was ridiculous for Ferguson to say that Prohibition was not an issue, and that, in fact, Ferguson was a "wet" who was supported by the liquor industry. Ball portrayed himself as a Wilson progressive, accusing Ferguson of being out of touch with reality; but Ball and his supporters never fully appreciated the power of Ferguson's appeal. In pursuing issues that were significant to the small farmers and tenants, such as rental rates and income, Ferguson was able to tap a latent source of support, and it carried him to victory: in the July primary he won by more than 40,000 votes, and he was easily swept into office in November.

During his first term, Ferguson promoted a fair number of progressive ideas. He called for legislation to protect children in the work place, prohibit price-fixing on agricultural materials, provide liberally for education, construct highways, and make land more easily available

James E. Ferguson

for purchase by tenant farmers. The legislature responded by passing a compulsory school attendance law and providing for the establishment of rural high schools. It also passed a farm tenant bill that limited rent on Texas farms to one-fourth the value of cotton or one-third the value of grain produced. Never effectively enforced, however, this law was struck down by the courts in 1921.

Ferguson was quite popular at the end of his first term and expected to be easily reelected. He was opposed, however, by Charles H. Morris, a wealthy East Texas banker and avowed Prohibitionist. In the campaign Morris set the cornerstones of his own policies by calling for the reduction of taxes and state expenses while accusing Ferguson of mismanagement and misappropriation of public funds. Morris's specific charges of unethical financial practices were not taken seriously at first and played little role in the outcome of the primary election of 1916, but later they came back to haunt Ferguson.

Morris claimed that Ferguson had used public funds, earmarked for other purposes, to buy groceries; had been secretly financed by a Houston brewery in his 1914 campaign; and had deposited more than $100,000 of the state's money in his (Ferguson's) bank in Temple and had kept it there for a considerable period of time without paying any interest to the state. In was also revealed that Ferguson was deeply in debt to the Temple State Bank, having taken out more than $150,000 in the form of overdrafts. Ferguson admitted that he had purchased groceries for the mansion with state money and, in fact, declared that he would do it again. He either denied or avoided discussing all the other charges, and his defense was accepted by the people. He defeated Morris in the primary election by more than 60,000 votes.

Ferguson's problems began in earnest during his second term, when he became embroiled in controversy with the University of Texas. Although Jim had always been an advocate of education, he made a distinction between the public school and the university. He regarded the latter as elitist and undemocratic, believing that more support should be diverted toward the education of "the masses." Hence, he was ready and willing to do battle with the university, and the occasion to do so arose in 1915, when Ferguson questioned certain aspects of the university's budget request and received unsatisfactory answers. The governor decided that the institution was controlled by an arrogant clique and resolved to purge it. By the spring of 1916, he had focused upon several specific targets, including Acting Pres. William J.

Battle and Faculty Secy. John A. Lomax. When the regents named Robert E. Vinson to the presidency without consulting Ferguson, he became even more disturbed and demanded Vinson's dismissal.

Ferguson's specific charges against the university were based on allegations that some of the faculty had engaged in inappropriate political activities; Battle had lied to him about the appropriations bill; faculty members had padded their expense accounts and forced students to buy books they had written; and the university had several deceased individuals on the active payroll. The regents and the administration made efforts to placate him but to no avail. Ferguson was now obsessed with his desire to humble the university, but as tensions mounted in early 1917, friends of the institution struck back. Based on the allegations made public by Charles H. Morris during the campaign of the previous year, Sen. W. A. Johnson introduced a resolution calling for an investigation of Ferguson's behavior. At first there was opposition to Johnson's proposal, but as Ferguson's war with the university intensified, the opposition faded and a formal investigation was undertaken in March. The inquiry revealed that most of the charges against the governor were true; however, no recommendation for impeachment resulted from the findings. Meanwhile, a resolution, offered by Sen. George W. Dayton and stating that the university had dealt satisfactorily with the charges raised by the governor, was adopted, and everyone assumed that the matter was closed. It was not. For reasons that have never been fully explored or explained, Ferguson vetoed the entire university budget in May, 1917, apparently hoping that he could somehow gain control of the institution as a result. Unfortunately for the governor, his ploy backfired, triggering a broad-based reaction against him that led to his undoing. Speaker of the House F. O. Fuller now threatened to call a special session of the legislature to consider impeachment, but in an effort to head off even greater criticism, Ferguson called one himself.

During the month of August, the Texas house examined all the charges against Ferguson relating to his misuse of state funds and his dispute with the university. Ferguson testified in his own defense and made an excellent presentation; in fact, it appeared for a while that the efforts to impeach him might fail. But then, toward the end of his testimony, he volunteered the information that he had borrowed money from friends to pay off his obligations to the Temple State Bank, and when he was asked to identify his benefactors, he refused. The loan had come, in fact, from Houston brewers, and by refusing to identify them, Ferguson created the impression that he had something to hide. The tide now turned against him: twenty-one articles of impeachment were turned over to the state senate, and Ferguson was put on trial. Once again he testified in his own defense and hurt himself in the process by once more refusing to identify the source of his loan. On September 24, 1917, the senate found the governor guilty on ten counts, and on the same day Ferguson resigned. The senate then issued a ruling that he was forever disqualified from holding public office in Texas again.

Despite his impeachment, James E. Ferguson played an important role in Texas politics for another twenty years. In spite of the censure against him, he ran unsuccessfully for governor in 1918 and for the U.S. Senate in 1922. He continued to insist that his resignation had come before the Texas senate ruling declaring him ineligible for office in the future. More importantly, he was *de facto* governor of the state while his wife was in office for two terms, 1925–27 and 1933–35. Unfortunately, his influence during that long period of time was almost entirely negative. He had begun his political career as a reformer, but his arrogance and rigid behavior had caused his downfall and he became bitter and vindictive thereafter. Ferguson died in 1944, and is buried beside his wife in the state cemetery at Austin.

WILLIAM P. HOBBY ☆ 1917–21

William Pettis Hobby was born at Moscow in Polk County, Texas, on March 26, 1878. His father was Edwin Hobby, who had served in the state senate and later as a judge of the court of appeals. Young Hobby received his education in the Houston public schools, and at the age of seventeen began his career in journalism under the tutelage of Col. R. M. Johnston, publisher of the *Houston Post*. Over the years Hobby advanced until, at length, he became first head of the news department and then managing editor. In 1907, he became publisher and editor of the Beaumont *Enterprise and Journal,* and finding success in this venture, he prospered. He also became interested in politics, and (through his marriage to the daughter of S. B. Cooper, a member of Congress, and his friendships with R. M. Johnson, John H. Kirby, and Frank Andrews) he became aligned with the conservative wing of the Democratic party. Hobby's first venture into elective politics came in 1914, when he was elected lieutenant governor on the same ticket with James E. Ferguson. He served as acting governor while Ferguson was on trial and became governor in his own right when Ferguson resigned on September 24, 1917.

The United States had been at war for six months when Hobby took office, and the Prohibitionists were trying enthusiastically to use the conflict as an excuse to promote their cause. They argued that statewide Prohibition was essential to protect the many young soldiers stationed in Texas from sin and perdition. Great pressure was placed upon Hobby to call a special session to consider the matter. Reluctant at first, he finally gave in and summoned the lawmakers to Austin in late February, 1918. The special session was obviously controlled by the Prohibitionists, and they ratified the Eighteenth Amendment to the U.S. Constitution. They also passed laws to prevent prostitution near army bases and a bill calling for statewide Prohibition; after some hesitation, Hobby signed this last measure into law. During this session the legislators also granted voting rights to women in primary elections.

Jim Ferguson was out of office, but by no means out of politics. He had threatened to run for reelection in 1918 and, despite the legislative prohibition against his holding office, he made good his threat. Since the state executive committee of the Democratic party was still controlled by his friends, they placed his name on the primary ballot. The primary campaign of 1918 was one of the most vicious in the history of the state. All the old charges were trotted out against Ferguson, many prominent leaders opposed him, and the Prohibitionists mounted an especially effective assault. One of the most outrageous charges made against Ferguson was that he had received a controversial $156,500 loan from the German government in exchange for his opposition to the draft. This charge was utterly false, of course, and it prompted Ferguson's brewery friends in Houston to admit that they had provided the money; yet their revelation had no effect on the outcome of the election.

Ferguson, not to be outdone by the Hobby camp, attacked the University of Texas, ridiculing its research work and calling its leaders crooks and grafters. He criticized Hobby for appointing "full-blooded Germans" to office, alleged that the governor was a drunk, and declared that ex-governors Campbell and Colquitt, who supported Hobby, were "ignorant fools." Nevertheless, Hobby easily prevailed in the primary election, overwhelming Ferguson by a vote of 461,479 to 217,021. The people showed little interest in the November election,

William P. Hobby

and there Hobby defeated his Republican opponent by a vote of 148,982 to 26,713.

Addressing the legislature in early 1919, Hobby emphasized the need to support education. He urged a generous appropriation for higher education, higher salaries for public school teachers, and increased state support for small school districts. He also urged the creation of a state fund to support home loans, revision of the jurisdiction of the higher courts, tax levies on oil and gas products, and a convention to revise the constitution of 1876.

There were no great controversies during either the regular session or the four special sessions that followed, but not all of Hobby's recommendations became law. While Hobby was governor, the legislature approved his education proposals, imposed a tax on oil production, and adopted constitutional amendments calling for Prohibition, women's suffrage, a home loan system, and a constitutional convention. On a referendum which followed, Prohibition was approved, but the home loan program and women's suffrage lost. In a separate vote in November, 1919, the people overwhelmingly defeated the proposed constitutional convention.

Hobby declined to run for a second full term in 1920, but he did serve as chair of the Texas delegation to the Democratic National Convention in San Francisco and was vice chair of the entire convention. Returning to his home in 1921, he devoted himself to his newspaper interests in Beaumont and his business interests in Houston. Meanwhile, Governor Pat M. Neff appointed him to the first board of regents of Texas Tech, and he was instrumental in the organization of that institution.

Hobby's first wife died in 1929, and on February 23, 1931, he married Oveta Culp, the daughter of I. W. Culp, a prominent Bell County attorney and politician. She joined in the administration of his business interests and eventually became executive president of the *Houston Post*. Always very active in politics, she was named secretary of health, education, and welfare by President Eisenhower in 1953, and served until 1955, when her husband's failing health prompted her to retire.

Two children were born to the Hobbys, Jesse Oveta and William Pettis Hobby, Jr. Later, Bill Hobby would forge a distinguished record of public service on his own account and served as lieutenant governor from 1973 to 1991. Although the elder Hobby retained an interest in politics throughout his life, he never ran for office again after retiring in 1921. He died on June 6, 1964, and was buried in Glenwood Cemetery at Houston.

Notes

1. James T. DeShields, *They Sat in High Places: The Presidents and Governors of Texas* (San Antonio: The Naylor Company, 1940), 387.

2. Janet Schmelzer, "Reform Was His Battle Cry: Governor Thomas Mitchell Campbell of Texas," unpublished Ph.D diss. (Fort Worth: Texas Christian University, 1982), 123.

3. Ross Phares, *The Governors of Texas* (Gretna, La.: Pelican Publishing Company, 1976), 131–32.

Sources and Further Reading

Acheson, S. *Joe Bailey: The Last Democrat.* Freeport, New York: Books for Libraries Press, 1932.

Anders, Evan. *Boss Rule in South Texas: The Progressive Era.* Austin: University of Texas Press, 1982.

Clark, James A., with Weldon Hart. *The Tactful Texan: A Biography of Governor Will Hobby.* New York: Random House, 1958.

Cumberland, C. C. "Border Raids in the Lower Rio Grande Valley, 1915." *Southwestern Historical Quarterly* 57 (1954): 285–311.

Gould, Lewis L. *Progressives and Prohibitionists: Texas Democrats in the Wilson Era.* Austin: University of Texas Press, 1973.

———. "The University Becomes Politicized: The War with Jim Ferguson, 1915–1918." *Southwestern Historical Quarterly* 86 (1982): 255–76.

McKay, Seth A. *Texas Politics, 1906–1944.* Lubbock: Texas Tech Press, 1952.

Nalle, Ouida F. *The Fergusons of Texas.* Austin: Naylor, 1946.

Phares, Ross. *The Governors of Texas.* Gretna, La.: Pelican Publishing Company, 1976.

Schmelzer, Janet. "Reform Was His Battle Cry: Governor Thomas Mitchell Campbell of Texas." Unpublished Ph.D diss. Fort Worth: Texas Christian University 1982.

———. "Thomas M. Campbell: Progressive Governor of Texas." *Red River Valley Historical Review* 3 (1978): 52–64.

Steen, Ralph. "The Ferguson War on the University of Texas." *Southwestern Social Science Quarterly* 35 (1955): 356–62.

Tinsley, James A. "The Progressive Movement in Texas." Ph.D. diss., University of Wisconsin, 1953.

Chapter ten

THE TWENTIES

1921–31

Three issues dominated politics in Texas during the Jazz Age: the Ku Klux Klan, Prohibition, and "Fergusonism." For a time the Klan practically controlled Democratic party politics, and most state elections featured at least one candidate for major office backed by that organization. In 1922, a Klan candidate, Earle B. Mayfield, was actually sent to the U.S. Senate.

Jim Ferguson held no office during this period, but his wife Miriam served as governor for one term and ran for the office on two other occasions. The Fergusons represented a paradox: in spite of obvious ethics violations throughout their career, they continued to be immensely popular with many people, especially small farmers and workers. Their implacable hostility to the Klan also contributed to their popularity, but the Fergusons were by no means reformers. There were some real efforts, most notably by Governors Neff and Moody, to promote change (indicating that progressivism was not entirely dead), but these efforts met with stiff resistance in the legislature and, consequently, very little was accomplished. As for Prohibition, it was now the law of the land; but questions about its permanence, efficacy, and enforcement cropped up throughout the decade as it continued to be a divisive issue among Texas politicians.

Though reform was now dormant, this was a period of change in Texas. The population increased rapidly, and technology altered the lives of many people, especially those living in the cities. There were changes in education characterized by consolidation of many rural districts, altered curricula, and the founding of several new junior colleges and four year institutions. Despite all these developments, however, the decade of the 1920s remained a period of complacency. Most people seemed satisfied with prevailing conditions and gave no indication of a desire to seek new directions.

The governors during this period were Pat M. Neff, 1921–25; Miriam A. Ferguson, 1925–27; and Dan Moody, 1927–31.

PAT M. NEFF ☆ 1921–25

Pat Neff's parents migrated from Virginia to Texas in 1852 as newlyweds. They settled on a tract of land granted by Governor Pease in McLennan County and began their household and family. Neff's father farmed and served part-time in the Texas Rangers, while his mother cared for the home and family, which eventually included nine children. Although his father died in 1882, Neff's mother continued to own the tract and willed it to him upon her death in 1921. Later, Neff donated it to the state, and on May 14, 1939, it was dedicated as Mother Neff State Park – the first state park in Texas.

Pat Neff was born on the farm on November 26, 1871, and he grew up working with his father and brothers and occasionally attending the small settlement school. Eventually Neff attended McGregor High School and Baylor University, from which he graduated in 1893. After teaching school for two years, he entered the University of Texas Law School, and upon passing the bar, he settled in Waco to practice law. Neff soon entered politics and served several terms in the Texas house of which, during the 1903 session, he became speaker. In addition, he was McLennan County attorney for several years, president of the Texas Conference for Education, and grand chancellor

Pat M. Neff

of the Knights of Pythias of Texas in 1918 and 1919. In 1920, he was elected governor.

The campaign for governor in 1920 attracted more than ordinary interest. First in the field as a candidate was ex-Sen. Joseph Weldon Bailey, who had been out of politics for eight years. An outspoken opponent of Wilsonian progressivism, Bailey believed that politicians like Governors Campbell and Hobby were leading Texas down the path of destruction and that only he possessed the personal and political traits necessary to save the state. Although he generally agreed with the views of James "Pa" Ferguson, he declined to join Ferguson's new American party, founded in August, 1919, preferring instead to "Save the Democracy." In fact, responding to Ferguson's move, a number of Bailey's friends sought to organize a "Bailey Democratic party" at a meeting in Fort Worth late in the summer of 1919. Bailey attended the function, and in his address to his followers he denounced regulation, socialism, monopoly, class legislation, and the League of Nations; but he admonished his friends to continue to work through the regular channels of the Democratic party. Later he said he would lead the fight for "reform" but declined to run for office.

During the fall Bailey changed his mind and announced that he might run for governor. Dallas newspapers predicted that he would announce on February 13, 1920, and speaking before a throng of supporters at Gainesville five days later, he declared himself a candidate. In a long and rambling speech, he promised to save the party and the state from what he called the "poisonous politicians prevailing throughout the country."[1] More specifically, he advocated a reduction of government spending, tax reduction, states' rights, the separation of church and state, and better education. He denounced labor unions, Prohibition, women's suffrage, socialism, monopoly, the League of Nations, and President Wilson.

Soon, two more viable candidates in addition to Neff entered the race. The first was Robert E. Thompson of Gainesville, a well-known lawyer who had served as district attorney and, at the time of the election, was speaker of the Texas house. Also announcing was Ben F. Looney of Marion County, who had served two terms in the Texas house, one in the senate, and had been attorney general from 1913 to 1919. Like Neff, these men were essentially progressives. They all supported President Wilson; all favored women's suffrage and Prohibition, while at the same time calling for economy in government, lower taxes, and improved education.

Bailey's first setback came with his effort to force the selection of an anti-Wilson delegation to the national convention. After suffering shattering defeats at the precinct and county levels, only forty-two delegates to the state convention out of a total of 1,409 elected were avowed Bailey supporters. So humiliated was the ex-senator that he left the state without comment, leading some observers to believe that he had abandoned the campaign; but he returned in June to renew his efforts.

The first primary was fairly close, with Neff and Bailey barely three thousand votes apart and Thompson and Looney running a distant third and fourth. This set the stage for the first runoff under the revised election law of 1918. Bailey continued his attacks as before, claiming the state party was dominated by a selfish clique and pleading for a return to "old fashioned" values. Neff declared that Bailey represented stagnation and reaction and had no place in modern Texas government. Apparently the voters agreed, for Neff crushed Bailey in the August runoff by a vote of 264,075 to 184,702. He was easily elected in November over his Republican and American party opponents.

Neff's apparent popularity as reflected in the election returns did not carry over to his relationship with the state legislature. During his first term he proposed many reforms, all of which were rejected. To save money he urged the consolidation or elimination of several state agencies; for example, he proposed that the Texas Pure Food and Drug Department be combined with the health department, and he urged that both the tax board and the tax commission office be abolished and their duties absorbed into the state comptroller's office. He also called for transferring the duties of the mining inspector to the Texas Department of Labor. All of this, he argued, would save the state over $100,000 a year.

Neff called for better law enforcement, as well as improvement of the prison system, highways, schools, water conservation, and better health programs. All these proposals were either rejected or ignored. To make matters worse, the legislature adjourned the regular session of 1921 without passing an appropriations bill, and two special sessions were required before lawmakers finally provided the funds required to operate state government.

The legislature Neff dealt with represented in some ways a cross section of the state, for not only did it include lawyers, but teachers, doctors, farmers, ranchers, bankers, merchants, and journalists as well.

Most of the lawmakers were sixty years of age or older and might be assumed to have been conservative; yet, at the beginning of Neff's term, there was no indication that he would have problems with this group. In fact, the speaker of the house said that he expected both houses to work in perfect harmony with the governor. It was Neff's position on law enforcement that triggered his break with the lawmakers. Neff favored a bill that would allow the state to bring *quo warranto* proceedings against local agencies that failed to enforce state laws. Neff was outraged when the bill failed to pass, saying it was a victory for lawless elements, especially bootleggers. Many legislators resented his remarks, declaring they had acted in good faith, and an impasse between the branches of government developed. Nothing further was accomplished during the balance of the regular session, and the lawmakers adjourned at the end of sixty days since, by statute, their *per diem* dropped from $5.00 to $2.00 at that time; during a special session it would again be $5.00.

Prior to the special session, the governor made several speeches around the state in which he criticized the legislature, so tensions still ran high when it reassembled in July. Neff called upon them to appropriate funds for the operation of state government with available revenue, provide adequate funding for the public schools, and redistrict the state. The lawmakers considered his calls for economy, but in the process they made severe cuts in the budget for higher education, prompting one observer to comment that things had not been so bad since the days of James E. Ferguson. Relations between Neff and the lawmakers were not improved when, also during this special session, they passed measures aimed at prison reform and he vetoed the measures on the grounds that "existing laws and regulations cover the situation."[2]

Although Neff's opponents believed that the failure of the governor's program would weaken his reelection bid and sought a viable candidate to oppose him, no one of high quality seemed interested. Among those who did announce were Fred Rogers, a farmer and labor leader from Bonham, Harry T. Warner, editor of the Paris *Morning News,* and several others who made ineffectual efforts and then withdrew from the race. During the primary campaign, Neff ignored his opponents and spent all of his time and energy defending his programs. Time and time again he described for the voters the urgent need for real change in the prison system, law enforcement, and education, and for improvements in the public schools, the highway system, and taxation.

Neff won the primary without a runoff and was reelected in November without campaigning. He defeated Judge William H. Atwell, the able but hapless Republican candidate, by a margin of nearly five to one. Clearly, he was still popular with the people, but as before, his popularity did not carry over to the legislature. He repeated most of his earlier calls for reform and added a proposal for replacement of the state constitution, saying the fundamental law of 1876 was outmoded and obsolete. Neff also offered a detailed proposal for school reform that called for the creation of a state board of education and an increase in the per capita expenditures on education to fifty dollars per child. However, the break between the governor and the legislature that had marred his first term was not sufficiently healed, and as a result almost none of his policies were implemented.

At the end of his second term in office, Governor Neff returned to Waco to practice law, but his career in public service was not over. Between 1927 and 1929, he served on the U.S. Board of Mediation. Immediately thereafter, he was elected to the Texas Railroad Commission and chaired that body from 1929 to 1931. He left the commission to become president of Baylor University and remained in that office until 1947. In addition to his work in state government and higher education, he was also very active in church and fraternal organizations. He was president of the Baptist Convention of Texas, president of the Southern Baptist Convention, and grand master of the Masonic Lodge of Texas, to name only three of his many offices and honors. Pat Neff died on January 20, 1952, in Waco and is buried there.

MIRIAM A. FERGUSON ☆ 1925–27; 1933–35

Miriam Amanda Wallace, daughter of Joseph and Eliza Garrison Ferguson Wallace, was born on June 13, 1875. The family had substantial land holdings in Bell County, so Miriam lived comfortably as a child, receiving her primary and secondary education both in the public schools and from private tutors. Later she attended Salado College and the Baylor College for Women, but she did not graduate from either institution. She began a courtship with James E. Ferguson shortly after her father died in 1898, and on New Year's Eve, 1899, she and James were married. Two daughters, Ouida and Dorias, were born from this union. The Fergusons moved to Temple in 1907, where Jim founded the Temple State Bank. For several years he had practiced law successfully, invested in land, and prospered, so that by this time the couple were relatively well-to-do. In 1914, Jim ran for governor and, to the surprise of many, he was elected.

In 1915, there were three distinct factions in Austin society – the old families, the politicians, and the university people – all of whom hated each other. Although she had always despised socializing, Miriam found it necessary to deal with these groups in her position as first lady of the state. To do this successfully, she hired a social secretary (and was soundly criticized for doing so), but this had no effect upon her husband's administration. With her secretary's help, Mrs. Ferguson presided as best she could at necessary social functions, but she was a dedicated Prohibitionist, and no alcohol was ever served at the mansion while she was there.

Jim Ferguson was reelected in 1916, but the following year he was impeached, removed from office (on the grounds that he had committed numerous financial irregularities), and declared ineligible to ever hold public office again. In the fall of 1917, the Fergusons returned to Temple, having suffered serious financial as well as political losses – yet they were by no means destitute. Ferguson founded a newspaper, which he called the *Ferguson Forum,* and used it in part to keep his name before the public.

In 1918, despite his "ineligibility" to run for public office, Jim Ferguson ran for governor again. He was defeated in a vicious campaign by incumbent William P. Hobby, who had succeeded him after the impeachment. Two years later Ferguson organized his own American party and ran for president, but this gained him nothing except to keep his name before the public. In 1922, he and Miriam both announced as candidates for the U.S. Senate. After a while Miriam withdrew, but Jim continued in the race and lost the primary to Earle B. Mayfield, the ultimate winner of the Senate seat. By this time it was generally accepted that one of the Fergusons would run for governor in 1924.

As predicted, early that year Jim announced as a candidate, but the court ruled him ineligible and Miriam immediately took his place, declaring that it was her mission to vindicate the family name. In her initial platform she attacked the Klan and promised to improve the prisons, highways, and schools, veto all liquor legislation, and reduce

Miriam A. Ferguson

state expenditures by fifteen million dollars. She never hid the fact that Jim would rule with her if she were elected, and, in fact, the Fergusons often said that a vote for Miriam would give the people "two governors for the price of one."[3]

Nine people entered the Democratic primary in 1924, but only four were major candidates: Miriam Ferguson; T. W. Davidson, the incumbent lieutenant governor; Lynch Davidson, a former lieutenant governor; and Judge Felix D. Robertson, who was believed by practically everyone to be the Klan's candidate. In the campaign the Fergusons usually appeared together, but Jim did most of the talking. He blasted the Klan and his political enemies and harangued the people about the wisdom of putting a Ferguson back in office. Meanwhile, Miriam spent a lot of time posing, and even though the press generally favored one or the other of the Davidsons, Miriam got substantial coverage by virtue of her gender. There were many stories about her, accompanied by photographs in domestic settings, and often she was shown in a bonnet (although, as a personal preference, she normally did not wear one). Soon the papers began to refer to her as "Ma" and to Jim as "Pa," and there appeared campaign posters and bumper stickers proclaiming "Me for Ma" and others which countered, "No Ma for Me – Too Much Pa."

Robertson led in the July primary with slightly more than 193,000 votes, "Ma" was second with 164,424, Lynch Davidson polled 141,208, and T. W. Davidson racked up 125,000. Many observers believed that voters failed to distinguish one Davidson from the other and that the outcome might have been quite different if only one Davidson had been in the race. The runoff between Miriam and Robertson featured continued attacks upon the Klan by Jim along with promises of efficient and economical government if Miriam were elected. When the votes were counted, "Ma" won by a substantial margin (413,751 to 316,019), but success was by no means assured; she still had to face the general election in November.

The Republicans saw 1924 as their best chance since Reconstruction to elect a governor, and so they chose a formidable candidate, Dr. George C. Butte, dean of the University of Texas School of Law, who resigned his position to run a strenuous campaign. He argued that the contest was one for responsible government, which only he could provide and stressed that, if "Ma" were elected, she would be a mere figurehead for Jim, who was corrupt. Meanwhile, Jim Ferguson attacked Butte as a tool of the Klan (though Butte denied the accusation), defended his own record, and promised that his wife would be a good governor. He said that he and Ma favored higher education, and that Butte's greatest contribution to the university – which Ferguson claimed was controlled by elitists – had been to resign his position as dean of the law school. When the people went to the polls, they demonstrated that the Republicans had miscalculated, for Ma defeated Dr. Butte by a vote of 422,528 to 294,970.

Addressing the legislature early in her administration, Governor Ferguson, pointing out a projected shortfall of two million dollars in revenues, called for economy. She also called for investigations of various departments (including those dealing with banking, highways, and the prison system), demanded adequate support for education, and recommended small taxes on gasoline and tobacco to help balance the budget. The legislature, however, gave her recommendations little attention. The prison system and the highway department were investigated, but the lawmakers took no action and imposed no new taxes. They kept the budget within the limits of projected revenue, but this was accomplished by killing a proposal to make a needed addition to the school fund. On the other hand, Governor Ferguson did not reduce state expenditures by fifteen million dollars as promised in the campaign. As everyone had expected, Jim Ferguson played a major role in the administration, and his antics cast an aura of corruption over the entire executive branch.

One controversy centered on the *Ferguson Forum*. There were no standard rates for advertising in the paper, and many people found that the more they paid to advertise, the more likely they were to receive favors from the governor. In some cases, Jim Ferguson actually solicited business on official stationery. A greater source for controversy involved textbook selection for the public schools. Jim was clerk of the textbook commission, and under his influence, the commission negotiated a contract with the American Book Company for the purchase of thousands of spellers at no discount. In fact, later investigations revealed that Texas paid more than the retail price for a single copy than did other states. Jim's most outrageous actions, however, derived from his influence over the highway commission. Although he had no official connection with the commission, he met with it regularly and influenced the awarding of contracts. Later it was found that contracts with the American Road Company and the Hoffman Construction Company were awarded without bids and that these firms received excessive fees for their work (in some cases 200 percent more than the estimated value of the project).

Governor Ferguson's pardon policy strained credulity. She had promised during the campaign that she would exercise the power of pardon liberally, and she kept her promise – with a vengeance. During her first two years in office, she issued more than three thousand pardons, and it was widely believed that clemency could be purchased. The Fergusons insisted that the vast majority of these pardons were issued to liquor law violators who were not really "criminals," but there were hundreds granted to violent felons as well.

Mercifully for the state, Miriam was defeated by Dan Moody in her bid for reelection in 1926. The attorney general won in part because he was able to demonstrate persuasively that the Ferguson administration had been utterly corrupt. Strangely, no charges were ever brought against the pair; in fact, they remained in Austin for the next four years while Jim did everything he could to thwart Moody's reform efforts.

Miriam ran for governor again in 1930 against Ross Sterling, chair of the highway commission; state Sen. Clint Small; former Sen. Earle B. Mayfield, the Klan candidate; Lieut. Gov. Barry Miller; and conservative entrepreneur and Prohibitionist Thomas B. Love of Dallas. Because the Fergusons still had considerable support from the small farmers and workers, the former governor ran first in the July primary, but Sterling defeated her in the runoff to win the November election. Two years later and having determined that the Depression made 1932 a very good Ferguson year, Ma was back again to challenge Governor Sterling for his office. She announced her candidacy in February, offering a platform that called for tax reduction. During the primary campaign, the Fergusons accused Sterling of excessive spending and being under the influence of big business, while Sterling repeatedly asked the people whether or not they wanted honest, responsible government or the alternative, the Fergusons.

Ma won a plurality over Sterling and the third candidate, Tom Hunter, a conservative oilman from Wichita Falls, in the July primary. In the runoff campaign, the candidates continued to snipe away at each other with charges of corruption and inefficiency. The poll in August, which featured a great deal of fraudulent voting (especially in counties that were Ferguson strongholds), produced a razor-thin victory for Ma. She defeated Sterling by fewer than four thousand votes, and the governor demanded a recount. A special session of the legislature considered an investigation, but these proposals were killed, and Ma was officially declared to be the Democratic party nominee. Orville Bullington of Wichita Falls, the Republican candidate for governor, opposed Miriam in the November election. He appealed to everyone to place citizenship above party and elect him in order to promote honest, effective government. Bullington conducted an elaborate campaign, but the Depression made 1932 a terrible year for Republicans, and Ma achieved victory by a vote of 522,395 to 317,590.

In her inaugural address on January 17, 1933, Ma pointed out that the state was in a financial mess, and she recommended a sales tax to cover the budget deficit. This proposal attracted much attention, and there was considerable discussion in the legislature of both the sales tax idea and a possible income tax; in the final analysis, however, the lawmakers did nothing except to raise the oil tax from one-half cent to two cents per barrel, cut appropriations, and authorize the sale of twenty million dollars worth of relief bonds. There was much less controversy over Ma's executive actions during her second term. She continued her liberal pardon policy, now known as the "Texas Open Door," but there were no outrageous actions to compare with the earlier textbook and highway scandals. Despite this relatively peaceful administration, Ma did not run for reelection in 1934.

Most people believed that the Fergusons were now out of politics for good, so many were surprised when Ma entered the race for governor in 1940. The old magic was gone, however, and she ran fourth in a field of eight. Pa Ferguson died in 1944, and Ma lived quietly thereafter in Austin until her own passing on June 25, 1961. She is buried in the state cemetery beside her husband.

DAN MOODY ☆ 1927–31

Taylor, in Williamson County, was the site of Dan Moody's birth on June 1, 1893. He was the son of David James, who was sixty years of age when Dan was born, and Nancy Robertson Moody. The family was originally from Virginia, but in the mid-nineteenth century, Dan's grandfather migrated first to Tennessee and then to Missouri. Dan's father, who had come to the state on several earlier occasions as a cattle drover, settled in Texas in 1876, where he worked for the Illinois & Great Northern Railroad and entered politics. Elected in 1892, he was the first mayor of Taylor, and he later served as the town's justice of the peace. He also dabbled in the insurance and building and loan businesses.

Business losses caused by a depression impoverished the family in 1895, and life was hard for the next several years. Dan went to work delivering milk at the age of nine, but he still found time to go to school. While completing his secondary education, he worked at various jobs, including as a grocery delivery boy, a cashier, and as a lineman for the local power company. When he was sixteen, Dan became a member of the electrical workers union, and from 1910 to 1914 he attended the University of Texas, paying his expenses by means of summer work as an electrical contractor. Although he never graduated from the university, Moody passed the bar and set up a law practice in Taylor before World War I.

When the United States entered the war in 1917, Moody volunteered for the service. He was rejected, so instead he joined the Texas National Guard and was in training at Little Rock when the war ended. He then returned to Taylor to practice law but soon decided to enter public service and was elected Williamson County attorney in 1920. Two years later he became district attorney, and in this capacity he worked vigorously against the Ku Klux Klan, an effort that brought him statewide attention and led him to be elected attorney general in 1924. At the age of thirty-one, he became the youngest attorney general in the history of the state. Attorney General Moody attacked the corruption that embroiled the state's highway construction and maintenance program, bringing suit against the American Road Company and the Hoffman Construction Company and showing their contracts to be grossly inflated. As a result of his efforts, these contracts were soon modified and, in some cases, canceled altogether.

In 1926, Moody's friends urged him to run for governor and he consented, hoping to displace the incompetent regime of Miriam Ferguson. Moody blamed practically all the corruption and inefficiency in state government on Governor Ferguson and her husband, and he charged that Jim was actually running the state, an unconscionable practice which he termed "Fergusonism." When he opened his campaign for governor in March, 1926, he aimed five specific charges at Jim: the ex-governor, Moody declared, was a paid employee of the railroad commission while at the same time serving as chief adviser to the governor, his wife. Moody also charged that Jim controlled the

Dan Moody

highway and textbook commissions and that his newspaper in Temple advertised for numerous corporations while legislation affecting them was under consideration. Moody pledged that if he were elected, he would end corruption in state government, enforce the law, improve the highways and schools by honest means, and support judicial reform.

In addition to Moody and Mrs. Ferguson, there were several other candidates in the primary race, but only ex-Lieut. Gov. Lynch Davidson was a serious contender. As it turned out, however, even his effort was overshadowed by the bitter struggle between Moody and the Fergusons. Moody, of course, continued to stress corruption and incompetence in his attacks upon the Fergusons, giving most of his attention to the highway and textbook scandals as well as Governor Ferguson's pardon policy.

Although Miriam Ferguson campaigned very little, preferring to confine herself to "thank you" visits to various parts of the state, Jim worked tirelessly to discredit Moody. When the young attorney general married on April 20, 1926, Jim said that if Moody were elected, Texas would be governed by "Jiggs and Maggie," and he depicted the wife pursuing the governor around the mansion with a rolling pin. He also attempted to convince the voters that Moody was secretly backed by the Klan and the big oil companies. With respect to the choice of textbooks for the state, Jim alleged that the controversy was really about evolution, and that Miriam had protected the children of Texas from being confronted with this sordid theory. If Moody were elected, alleged Jim, education would come under the control of those "monkey faced" Baptists at Baylor.

Centers of support for Moody in the campaign proved to be in the cities, especially in North, West, and South Texas. Ferguson's support came mostly from rural areas and East Texas, as well as from those who opposed Prohibition (even though she was considered a "dry"). Declaring her confidence in reelection, Mrs. Ferguson said that if she lost the primary to Moody she would resign. Her bluff was called because Moody not only prevailed, he came within 1,770 votes of a clear majority. After some hesitation, the governor went back on her word, declaring that she had a mission to rid the state of Klan domination and was in the fight to the end. The second primary election in August resulted in a decisive victory for Moody, who defeated the governor by a vote of 495,723 to 270,595. Moody did not bother to campaign for the November election, and in a very light turnout he defeated the Republican candidate, H. H. Haires, by a vote of 233,068 to 31,531.

When Dan Moody was inaugurated on January 18, 1927, he became the youngest governor in the history of the state and had the youngest wife ever to live in the governor's mansion. His was the first inaugural held outdoors and was attended by the largest crowd in history. In his inaugural address he called for honesty, efficiency, and economy in state government. Specifically, he asked for tax reform, judicial reform, increased support for education, better highways, the adoption of a uniform accounting system, and the creation of a state civil service system.

Although the legislature was dominated by those who claimed to be friends of the governor, and though the rancor that had characterized Pat Neff's relations with the lawmakers was absent, only about half of Moody's proposals became law. Education benefited by increased *per capita* appropriations and special appropriations for colleges. The textbook scandal was cleared up, taxes were reduced, many new miles of highways were laid, and there was some improvement in the administration of the prison system. On the other hand, there was no fundamental tax reform, no change in the judicial system, no new civil service program, and no unified accounting system. Moreover, no effort was made to bring about fundamental changes in the prison system or the comprehensive development of a modern highway system.

During his first term Moody received some national publicity because he headed the Texas delegation to the Democratic National Convention in Houston. Moody was thought by some to be a viable choice for the vice presidency, but at length he declared that he would run again for governor. At the convention, however, Moody was an active member of the platform committee and attempted without success to introduce a Prohibition plank. Even though they differed on the Prohibition question, Moody announced that he would support Al Smith, the anti-Prohibitionist candidate for president, and this led to the rise of considerable opposition to the governor.

Moody's most serious opponent in 1928 was L. J. Wardlaw of Fort Worth, who was a close friend of the Fergusons. Wardlaw had support from both the pro- and anti-Prohibition camps, from many of Ferguson's diehard supporters, and even from the Klan. In his campaign Wardlaw argued that Moody was inefficient and that he had broken most of his promises. Moody, however, did not regard Wardlaw as a serious threat and campaigned very little. In the July primary, Wardlaw polled an impressive 245,000 votes, but Moody won easily with 442,080.

The contest in November attracted relatively little attention, and Moody was easily reelected. In his inaugural he asked the legislature to consider those reforms he had called for two years earlier, but it paid him little heed. Moody made a special effort to promote prison reform, declaring that the prison system was too decentralized, overcrowded, a breeding ground for disease, had no effective reform program, and that the main facility at Huntsville was a firetrap. The governor wanted to reduce the emphasis on farming, sell prison-owned farmland, increase industrialization, and improve facilities. The response of the legislature was to authorize the appointment of a commission to investigate the system and make recommendations to improve it. At length the commission reported but was divided in its recommendations: the majority report called for the construction of a new prison, with manufacturing as its primary activity, while the minority report called for improving the existing facilities. The legislature adopted the minority report, much to the governor's disgust, but he allowed the bill reflecting that decision to become law without his signature.

Moody exercised his veto power more readily on other matters than during his first term. He refused to approve appropriations that exceeded revenues, and in all he vetoed more than one hundred measures. On the other hand, in an effort to force the enactment of more features of his program, he called five special sessions, an all-time record, during his second term. Sadly for him, the strategy achieved little save the passage of a law allowing the governor to appoint a state auditor.

The failure of Moody's reforms resulted from several causes. First was the natural tendency of state officials to oppose change in the *status quo* and their exercising influence upon the legislature. Second was the fact that Texans were still rural and conservative in their thinking, even though the population of the state was rapidly increasing and urbanizing. Finally, big business opposed many of Moody's reforms and worked hard to prevent their adoption. Even though most of Moody's reform proposals were not adopted, his administration was by no means a failure. His reform of the highway department and his reversal of the Fergusonses' pardoning and textbook policies were all noteworthy achievements. All in all, Moody had nothing to be ashamed of when he left office in 1931.

Still a young man when he retired, Moody remained in Austin to practice law, and there was much speculation about his future in politics. He ran for the Senate in 1942, but was defeated and, in fact, was never again elected to public office. He died on May 22, 1966, and was buried in the state cemetery at Austin.

Notes

1. Seth S. McKay, *Texas Politics, 1906–1944* (Lubbock: Texas Tech Press, 1952), 91.

2. Ibid., 105–107.

3. Ross Phares, *The Governors of Texas* (Gretna, La.: Pelican Publishing Company, 1976), 131–32.

Sources and Further Reading

Alexander, C. C. *Crusade for Conformity: The Ku Klux Klan in Texas, 1920–1930.* Houston: Texas Gulf Coast Historical Association, 1962.

Brown, Norman. *Hood, Bonnet and Little Brown Jug.* College Station: Texas A&M University Press, 1989.

DeShields, James T. *They Sat in High Places: The Presidents and Governors of Texas.* San Antonio: The Naylor Company, 1940.

McCarty, Jeanne B. *The Struggle for Sobriety: Protestants and Prohibition in Texas, 1919–1935.* El Paso: Texas Western Press, 1980.

MacCorkle, S. A. "The Pardoning Power in Texas." *Southwestern Social Science Quarterly* 15 (1934): 218–28.

McKay, Seth S. *Texas Politics, 1906–1944.* Lubbock: Texas Tech Press, 1952.

Phares, Ross. *The Governors of Texas.* Gretna, La.: Pelican Publishing Company, 1976.

Shirley, Emma M. *The Administration of Pat M. Neff, Governor of Texas, 1921–1925.* Waco: Baylor University Press, 1938).

Chapter eleven

DEPRESSION AND WORLD WAR II
1931–47

The worst effects of the Great Depression did not appear in Texas as early as in other areas of the country, but by 1933, unemployment, price collapses, agricultural dislocation, and bankruptcy had become commonplace. The oil industry and agriculture, mainstays of the Texas economy, were especially hard hit, and state government did little to alleviate these problems. It was not until the election of Franklin D. Roosevelt and the coming of the New Deal that improvements began to appear. Texans exhibited the characteristic individualism of their frontier heritage during the period by relying on themselves for help. Friends, relatives, and charitable organizations also assisted in relief efforts, but at length the intensity of the problem was much too great to be handled by private sources. The horrors of the Depression, though hard for Anglos, were felt more intensely among minorities, particularly African and Mexican Americans.

The politics of the Depression era in Texas were relatively conservative, though certain Texas politicians, like Lyndon Johnson, Sam Rayburn, and John Nance Garner, played roles of varying importance in the Roosevelt administration. Of the Texas governors who served during this period, only James V. Allred was even close to being a New Dealer. In fact, a schism began to develop within the Democratic party that would carry over into the war years and beyond. This break was caused by growing opposition among conservative Texas Democrats to the reform impetus of the New Deal, which intensified after 1935; the fight against the "court-packing scheme" of 1937; and President Roosevelt's subsequent effort to purge the party of his enemies in the 1938 primary election. Further animosity toward Roosevelt, generated by John Nance Garner's desire for the presidential nomination in 1940, which was thwarted by the president's decision to seek a third term, also contributed to the political tensions of the day. The conservatives came to be known as the Texas Regulars, while the liberals were styled "loyalists."

Amid the domestic political turmoil, war came suddenly in December, 1941, and the effects on Texas were profound. Prosperity returned and Texans responded to the call of patriotism, but farmers complained that their share of the restored prosperity was not equitable, labor unions were not satisfied with their lot, the schools remained underfinanced, and the disadvantaged minorities asked for more extensive assistance. Politically and culturally, the leadership was borderline reactionary, the split in the Democratic party became more pronounced, and tensions among minorities intensified.

The governors during this period were Ross S. Sterling, 1931–33; Miriam A. Ferguson, 1933–35; James V. Allred, 1935–39; W. Lee O'Daniel, 1939–41; and Coke R. Stevenson, 1941–47. For a discussion of the Ferguson administration, please see Chapter 10, The Twenties, 921–31.

ROSS S. STERLING ☆ 1931–33

Ross Shaw Sterling was born on a farm near Anahuac in February, 1875, and his family roots ran deep in Texas history. His mother's people were among Stephen F. Austin's early followers, and his father served as a captain in the Confederate Army during the Civil War. The elder Sterling supported his family as a carpenter, farmer, storekeeper, and self-educated country doctor, but he never achieved financial success and so Ross had to leave school at age twelve to work. In 1896, when he was twenty-one, he bought a small store from his father and operated it until 1900, when he entered the produce commission business in Galveston. He was doing well when his business was wiped out by the Galveston hurricane.

Sterling first became associated with the oil industry in 1903, when he opened a feed store at Sour Lake to provide grain and hay for the mules used in hauling supplies at the Sour Lake field. This business prospered, and over the next few years Sterling expanded his operations to several other towns. In 1907, he began buying banks in the towns where he had stores and used them to finance his expanding interests.

Late in 1909, Sterling began to invest directly in oil properties, beginning with two producing wells in the Humble field. Soon he took the lead in organizing a new business, and, along with several other operators, in January, 1911, the company incorporated under the name Humble Oil Company with a capital of $150,000. Humble Oil expanded and prospered over the next several years, Sterling became fabulously wealthy, and by 1922, he chaired the board of the company. But Humble Oil was only one of his many interests, which included various business investments, real estate, and charities. He was also vitally interested in public affairs and first became involved in state politics in 1924, when he joined with ex-Gov. William Hobby to support George C. Butte, the Republican candidate for governor.

After the election, Sterling resigned from the board of Humble and sold his stock to Standard of New Jersey so that he could devote all his time to politics and public service. He became chair of the Texas Highway Commission, and in 1930, he ran for governor against six other candidates. These included former governor Miriam Ferguson, former U.S. Sen. Earle B. Mayfield, state Sen. Thomas B. Love of Dallas, Lieut. Gov. Barry Miller, state Sen. Clint Small of Wellington, and James Young of Kaufman, a former member of Congress.

When Sterling opened his campaign late in the spring, he was met with enthusiastic approval from the business community. In many parts of the state, Sterling clubs sprang up, and in Houston, business magnate Jesse Jones, who would later name Sterling to the Reconstruction Finance Corporation (RFC), took up his cause. The commissioner's platform called for prison reform; improved conditions for

Ross S. Sterling

farmers, stockmen, and laborers; support for education; and taxes on oil, gas, and sulfur. One of his proposals for a major bond issue to finance highways, made before he entered the race, became the target of criticism from all his opponents, who claimed that it represented a conflict of interest and would be too expensive. As the campaign progressed, the bond question became the major issue, and Sterling was surprised by the vehemence of the attack. Nevertheless, he steadfastly continued to advocate the proposal.

Miriam Ferguson led the pack in the first primary with 242,969 votes, and Sterling was a distant second with 170,754. As the runoff campaign began, the defeated candidates chose sides. Small, Love, and Young urged their backers to support Sterling, while Mayfield and Miller favored Ma Ferguson. Governor Moody, who had remained impartial during the first primary, now began a major effort on behalf of Sterling, believing that the election of Ma Ferguson would be catastrophic for the state. The campaign was vigorous and bitter, with Jim Ferguson sending hecklers to trail both Sterling and Moody around the state in an effort to disrupt their rallies. Ferguson himself campaigned actively for his wife and usually drew large crowds, who cheered as he denounced Sterling and Moody as "aristocrats and elitists." But in the final analysis, the Fergusons' efforts were not enough, and Sterling won the runoff by a substantial margin, 473,371 to 384,402. In November, he easily defeated the Republican candidate, Col. W. E. Talbot of Dallas.

Arriving in office just as the worst effects of the Depression were descending upon the state, Sterling faced difficulties other governors had not had to face. As commodity prices fell, so did state income, yet expenses increased. In his first message to the legislature, Sterling offered a program based upon the Democratic party platform. This program included, among other things, calls for harmony in public life, economy, conservation, aid for the farmers, improved highways, support for education, enforcement of the law, prison reform, and a more equitable system of taxation. The lawmakers, although not hostile to the governor, did little to implement his proposals, and in fact, the regular session adjourned without much accomplished. There were minor adjustments in taxes, but in the end, appropriations substantially exceeded projected revenues, and Sterling felt compelled to veto several measures, most of which affected education.

The most vexing problem that Sterling faced was the overproduction of oil. Just before his election, Columbus "Dad" Joiner discovered the vast East Texas field, and it began to produce enormous quantities of petroleum. As a result, the price of oil practically collapsed, forecasting a potential catastrophe in state finances. The railroad commission attempted to limit production, but was enjoined from doing so by the courts. Sterling, declaring martial law, ordered the National Guard into the field near Kilgore and Longview, and for six months, from August, 1931, to February, 1932, the army controlled the field. During this period Sterling and the railroad commission were the targets of vicious attacks by many in the oil industry, especially "wildcatters" (or independents), but the governor's action succeeded to a limited degree in preventing a total collapse. The National Guard kept control of the East Texas fields until forced to withdraw by the courts. Subsequently, the proration policy advocated by the railroad commission was accepted by the courts and went into effect shortly after Sterling left office.

Cotton prices also plummeted during Sterling's administration, adding to the financial woes of the state. By August, 1931, the price had fallen to five cents a pound, and the governor took action. Sterling proposed, and the legislature passed, a bill calling for a 50 percent reduction in cotton acreage in 1932. The plan was challenged in the courts, however, and struck down as a violation of the Fourteenth Amendment. The price of cotton remained at an all time low as a result and did not begin to rebound until after the implementation of New Deal programs in 1933.

Defeated in his bid for reelection in 1932 by Miriam Ferguson, Sterling retired to private life. While serving the state as governor for two years, he had neglected his personal financial interests and suffered great losses. Taking advantage of his many contacts and utilizing his innate resourcefulness, however, he soon accumulated a second fortune from oil and agricultural endeavors. He died on March 25, 1949, and is buried in Houston.

JAMES V. ALLRED ☆ 1935–39

James V. Allred was born at Bowie, Texas, on March 29, 1899. The family was not well-off, and James began working when he was still quite young. He ran errands, shined shoes, sold newspapers, and worked as a janitor; on May 17, 1917, he graduated from Bowie High

School with honors and entered the Rice Institute the following fall. Although Rice was tuition free at that time, Allred still needed money for personal expenses, so he worked part-time at a filling station. After completing one year of college, "Jimmy" Allred enlisted in the navy and was stationed at San Francisco for the duration of the war. He was discharged in February, 1919.

Upon his return to Texas, Allred moved to Wichita Falls, where he found employment as a secretary in a law firm. In the fall of 1920, he enrolled in law school at Cumberland University in Tennessee and graduated after one year of classes. Admitted to the Texas bar in June, 1921, he joined the Wichita Falls law firm of Martin & Oneal. Two years later he was appointed district attorney and served in that office until 1926, when he resigned to run his first race for attorney general. Although he was defeated by the incumbent, Claude Pollard, he ran an effective campaign and lost by only four thousand votes. Allred returned to his law practice and remained in Wichita Falls until 1930, marrying Jo Betsy Miller on June 27, 1927. In 1930, he ran again for attorney general and defeated R. L. Bobbitt by an impressive majority; he was reelected in 1932. While serving as attorney general, Allred attracted much attention through his efforts to regulate monopolies and enforce antitrust laws.

In 1934, he entered the race for governor. There were six major planks in Allred's platform, including proposing the creation of a public utilities commission; submitting the question of Prohibition repeal to a popular vote; decreasing taxes and making the revenue system more efficient; creating a modern state police force; increasing the powers of the board of pardons and parole; and establishing effective controls over lobbyists.

Allred faced five important opponents in the primary race: Tom Hunter and C. C. McDonald (both from Wichita Falls), Edgar Witt of Waco, Clint Small of Amarillo, and Maury Hughes of Dallas. All of these men favored tax reduction and improved efficiency in government but sometimes differed from each other on other issues. Hunter was a wealthy lawyer who called for tax reduction, a "self-supporting" system of old age pensions, and adequate support for education; McDonald opposed Prohibition and was considered a bit radical by some because he favored the right of labor to organize and bargain collectively; and Small wanted to divest the railroad commission of the authority to regulate the oil and natural gas industries and create a new

James V. Allred

conservation commission for that purpose. The one distinguishing feature of Witt's platform was a call for the establishment of a revolving fund supported by relief bonds to enable people to obtain long-term, low-interest loans to buy homes.

Allred won a plurality in the July primary with 298,903 votes, followed by Hunter with 243,254, McDonald with 207,000, and Small with 125,324. During the runoff campaign, McDonald, Small, and Witt all supported Hunter, as did the Fergusons, and former governor Ross Sterling came out for Allred. The campaign was intense and at times nasty, with Hunter claiming that Allred had no program worth debating and Allred calling Hunter a Nazi. When true debate did occur, its primary issue was taxes. Allred prevailed in a close vote by a margin of approximately four thousand votes. Many observers believed that Hunter's cause was hurt more than helped by the endorsement he received from the Fergusons.

When Allred took office in 1935, the most difficult problem he faced involved old age pensions. There was a new amendment to the Texas Constitution that authorized payments to the old and needy, but it did not clearly specify who should be paid or how much they should receive. Though Allred and the legislature examined this problem, it was not solved during this period. Finance was the other principal issue, and the governor called for support of the New Deal, asking the lawmakers to issue additional relief bonds. He also called for the enactment of laws in support of his platform, which included adequate support for education, conservation, and state control of oil and gas production. On the question of taxation, Allred opposed a sales tax, on the grounds that it would be regressive, and declared that an income tax would be the best solution to the state's revenue problems.

Typical of its relationship with governors, the legislature passed a few measures but left many problems unsolved. Education received some support, the Texas Department of Public Safety was created, relief bonds were issued, the governor approved legislation designed to avoid federal regulation of the oil industry, and the Prohibition question was submitted to the people. There was no effective action on the questions of taxation and revenue, however, so in September of 1935, Allred called a special session to deal with the problem; but the session adjourned after thirty days, having accomplished nothing.

In the election of 1936, Allred was opposed by Hunter, F. W. Fischer of Tyler, Ray Sandersford of Belton, and Pierce Brooks of Dallas.

Allred was a popular governor, however, and he easily won the primary with a majority after only three weeks of campaigning. Allred called another special session during the campaign to deal with the pressing need to solve the old age pension problem. This session changed the existing law to apply only to the needy and passed appropriations – the money for which was to come from slightly increased taxes on petroleum products and liquor – to support the pensions.

Once again finance was the major problem facing Texas as the legislature assembled in 1937. Allred called for increases in property taxes and levies on the production of natural resources, but the legislature did nothing. At a special session in the fall of 1937, the senate passed a tax bill but the house failed to concur. Meanwhile, the legislat ure had substantially increased appropriations, and Allred was forced to veto numerous spending measures, including an effort to liberalize pensions.

In spite of his problems with the legislature, Allred's popularity remained high, and though he probably could have successfully broken tradition to run for a third term, he declined to do so. In a radio address explaining that he would not enter the race in 1938, he said: "Of course it is my nature to feel the tingle and desire for political conflict. . . . In the future, should the occasion arise, I always shall stand ready to give to the state I love."[1]

After his retirement from office Allred returned to his law practice, and in 1942, he ran for the U.S. Senate but was defeated by W. Lee O'Daniel. President Truman appointed Allred a judge of the U.S. District Court, Southern District of Texas, in 1951, and he served in that capacity in South Texas until his death on September 24, 1959. He is buried in Wichita Falls.

W. LEE O'DANIEL ☆ 1939–41

Undoubtedly one of the most incompetent individuals ever to hold the office of governor in Texas, W. Lee O'Daniel was first elected in 1938 and again in 1940. Following the death of Morris Sheppard in 1941, O'Daniel was elected to the U.S. Senate, where he humiliated the state – as he had as its governor – until he retired from office in 1948.

Of the thirteen men who originally filed for the Democratic primary in 1938, only four were viable candidates: Atty. Gen. William McCraw of Dallas, Ernest O. Thompson (former mayor of Amarillo, founding member of the American Legion, and famed chair of the

Texas Railroad Commission since 1932), and perennial candidate Tom Hunter, a veteran of the Wichita Falls business scene. The fourth candidate was O'Daniel.

A native of Ohio, O'Daniel had spent much of his life in Kansas before coming to Texas in 1925 to become manager of a Fort Worth milling company. In 1938, he organized his own firm and began a highly successful radio advertising campaign featuring a pitch for "Hillbilly Flour" and the music of a country and western band called the "Light Crust Doughboys." With O'Daniel himself as the announcer, the daily radio shows were soon expanded into a regular feature program that included a variety of music and discussions on such topics as religion, patriotism, and morals. O'Daniel soon became very popular and claimed on his radio show that his fans were urging him to run for governor. On Palm Sunday, 1938, he asked his listeners to write to him if they thought he should enter the race; nearly fifty-five thousand responses poured in, most of them positive, according to O'Daniel.

In opening their campaigns, McCraw, Thompson, and Hunter dealt with substantive issues. They called for economy in government, efforts to attract new industries, and lower utility rates; they opposed trusts and monopolies and pledged to honor the state social security obligation, while simultaneously opposing new taxes, especially an income tax. O'Daniel's platform was a little different. Claiming that his motto was the Golden Rule and his guiding principles the Ten Commandments, he called for state pensions of thirty dollars a month for all persons over sixty-five years old. He also called for elimination of the poll tax, tax reduction in general, economy in government, and a campaign to attract new businesses; his slogan was, "Less Johnson grass and politicians; more smoke stacks and business men." O'Daniel also told his followers that he had no money for the campaign so "you had better take down that old rocking chair and mortgage it and send the money in the manner you think best to get your pension."[2]

At first O'Daniel excited little attention outside the Fort Worth area, but when he took his campaign, featuring the "Light Crust Doughboys," on the road, things began to pick up. Opening his candidacy formally at Waco on June 12, O'Daniel proceeded on a speaking tour on the back of a flatbed truck, first in West Texas and then in other parts of the state. By the end of the month, the other candidates, who had at first ignored him, began to take him seriously and attack him personally. McCraw declared in one address that O'Daniel was no

W. Lee O'Daniel

more a hillbilly than he was a student of government. "[He] . . . talks a great deal about home and religion and the Ten Commandments and the fine women of our state, but he doesn't say a word . . . about gambling on horses, or selling liquor by the drink."[3] On another occasion and in a more pointed remark, McCraw wondered aloud how O'Daniel planned to raise the forty million dollars it would take to pay the pensions. In fact, O'Daniel was a charlatan who had no plan. His only concern being to win the election, he cared little for the common people and not at all for the elderly.

Nevertheless, he had credibility through his radio program, which gave him a tremendous advantage in the campaign. O'Daniel continued to attract ever larger crowds as the campaign went on, and at one meeting in Austin toward the end of the race, he spoke before a throng estimated at over thirty-eight thousand people. He told them that he would drive the professional politicians out of Austin, assemble a group of business-wise individuals to advise him, and tax oil, gas, sulphur, and other natural resources to pay for pensions and social security obligations. Apparently the people liked what they heard, for O'Daniel swamped his opposition in the July election. He polled 573,166 votes against a combined total of 501,102 for McCraw, Thompson, and Hunter. In the November general election, O'Daniel crushed oilman Alexander Boynton of San Antonio, the Republican candidate, by a vote of 473,526 to 10,940.

On the eve of his inauguration, speculation mounted as to how O'Daniel intended to finance social security and his pension plan. Rumors flew that he might go so far as to call for an income tax, but he astonished everyone by calling for a 1.6 percent tax on all business transactions and abandoning his promise of a thirty-dollar-a-month pension for all persons over sixty-five. Amidst a wave of indignation (emanating mostly from the business community and the elderly), the legislature met to ponder its response in early 1939. It soon became apparent that O'Daniel's transactions tax had little chance of passage, so he shifted his support to a combination of taxes on natural resources and retail sales. This plan, however, came under intense opposition from a group in the house, who came to be known as the "Immortal 56." The result was that no tax legislation of any kind passed during this session, thus making it impossible to finance either social security or the governor's pension plan. To make matters worse, even though O'Daniel vetoed several spending bills, the state deficit increased. After the legislature adjourned, there was considerable pressure brought to bear on O'Daniel to call a special session, but he refused.

Despite his failure to achieve anything during his first term, and in the face of substantial opposition from many in the business world and the elderly, O'Daniel ran for reelection in 1940. His platform was once again the Ten Commandments and, once again, he called for the passage of a transactions tax. Several well-known politicians entered the primary race against the governor: Ernest O. Thompson, Miriam Ferguson, Railroad Commissioner Jerry Sadler, and Highway Commissioner Harry Hines. They all admitted that some form of tax reform was necessary, but at the same time they all called for strict economy in state government. With the exception of Mrs. Ferguson, the candidates all advocated some form of levy upon the extraction of natural resources; her solution was a 0.5 percent gross receipts tax.

Governor O'Daniel campaigned very little. In fact, he made only one major speech, at Waco, in which he told people that he was very busy and also very upset that other state officials were traveling about criticizing him rather than helping him in his work. He said that, if he were reelected, he would clean house in Austin. His minimal efforts were crowned with success when the governor overwhelmed his opponents with over 54 percent of the vote, thus eliminating the need for a runoff. In November, O'Daniel faced no opposition since his Republican opponent, Dallas entrepreneur George C. Hopkins, did not campaign.

On April 9, 1941, Sen. Morris Sheppard died, and speculation turned to the question of who O'Daniel would appoint to fill out his term. Many well-known politicians, including Coke Stevenson, Lyndon Johnson, John Nance Garner, Wright Patman, Fritz Lanham, and Martin Dies were mentioned, but O'Daniel stupefied everyone by appointing eighty-seven-year-old Andrew Jackson Houston, the only surviving son of the Hero of San Jacinto. There was a storm of protest from all over the state because Houston was so old and feeble that he was literally incapable of doing anything. Clearly, O'Daniel had appointed him only because he knew there was no possibility the old man would oppose him in the special election set for June 28. Unfortunately, Mr. Houston's delicate health prevented him from going to Washington for several weeks, but he finally arrived to take the oath of office on June 2. After appearing in the Senate chamber three times, the oldest person ever to do so, he fell ill and was hospitalized in Baltimore, where he died on June 20.

Meanwhile, O'Daniel faced serious problems in Austin. There was very little support in the legislature for his tax proposals and, in fact, there was considerable talk around the state about reorganizing the government in order to cut costs. Still, the need to provide funding for the state's social security obligations was pressing and the "Fifty-Sixers" in the house proposed an omnibus bill calling for an increased tax on oil, gas, and the gross receipts of utility companies, along with a sales tax on certain items. O'Daniel opposed this proposal, but it passed by such a wide margin that a veto would have been useless.

With the great struggle over taxation finally at an end, everyone's attention turned to the special senatorial election. Many people wanted O'Daniel to run, some because they actually believed he would do a good job, others because they thought it would be wonderful to get him out of Texas. On April 21, 1941, O'Daniel addressed the legislature and offered them a five-point plan, saying that if they passed it, he would retire from office and run for the U.S. Senate. The plan called for forty million dollars in new revenues to be raised somehow, a state constitutional amendment prohibiting deficit spending, abolition of the poll tax, abolition of capital punishment, and the appointment of a state-audited budget director.

Only two of the five proposals became law, but O'Daniel decided to run for the U.S. Senate anyway, though he did not resign the governorship. He faced considerable opposition in his race for the Senate, for there were twenty announced candidates, four of whom were significant. These were, in addition to O'Daniel, Rep. Lyndon Johnson, Rep. Martin Dies, and Atty. Gen. Gerald Mann. The real fight proved to be between O'Daniel and Johnson, who seemingly was the victor. But, as the last returns trickled in four days after the election, O'Daniel prevailed by a mere thirteen hundred votes. Without doubt, fraud had played a role in the outcome.

From the outset O'Daniel made a fool of himself in the U.S. Senate. Having been vocally critical of the Washington establishment, he could not have expected to be fondly received, and he was not. When he made his first speech (on only his second day in the chamber), his new colleagues were profoundly shocked by both the incoherence and content of his utterance. For example, while proclaiming his support for President Roosevelt's war effort, O'Daniel simultaneously opposed the extension of the Selective Service Act.

Because of his initial performance O'Daniel was not popular, and the result was that every legislative proposal he introduced was rejected. His efforts included a proposal to amend the Interstate Commerce Act as it affected the regulation of pipelines, another to prohibit the sale of liquor near military camps, and yet another to investigate the production and distribution of fertilizer. He also introduced a series of antilabor bills, including one to prohibit strikes and another to eliminate overtime pay for workers in war industries. All were lost.

Claiming that he had been successful in his short term, O'Daniel announced in early 1942 that he intended to run again. His opponents were Dan Moody and James V. Allred, both former governors and both highly competent, and the campaign that followed can best be described as bizarre. Allred and Moody doggedly pointed out that O'Daniel had accomplished absolutely nothing, had been studiously ignored in the U.S. Senate, and, in fact, was still an isolationist (even though the country had been attacked and was at war). In contrast, the senator blithely informed his constituents that the war would soon be over because of his antistrike legislation (which had been rejected by the Senate), and that rationing of vital commodities, such as gasoline, would not be necessary; all this in spite of the fact that the Japanese had overrun the Philippines and other portions of the Far East and still controlled much of the Pacific; most of Europe had fallen to the Nazis; the salvation of the Soviet Union hung by a thread; and Britain was literally fighting for its life.

At first glance it would seem beyond the realm of credulity that a man like O'Daniel could have won this election; but he did win it, primarily by holding on to a great majority of the rural vote. He gained a plurality in the first primary, then defeated Allred by a close vote in the runoff. His victory is usually attributed to the fact that many people in Texas were hostile to the domestic policies of the Roosevelt administration and apparently indifferent to the rantings of the senator during the campaign.

O'Daniel remained ultraconservative and hopelessly out of step with reality while in the Senate and frequently voted with the Republicans. In 1944, he was invited to be the presidential candidate of the Democratic National Committee, an anti-New Deal group, but he declined. However, he was a premier campaigner for the anti-New Deal Texas Regulars, who received 13 percent of the vote. After the war he did all he could to obstruct President Truman's reconversion and foreign aid policies, and in 1947, he attempted to persuade Gen. Douglas MacArthur to run for president with himself as vice president.

In 1948, O'Daniel declared that he saw little hope that the country could be prevented from going entirely socialistic or communistic and declined to run for reelection. Perhaps he was also influenced by the fact that public opinion polls showed him with only 7 percent support from the electorate. Eight years later, however, he returned to politics, revived the hillbilly band, and ran for governor. Defeated, he tried once more in 1958 as an outspoken foe of integration. Mercifully, he was defeated and retired from politics for the final time. He died on May 11, 1969, and was buried at Hillcrest Memorial Park in Dallas.

COKE R. STEVENSON ☆ 1941–47

On March 20, 1888, in Mason County, Texas, Coke R. Stevenson was born in a log cabin. The family traced its history back to William Stevenson, who, in 1725, migrated from Ireland to America and settled in Pennsylvania. One of his descendants, also named William Stevenson, was born in South Carolina and later moved to Louisiana by way of Tennessee and Missouri. One of his sons, Joseph M. Stevenson, was born in Arkansas in 1827 and was Coke's grandfather. Joseph and his wife had five children, one of whom, Robert Milton, was born in Arkansas in 1854 and was Coke's father. Robert was very young when the family moved to Texarkana – just prior to the Civil War – and, except for a brief time in New Mexico, spent his entire life in the western part of the state after the family moved to Llano County.

Robert Stevenson and two of his brothers established a mercantile business in Kimble County in the early 1880s, and later he began a teaching career that continued for many years. In May, 1887, he married Sophia Virginia Hurley, and Coke, the first of their eight children, soon arrived. Though Robert was intelligent and industrious, he made very little money from his itinerant teaching and business activities, and Coke began his working life early by starting his own business, a freight line, when he was only sixteen. About a year later, he sold the little freight line and took a job in the First State Bank in Junction, where he began as a janitor and within two years advanced to cashier. While working in the bank, Stevenson also studied law and was admitted to the bar in 1913. Banking and studying did not take up all of Stevenson's time, however, and he invested in a number of businesses, including a grocery store, a meat market, a hardware store, a Ford dealership, and real estate. In 1913, he purchased his first interest in a

Coke R. Stevenson

ranching operation, and eventually his ranch would be one of the largest in Kimble County.

Stevenson's career in public service began in 1914, when he was appointed county attorney of Kimble County. In this office he worked hard to reduce livestock theft and improve county roads, and he was elected to a second term in 1916. Two years later, in 1918, he was elected county judge and served until 1920, when he retired from office in order to devote more time to his law practice.

Stevenson reentered public life in 1928, when he was elected to the state legislature. During his first term in the Texas house, he authored the bill to establish a state auditor's office and served on the penitentiary centralization committee. He was reelected in 1930 and during his second term, while Ross Sterling was governor, Stevenson participated in a major effort to improve state highways. The governor wanted to issue bonds to finance highway construction, but the conservatives, including Stevenson, wanted the state to build roads on a pay-as-you-go basis. Stevenson's crowd won out and the young legislator was very pleased. Moreover, the episode foreshadowed policies that Stevenson would follow years later as governor. During his third term in the house Stevenson was elected speaker, and upon reelection to a fourth term, he became the first person in the history of the state to succeed himself in the office of speaker.

While serving his fifth term in the house in 1938, Stevenson decided to run for lieutenant governor. He offered no program in his campaign for office, arguing that people simply should consider his past record and his ability to serve. He placed second in the primary election, then defeated Pierce Brooks of Dallas in the runoff; but his service as lieutenant governor was to be short-lived. When W. Lee O'Daniel was sent to the U.S. Senate in the special election of June 28, 1941, Stevenson became governor.

Throughout his political career, Stevenson had been an ultraconservative, and as governor he maintained this ideology. He exhibited no liberal tendencies at all and few that could even be described as constructive; he was reactionary, penurious, and in some cases downright cruel. He served during World War II, a time that required enlightened leadership, but he provided none. For example, Stevenson's economic policies were crude and shortsighted, and as the state's needs for increased revenues became ever more critical, the governor ignored pleas for higher taxes. He could have supported (and perhaps even secured) a hike in the wellhead oil tax to bring Texas policy more in line with those of neighboring oil producing states, but he chose not to. In fact, he saw to it that there were no tax increases of any kind during the war. Instead, Coke called upon all state agencies to tighten their belts and cut services at a time when services for the public were already barely adequate. On several occasions Stevenson was urged to call special sessions of the legislature to deal with pressing issues, but he steadfastly refused on the grounds that the cost for calling a special session could not be justified. Finally, he categorically ignored the critical need to raise the pay of state officials to attract higher quality applicants for public service, and the result of this shortsightedness was that many offices continued to be filled by less-than qualified individuals.

Stevenson owned a number of lucrative oil leases and many of his policies can be traced to this affiliation, for he not only opposed effective taxation, he also opposed regulation of any kind. Thus, in 1940, he endorsed the successful effort of the Texas oil fraternity to prevent ratification of the Anglo-American Petroleum Treaty on the grounds that it would endanger the Texas economy. In fact, the real reason for their opposition was the belief of those in the oil industry that the agreement might lead to increased imports from the Middle East and, thereby, the decline of domestic oil prices.

We can find a similar reason for Stevenson's attitude toward other wartime measures. He opposed all rationing of gasoline and rubber, arguing that rationing would "hurt the economy" and agreed with those who declared that the wartime shortages were imaginary. Yet, it was in the areas of civil liberties and human rights that Stevenson's policies went beyond mere absurdity and entered the realm of cruelty. One example of this can be seen in his handling of the race riots in Beaumont in the summer of 1943. The influx of thousands of African-American workers into the shipyards of the city had created housing shortages and other difficulties. The city exploded on the steamy night of June 15, 1943, when it was rumored that a black man had raped a white woman. At the time of the riot, Stevenson was on his way to Washington, D.C., and rather than return to seize control of a dangerous situation, he simply continued on his way.

Stevenson's attitude toward race relations is also reflected in his response to a savage lynching in 1942. When a black Texarkana man, Willie Vinson, was accused of assaulting a white woman, he was brutally lynched by a group of white vigilantes. Upon learning of the incident, U.S. Atty. Gen. Francis Biddle lodged a protest, but Governor Stevenson responded that even a white man would have been lynched for this crime. In any case, he concluded, African Americans often called violence down upon themselves by their own actions.

The governor's behavior with respect to Mexican Americans was only slightly more "humane." He instigated the state's Caucasian Race Resolution, which attempted to label Hispanics as Anglos and thus spare them the humiliation of being treated like black Texans. This "humanitarian" gesture was triggered by the threat of the Mexican government to forbid laborers (braceros) from entering the state any longer for harvesting. Stevenson also supported the creation of a Good Neighbor Commission as suggested by the State Department to investigate cases of discrimination, and this agency even functioned effectively for a short time during the war.

Perhaps the most damning criticism to be leveled at Governor Stevenson arose from his handling of the disturbing case of Dr. Homer P. Rainey, president of the University of Texas at Austin. In the late 1930s, a number of ultraconservatives, primarily made up of members of the oil industry and business types, were concerned about the "liberal" and "communistic" views of certain members of the University of Texas faculty, especially in the Economics Department. Among the most vocal were Orville Bullington, of Wichita Falls, and his friend Dan Harrison. These people and others prevailed upon Governors O'Daniel and Stevenson to appoint them to the Board of Regents of the University of Texas, and so, by 1941, they were in control and undertook a purging of the university. The regents did not pursue their goals subtly. They ordered Rainey to fire several tenured professors whom the regents considered undesirable because of their liberal views; they undertook to prohibit the use of certain reading materials at the university, including John Dos Passos's Pulitzer Prize–winning U.S.A.; and when Rainey protested their outrageous actions, they fired him.

Stevenson's reaction to these events was, quite simply, to do nothing about them. Secretly, he agreed with the regents, so he remained silent, even after Bullington declared that the university had a nest of homosexuals on the faculty. The result was that academic freedom at the university was diminished for several years, and a number of outstanding faculty members left in disgust.

All in all, Stevenson's administration was a disaster for the state. He thought of himself as a Jeffersonian, and he truly believed he needed no legislative program or to even attempt to lead his party. But Stevenson must not have studied Jefferson very carefully – otherwise, he would have known there was a substantial gap between Jefferson's rhetoric and his policies. When he left office in 1947, Stevenson was proud of the fact that the state budget was in the black. A deficit of thirty-four million dollars in 1941 had been transformed into a surplus of thirty-five million dollars, but the quality of state services had declined substantially in the process, and a pattern had been established that would last for many years.

Stevenson's last appearance on the public scene occurred in 1948, when he ran for the U.S. Senate against Lyndon Johnson. That he was still popular with many Texans in spite of his record was shown by the fact that he led Johnson in the first primary, even though Johnson carried on one of the most vigorous campaigns in the history of the state. In the runoff election, however, Johnson won as a result of fraud committed by the infamous Parr political machine in Duval County. Stevenson attempted to force a recount but failed, and after this debacle, he retired from politics.

Returning home to Kimble County after his defeat, Stevenson reopened his law practice and threw himself into working on his ranch. In 1954 and at the age of sixty-six, he married for the second time and fathered a daughter two years later. He enjoyed another two decades of relative health and vigor, but in early June, 1976, at the age of eighty-seven, he fell ill; he died of complications following surgery on June 28. He is buried on his ranch in Kimble County.

Notes

1. James T. DeShields, *They Sat in High Places: The Presidents and Governors of Texas* (San Antonio: The Naylor Company, 1940), 455.

2. Seth S. McKay, *Texas Politics, 1906–1944* (Lubbock: Texas Tech Press, 1952), 312.

3. Ibid., 315.

Sources and Further Reading

Atkinson, W. Eugene. "James V. Allred: A Political Biography." Ph.D. diss., Texas Tech University, 1978.

Burlage, Robb K. "James V. Allred: Texas's Liberal Governor." Unpublished seminar paper, University of Texas, 1959.

Green, George N. *The Establishment in Texas Politics, The Primitive Years.* Westpoint: Greenwood, 1979.

Hart, James P. "Oil, the Courts, and the Railroad Commission." *Southwestern Historical Quarterly* 44 (1941): 303–20.

Larson, Henrietta M., and Kenneth W. Porter. *History of the Humble Oil and Refining Company.* New York: Harper and Brothers, 1959.

McKay, Seth S. *Texas Politics, 1906–1944.* Lubbock: Texas Tech Press, 1952.

———. *W. Lee O'Daniel and Texas Politics.* Lubbock: Texas Tech Press, 1945.

Patenaude, Lionel V. *Texans, Politics and the New Deal.* New York: Garland, 1983.

Phares, Ross. *The Governors of Texas.* Gretna, La.: Pelican Publishing Company, 1976.

Wyatt, Frederica Burt, and Shelton Hooper. *Coke R. Stevenson: A Texas Legend.* Junction, Texas: Shelton Press, 1976.

Chapter twelve

TEXAS AT MIDCENTURY AND BEYOND

1947–69

The political scene in Texas at midcentury featured continued conservatism and reaction. The people and their leaders were attempting to deal with rapid social and economic changes and internal political discord at home, while at the same time the federal government became more deeply involved in the state's affairs. There were three major issues that, over a period of several years, defined the state's growing animosity toward Washington: the tidelands question, desegregation, and President Johnson's Great Society policy. All seemed to portend ever greater interference by outside forces in the affairs of the state.

Meanwhile, the civil rights movement began to mature, political scandals rocked the Democratic party to its foundations, the "Red Scare" appeared to challenge the exercise of civil liberties by many citizens, and a resurgent Republican party showed signs of coming into its own. The governors of this period played significant roles in all these matters, but only one, John B. Connally, Jr. (1963–69), showed any characteristics of greatness. The others were Beauford H. Jester, 1947–49; Allan Shivers, 1949–57; and Price Daniel, 1957–63.

BEAUFORD H. JESTER ☆ 1947–49

George and Frances Jester were civic and religious leaders in Corsicana when their son Beauford was born on January 12, 1893. The family was not wealthy, however, and as a boy Beauford delivered milk to earn extra money. He received a good education and attended the University of Texas at Austin, where he completed his B.A. After serving in the armed forces during World War I, he finished his law degree and was admitted to the bar in June, 1920. He acquired substantial wealth over the next two decades representing various oil interests, and in 1942, he was appointed to the railroad commission. Two years later he ran unopposed for a second term.

Jester's race for governor in 1946 exhibited certain bizarre qualities. In addition to the commissioner, the other major candidates were Lieut. Gov. John Lee Smith, former Railroad Commissioner Jerry Sadler, Atty. Gen. Grover Sellers, and Homer P. Rainey, the deposed president of the University of Texas. All, save Rainey, were either conservatives or reactionaries, with Smith being the most reactionary by far. Smith had hoped to ride a wave of patriotism to the governor's mansion in Austin by criticizing labor unions and accusing liberals of being communists. At first he had the support of those in the business community and several ultrarich oil executives, but, as his views became more and more extreme, he began to lose support. Ultimately, he finished last among the five leading candidates.

Jester shrewdly adopted a moderate position between Smith (and other right wingers) and the liberal, Rainey. This strategy worked well, and Jester polled a large plurality in the first primary. Jester attacked Rainey more vigorously in the runoff campaign, charging that the liberal was stirring up social tensions and that he intended to raise taxes. Jester prevailed, polling almost twice as many votes as the professor.

During his administration Jester sought to follow a moderate policy, especially with regard to organized labor, but he was not entirely successful. In 1946, the Congress of Industrial Organizations (CIO) began a massive organizational effort in Texas, which triggered an

Beauford H. Jester

equally intense reaction from business. Jester wanted legislation that would promote arbitration and mediation, but instead the lawmakers presented him with an array of repressive measures. Under pressure from the Texas Manufacturers Association (TMA) and other groups, he signed most of these laws, some of which prohibited the check off (the deduction of union dues from a worker's paycheck), strikes by public employees, picketing, and boycotts; also in the package was a right-to-work law that made it illegal to require a worker to join a union.

Governor Jester also faced problems in the Democratic party as the Texas Regulars (the anti-New Deal reactionaries) and the liberals battled for control. Here, Jester was more successful and must be given some credit for holding the party together. Although he opposed President Truman's civil rights plans and favored state control of tidelands, he was not prepared to bolt the party; he wanted to fight Truman from within. At the state convention of 1948, Jester successfully engineered the nomination of an uninstructed delegation to the national convention. In spite of bitter criticism from the right wing he stood his ground, and his actions undoubtedly helped keep many conservatives in the party.

Perhaps the most significant and controversial piece of legislation passed during Jester's administration was the Gilmer-Aiken Law, designed to reform the educational system. It streamlined administration, consolidated many school districts and placed controls over the selection of textbooks. It also changed the state board of education from an appointed to an elected body and the state commissioner of education from an elected to an appointed office. Financed by consumer taxes, the law had the support of the TMA and many conservatives.

Governor Jester easily won reelection in 1948, but his second term was cut short, for on July 11, 1949, he died suddenly of a heart attack and was interred at Oakwood Cemetery in Corsicana. Had he lived, perhaps he would have continued to exert a moderating influence on Texas politics. Jester was succeeded by Lieut. Gov. Allan Shivers, whose commitment to reaction was much greater than his sense of loyalty to the national Democratic party.

ALLAN SHIVERS ☆ 1949–57

Born on October 5, 1907, in Lufkin, Robert Allan Shivers was the son of Robert A. and Ester Shivers. Lufkin, therefore, boasts that

Shivers was a native son, but since the family moved to Woodville when the lad was only ten months old, the latter community really has a better claim (though this one too is tenuous, since the family soon moved again, this time to Port Arthur). Allan, who started going by his middle name when he got to college, was introduced to the world of politics early in life because his father was a lawyer and county judge. At the family table talk frequently turned to public affairs.

Like so many of Texas' political leaders before him, Shivers came from a family that was not well-to-do, so he worked while in school, his first real job being that of a soda jerk in a local drugstore. He graduated from Port Arthur High School in 1924 and began college that fall at the University of Texas. Because of family financial problems, he had to drop out in 1925, but he returned after a period of work and graduated in 1931. His political career really began while he was in college, where he became president of the student body during his senior year.

Soon after graduation Shivers passed the bar exam, even though he had not attended law school. Later, he went back to school at the University of Texas and completed his law degree in 1933. Then he returned to Port Arthur hoping to practice and get into politics as soon as possible – it did not take long. In 1934, he ran for state senator on a platform supporting old age pensions and relief bonds. Skillfully exploiting every opportunity during the campaign, he defeated an entrenched incumbent in the primary and went on to an easy victory in November – at the age of twenty-seven, he was the youngest senator in the history of the state.

During his first two years in office, Shivers established himself as an effective legislator. He seldom took part in floor debates but accomplished a great deal in the cloak room and in conference committees. Many colleagues soon came to have confidence that they could follow his lead on even the most complicated legislation. In 1935, Shivers met Marialice Shary, daughter of a fabulously wealthy Rio Grande Valley land developer, and they were married in 1937. From that point on in his career, Shivers had no financial worries; he could devote himself wholly to politics without ever having to practice law again.

In 1938, Shivers was elected to a second term in the state senate and to a third in 1942. During that time he watched in amazement as W. Lee O'Daniel worked his spell on the people. Shivers recognized that

Allan Shivers

O'Daniel had very few political scruples, but, impressed by the governor's ability to cultivate and maintain popular support, he learned from O'Daniel and filed away the lesson for later reference.

In early 1943, Shivers interrupted his political career to enter the service; he applied for and received a direct commission in the army. While he served overseas for slightly more than two years, a movement got underway to elect him lieutenant governor, and in 1946, shortly after his return, he won that office. Earlier his father-in-law had died and left him in charge of the vast Shary estates, and the experience of managing great wealth affected his political views. He began to move away from his earlier moderate-liberal position on social issues and the federal system and toward a states' rights-conservative view. Eventually he would emerge as an outright reactionary, but in the meantime he worked hard to get the state to recognize its responsibilities more fully.

While serving as lieutenant governor, Shivers once again proved himself a skillful political manager. During his second term alone he promoted legislation that, among other things, produced the creation of a board to administer state hospitals and schools; the adoption of the Gilmer-Aiken School law; constitutional amendments dealing with annual legislative sessions, salaries for legislators, and repealing the poll tax (all of which were defeated by the voters); a water needs study group; decent pay for state employees; an antilynching law; and the expansion of higher education. Under his guidance though, the lawmakers also passed several antilabor laws and scuttled a gas tax that had been passed by the house.

Rather suddenly, Shivers became governor on July 11, 1949, after Beauford Jester died of a heart attack. He was to serve as governor until 1957, longer than any other person in Texas history. One of Shivers's first problems was to deal with the looming financial crisis that Jester had been hoping to avoid. He called in business leaders to point out that taxes would have to be raised in some fashion. Major budget cuts, as proposed by the Texas Manufacturers Association and other conservative groups, would not be acceptable. Prior to calling a special session in 1950, Shivers was able to convince the major industry lobbyists to accept his program, which for the most part involved increased consumer taxes to support the growing needs of education, salaries, retirement benefits, highways, and humanitarian institutions.

These were reasonable achievements, but there was a darker side to the early years of the Shivers administration. He gutted the effectiveness of the Good Neighbor Commission, probably because as a Valley landlord he was embarrassed by any activity that called attention to the deplorable conditions experienced by Mexican and Mexican-American workers, and he exploited the Red Scare by stating explicitly that labor unions, the NAACP, and other liberal or reform organizations were infiltrated or controlled by communists.

Shivers won reelection easily in 1950 and again in 1952, and was able to control the machinery of the Democratic party effectively in the process. As the tidelands issue loomed and his political difficulties intensified, Shivers's party loyalty began to falter. The problem was that both President Truman and Democratic candidate Adlai Stevenson opposed state control of offshore land. Since Texas' "tidelands" were rich with petroleum, the oil lobby demanded that something be done. Sen. Price Daniel was already in the fray, and Shivers could not ignore the pressure. In 1952, he was one of three Southern governors supporting the candidacy of Dwight Eisenhower, who favored state control, and his actions caused a breach in the Democratic party that was difficult to repair.

Shivers was the first Texas governor to break tradition and seek a third term. His opponent in the 1954 primary was Ralph Yarborough, who represented the liberal faction of the Democratic party. Shivers was sufficiently fearful of Yarborough that he called upon his supporters in big business – the oil, gas, sulphur, and liquor industries – to sit still for tax increases to support increased appropriations for schools and social services. Otherwise, he warned, Yarborough might win the election. This possibility so frightened the business moguls that they approved Shivers's demands.

Yarborough began the campaign by talking about issues, but soon found that it would be more productive to attack the governor's involvement in certain questionable activities. The fact was that, while during his first four years in office Shivers had run what appeared to be a relatively clean administration, the shadow of scandal now hung heavily over Shivers and many of those around him. Among the questions that Yarborough raised were those having to do with the outrageous behavior of the insurance industry in the state, which Shivers seemingly ignored, and a questionable land deal in 1946 (whereby Shivers had parlayed the purchase of a $25,000 option on 13,500 acres in the Valley into a $450,000 sale). These revelations could have been so damaging as to destroy Shivers's chances, but he used the Red Scare issue adroitly to salvage a victory. He accused Yarborough of being an outright desegregationist (which he was not) and a communist dupe in his support of the rights of labor. In the hysterical atmosphere of the early 1950s, these charges were enough to turn the tide. Shivers won a plurality in the July primary with a 23,000-vote lead over Yarborough and then claimed a decisive victory in the runoff.

Regrettably, Shivers's third term was marred by scandal. Not only was he unable to answer satisfactorily the questions raised about the insurance industry and the land deal, but he now became embroiled in an even deeper scandal involving the state land commissioner, Bascom Giles. After the war a program had been established in Texas to help veterans buy land cheaply: in a nutshell, the state land office was to purchase land for resale to veterans on low-interest, long-term notes. But in 1955, an investigation by Kenneth Towery, a Cuero news reporter, revealed that crooked promoters were selling land to the state for resale to veterans at prices much higher than it was worth. Supposedly, the program was under the supervision of a board composed of Commissioner Giles, Atty. Gen. John Ben Sheppard, and Governor Shivers. Admitting his involvement in the scheme, Giles resigned and, although Shivers and Sheppard were never formally implicated, many assumed they were guilty. Shivers's problems were compounded in 1957 when there were further revelations concerning illegalities in his dealings with the insurance industry.

Shivers left office in 1957 with his reputation badly damaged and returned to his law practice and the management of his many business interests. He died on January 16, 1985, and is buried in the state cemetery at Austin.

PRICE DANIEL ☆ 1957–63

Born Marion Price Daniel on October 10, 1910, in Liberty, Daniel was to become the only person ever to hold four of the top five positions in Texas government. At various times in his career, he was a speaker of the Texas house, attorney general, U.S. senator, and governor. Daniel was educated in the Fort Worth public schools and graduated in 1926. In the fall of the same year, he enrolled at Baylor and was active in campus politics from the beginning, being elected president of the freshman class and later president of the senior class. In 1931, he received his bachelor's degree and entered law school. Admitted to the bar in 1932, he set up his practice in Liberty, and his first successful effort in state politics came in 1938, when he was elected to the house. Subsequently, he served three terms and during the third, he was elected speaker.

When the United States entered World War II in 1941, Daniel left office to enlist in the army. Although he joined as a private, he was soon granted a commission in the judge advocate general's office and served there until 1946. While he was still in the service, Daniel's supporters in Texas began to promote him as a candidate for attorney general, and upon his return, he waged a vigorous campaign against Pat Neff, Jr., and was elected.

Daniel served three terms as attorney general, during which time be became notable for his attacks upon organized crime. Yet, he was to become most famous for his efforts in the tidelands controversy. When, on June 23, 1947, the U.S. Supreme Court handed down its ruling in the case of *United States* v. *California* – in which the court decreed that the federal government, not California, had dominion over the submerged land out to the three-mile limit – Daniel correctly surmised that the decision would have repercussions in Texas and other coastal states. Daniel argued that, since Texas had retained control of all its public land when it entered the Union of 1845, the Court's ruling could not apply to the Lone Star State. Daniel researched the question thoroughly, becoming an authority on the subject of submerged land ownership, and when Texas' case came before the Supreme Court in 1950, he argued his position effectively. Nevertheless, he lost the decision by a vote of four to three.

In 1952, and with substantial backing from the oil and gas industry, Daniel ran for the U.S. Senate. At first he thought that he would face an uphill battle against incumbent Tom Connally, but when the old senator found that most of his support in the state had withered away over the years, he retired from the race and Daniel was easily elected. Because many Texas Regulars opposed President Truman's policies on practically all fronts (and because the Democratic candidate, Adlai Stevenson, opposed state control of tidelands), Daniel and Gov. Allan Shivers supported the Republican candidate, Dwight Eisenhower, in the November election.

As a result, the Democratic National Committee threatened the new senator with reprisals, but he was saved by the actions of Majority

Price Daniel

Leader Lyndon Baines Johnson and given a place on both the Senate Interior and Insular Affairs committees. Daniel cosponsored Joint Resolution 13, which called for restoration of the tidelands to the states. It was successfully shepherded through the legislative process, and Eisenhower signed it on May 22, 1953. Though Daniel sponsored other legislation, he was, after winning the tidelands battle, no longer interested in the Senate and turned his attention instead to his lifelong dream of becoming governor of Texas.

Because his administration had been racked by scandals, Allan Shivers was forced to withdraw from the primary race in 1956, thus paving the way for a battle royal between the liberal and conservative factions of the Democratic party for control of the state. The liberals were represented by Ralph Yarborough and the conservatives by Senator Daniel in the ensuing campaign. There were also some reactionaries in the race, including former Governor O'Daniel and J. Evetts Haley, the eccentric rancher, both of whose campaigns consisted primarily of accusing all their opponents of being communists.

Daniel had the backing of big oil and the major corporate interests of the state in the campaign. He tried to frighten people by pointing to the threat of organized labor, but he also called for lobby control, school improvement, narcotics control, old-age pensions, and water conservation. Yarborough's platform was actually very similar to Daniel's, but he was hurt by his identification with the forces of desegregation (even though he had specifically come out against "forced integration"). Daniel ran first with a substantial plurality in the July primary and, thus, was heavily favored to win the runoff in August. Yarborough campaigned effectively, however, and almost won; the final vote was 698,000 to 694,830. Subsequently, Daniel was reelected in 1958 and 1960.

Measured by his success in getting his programs passed by the legislature, Daniel must be judged to have been one of Texas' most effective governors. In one regular and three special sessions, the fifty-fifth legislature considered fifty-seven specific proposals offered by the governor and passed fifty-three of them. Among the most important were laws that regulated the activities of lobbyists, created a water planning board, and increased teachers' salaries – all without any increase in taxes.

When Daniel addressed the legislature on January 21, 1959, at the beginning of his second term, the state faced a substantial deficit caused by a combination of increased population and declining oil revenues. Daniel was less successful than during his first term in his efforts to deal with this problem. In one regular and three special sessions, the legislature hesitated to accept most of his financial proposals, which involved tax increases on natural resources, motor vehicle sales, and liquor. The legislative opposition resulted largely from substantial pressure brought to bear by the oil and gas lobby. Finally, in the third special session, a gas severance tax was passed, but a hostile amendment rendered it unconstitutional. In the final analysis, Daniel's only successes were to bring about a small increase in both the franchise tax and the taxes on tobacco, automobiles, and liquor; yet, these increases did not produce sufficient revenues to balance the budget.

The tax controversy reached its climax in Daniel's third term when proposals were offered for a retail sales tax and an income tax, both of which the governor opposed. Early in the session of the fifty-seventh legislature, Daniel proposed a tax package that included increases in the gas severance tax and the corporate franchise tax, as well as escheat legislation, and immediately the oil and gas industry and some large business concerns began to lobby against the proposal. At the same time, an organization calling itself "Citizens for a Sales Tax" emerged. This was in reality a front for lobbyists – representing the oil and gas industry, the TMA, and the Texas Industrial Conference – led by Tom Sealy of Midland and Searcy Bracewell of Houston, both of whom had close connections with big business.

Daniel countered these forces with a lobbying effort of his own. Two of his staff assistants, George Christian and John Goldson, worked closely with several key members of the legislature, and Daniel coordinated his efforts with Speaker James Turman, who was instrumental in keeping several of the governor's proposals alive in the house. Moreover, in a strange turn of events, Daniel was indirectly assisted by the liberals in the house led by Henry Gonzales of San Antonio, who engineered delays and gave Daniel's forces time to prepare amendments to the sales tax measure.

The battle resulted in a draw. No significant tax legislation was passed during the regular session, and, thus, a special session was required. Here Daniel found that the lobbying pressures were too great to resist, and he gave in to a compromise. When the legislature, after considerable wrangling, passed a sales tax bill, the governor allowed it to become law without his signature. In its original form, this bill called for a 2 percent tax on all sales of 25 cents or more, with the exceptions of food, agricultural implements, and clothing under ten dollars.

After passage of the tax measure, the governor and the legislature turned to education. No new funds were appropriated for education during the regular session, although they were desperately needed, nor was anything significant achieved during the first called session. However, during the second session Daniel was able to mobilize sufficient support to get something done, and two bills, drafted with the support of the Texas State Teachers Association, were submitted and passed. These provided for salary increases and increased funds for operations.

Finally during the fifty-seventh legislature, the lawmakers took another important step, this time in the area of water resource management, by creating the Texas Water Pollution Control Board. This agency was given the power to grant or deny waste disposal permits, issue regulations concerning pollution, and enforce its decisions. Again, Daniel used his influence and political skills to shepherd this significant law through the legislature.

Although he suffered some reversals, Daniel was able to steer 80 percent of his proposals into law during his six-year tenure as governor of Texas. This impressive record resulted largely from Daniel's skillful use of his limited powers, his ability to cultivate support from other politicians (even those who opposed him), and his ability to generate support from both special interest groups and the citizenry. However, Daniel did not use his administrative skills on behalf of social reform. While in the Senate, he opposed desegregation and was a signatory to the infamous Southern Manifesto, which denounced the Brown decision of 1954; and as governor he did nothing to promote integration. When he left office, the racial situation in Texas was no better than when he had entered.

After leaving office Daniel returned to private law practice until he joined the Johnson administration in 1967 as assistant to the president for state-federal relations. Before Johnson left office, Daniel also served him as director of the Office of Emergency Preparedness and as a member of the National Security Council. On January 1, 1971, he became a member of the Texas supreme court and served there until his retirement in 1978. He died at his ranch near Liberty on August 27, 1988, and was buried there.

John Bowden Connally, Jr., was born on February 27, 1917, at Floresville, in Wilson County, the son of tenant farmer and sometime politician, John B. Connally, and Lela Wright Connally. There were six other children in the family, and one of them, the firstborn son Wyatt, burned to death in the family home before reaching one year of age. Life was hard for the Connally family, and John was required to go to work early. By the time he was five years old, he was already working in the cotton fields alongside his parents, brothers, and sisters. In 1926, the elder Connally tired of farming and moved his family to San Antonio, where he initiated a "bus line" with one old Buick. They settled in Harlandale, a suburb of the Alamo City, where they enjoyed electricity and indoor plumbing for the first time. Young John attended high school in Harlandale, where he excelled in debate and oratory. He developed into a handsome, exuberant young man known for his fastidiousness and oratorical skills.

The family returned to Wilson County in 1932, and, using money realized from the sale of the bus company, the senior Connally bought a twelve-hundred acre ranch and began a new career breeding Hereford cattle. Soon he also entered politics and was elected clerk of Wilson County. Meanwhile, in 1934, young John entered the University of Texas at Austin and threw himself into drama, oratory, and campus politics. He joined the prestigious Athenaeum Society and soon became its president. Later, he was elected president of the senior class, a position he took very seriously. Campus politics became his passion, in fact, and he sacrificed his grades to his extracurricular activities. As a result he failed two courses and was required to resign his position as class president. By this time he had decided upon a career in law, but he would not complete his degree until 1941.

In 1939, Connally applied to become secretary to Rep. Lyndon B. Johnson, who had been elected to Congress in 1937. Although he was only nine years Connally's senior, Johnson had already gained a reputation as a wheeler-dealer and a politician on the make. He referred to Connally as "my boy," and their relationship was to last, more or less, for the rest of Johnson's life. Even though they were different in many ways, Connally learned much from Johnson and contributed a great deal to his career, beginning with the management of his 1941 senatorial campaign.

John B. Connally, Jr.

Shortly after Connally finished his law degree, the United States entered World War II, and Connally and his boss entered the navy. Johnson was to serve for only eighteen months and would be awarded the Silver Star for being a passenger on one mission over enemy territory. Connally, on the other hand, remained in the service for the duration of the war and saw considerable combat. He was flight director on the carriers *Essex* and *Bennington* during some of the heaviest fighting in the Pacific, when American warships were coming under kamikaze attacks from the Japanese Imperial Air Force. Connally won the bronze star for his heroism and was always a little miffed that Johnson received greater recognition.

Johnson tried to coax Connally back into his service in Washington at the end of the war, but Connally declined at first in order to enter private business. From 1946 until 1948, he was manager of radio station KVET in Austin, but in the latter year he finally gave in to Johnson's entreaties and joined him as campaign manager in his quest for the Democratic senatorial nomination. After Johnson defeated Coke Stevenson by those infamous eighty-seven votes and swamped his Republican opponent in the general election, Connally joined his staff briefly as an aide. Following a short stint with Johnson, Connally decided to return to private life to practice law. His big financial break came in 1952, when he became counsel to Fort Worth multi-millionaires Sid Richardson and Perry Bass. This move brought him into the presence of enormous wealth and made possible a life of ease and a career in politics.

After Kennedy and Johnson were elected in 1960, the vice president recommended Connally for a cabinet position. His wartime experience, combined with his connections to the oil fraternity, made him a natural for the office of secretary of the navy, and the president duly appointed him in 1961. By this time, however, his ambition was to be governor of Texas, and after a few months in office, he resigned to pursue that goal. He was selected as a candidate by a small group of millionaires and conservatives who convened at Dolph Briscoe's ranch in 1961. They feared that Texas was drifting out of the hands of the conservative Democrats, and they wanted to reverse that trend.

At first Connally was not the front-running candidate and, in fact, in early 1962 only 4 percent of the voters favored his making the race. Still, he had a fair amount of name recognition and the timing was right. Governor Daniel, who really wanted a fourth term, had lost much of his support in the business community because he had op-posed the sales tax, and there was a very good chance that he could not win. In all, five candidates entered the 1962 primary: in addition to Connally and Daniel, Atty. Gen. Will Wilson made the race, as did Marshall Formby of Plainview, who formerly chaired the highway commission. The fifth contender was liberal lawyer Don Yarborough of Houston, who was running as a Kennedy Democrat.

As the contest developed, Connally became the leader with consid-erable moderate and conservative support. His strongest argument was that Texas was losing millions of dollars because it had a second-rate educational system and, thus, could not attract first-rate scholars who, in turn, could attract federal research dollars and new industries. Connally said this disgraceful situation had to change and many agreed. When the ballots were cast on May 5, Connally led with 431,490 votes to 317,986 for Yarborough. Daniel was third, with Wilson and Formby far behind. In the runoff Connally narrowly squeezed by Yarborough with only 26,250 votes to spare. Obviously, many Republicans and ultraconservatives voted for Yarborough, reasoning that he would be easier to defeat in November than Connally.

The Republican candidate was Jack Cox, a former Democrat who had switched parties. Cox was a *bona fide* contender and could not be ignored, so Connally conducted a vigorous campaign. He continued to emphasize the themes that had won him the primary, and toward the end of the campaign, he conducted an LBJ-style airplane blitz of the state that took him to thirty-one cities in forty-eight hours. In the voting on November 3, Connally won with 847,038 to Cox's 715,025 votes. The Republican candidate was defeated, but he had received 46 percent of the vote, indicating both that conservatism was gaining ever greater support in the state and the Republican party was no longer a joke. This should not have surprised anyone, since John Tower had been sent to the U.S. Senate in a special election to replace Lyndon Johnson only one year earlier.

When Connally became governor of Texas in 1963, the state faced daunting problems. In spite of its fabulous oil wealth, Texas ranked thirty-third in the nation in per capita income, forty-fourth in adult literacy, and last in *per capita* expenditures for child welfare. Moreover, the educational system was one of the worst in the nation, and social attitudes were Paleolithic. Even though nine years had passed since the Brown decision on desegregation, only 2 percent of the state's African-

American children had been integrated, and Mexican Americans continued to suffer from discrimination in practically every aspect of social and economic life.

Here were opportunities for a governor of stature to accomplish many things. The state had a lot of money and, as Connally had said, "I want to do something really big as governor."[1] He knew that race, welfare, and education were the three issues upon which he could focus his attention; but as indicated by his emphasis during the campaign, he had already focused on education. He had convinced himself that major improvements in that area would make it possible for other problems to take care of themselves.

Connally set forth his ambitions in his first message to the legislature. He proposed the creation of a special commission to study higher education and make recommendations to improve the system. Styled the Governor's Committee on Education beyond High School, this group reported in July, 1963, calling for the expenditure of $100 million on salaries, libraries, research, and new graduate programs. Connally enthusiastically agreed, for even before the report was produced, he had begun acting on his own. During the legislative session, he presented a $32.9 million tax package to provide funds for educational improvements. This proposal had considerable support from many lawmakers, but Lieut. Gov. Preston Smith, an ultraconservative used car entrepreneur from Lubbock, and Speaker of the House Byron Tunnell opposed it. Because of their influence Connally was forced to agree to cut $13 million from his higher education budget. After that, the appropriations bill passed, but Connally then vetoed $12.5 million from other areas in order, as he put it, "to provide a sort of layaway plan on a substantial down payment on excellence in education."[2]

Education was clearly the major focus of Connally's administration, but it was not the only issue he faced. Few tourists came to Texas because the state's attractions were little known, and to remedy this, Connally proposed the creation of a Texas Tourist Development Agency. The creation of this agency was a significant step, and the beginning of a new era for the Texas economy – over the next thirty years, tourism developed into a major industry.

Although he was by no means a liberal on social issues, Connally also proposed the repeal of the poll tax. The legislature agreed, but this move required a constitutional amendment, and the voters rejected it in November.

By the end of the legislative session in the summer of 1963, Connally was generally satisfied with his achievements and was already looking forward to a second term, during which he hoped to do even more. Fate intervened, however, and the governor nearly lost his life. President Kennedy came to Texas in late November, 1963, on a Democratic fence-mending junket, and Connally, who was in the same car with Kennedy on November 22, was severely wounded in the back, leg, and arm. Later, the Warren Commission concluded that Lee Harvey Oswald, acting alone, had killed President Kennedy and wounded the governor, but Connally, like some others, had his own unanswered questions about the incident. He was convinced that, whether or not Oswald acted alone, it was not possible for the "single bullet theory" to be true. He did not believe that the bullet that struck him had hit the president first.

As Connally gradually recovered his health in 1964, he found his political future certain. Not only was he a popular governor, he was able to use the sympathy generated by the assassination attempt to gain practically anything he wanted from the legislature. Easily re-elected in 1964 and again in 1966, and with his friend Ben Barnes now installed as speaker of the house, Connally went on to build a string of legislative successes over the next few years even more impressive than those of Allan Shivers and Price Daniel. His emphasis on education continued with the creation of the Texas Commission on Higher Education, which ultimately evolved into the Coordinating Board, Texas Higher Education. This agency has served admirably over the years to bring balance and fairness into the state system of higher education. Appropriations were increased, salaries continued to grow, building funds expanded, student loan programs sprang into being, more junior colleges appeared, the University of Houston was made a state university, and both Angelo State and Pan American College became four-year institutions. Connally got almost everything he wanted from the legislature regarding higher education, and for the first time in history the Texas college and university system approached competitiveness with systems in other large states. Tragically, since Connally's day, many of these gains have been lost due to the penuriousness of the state's political leaders.

Connally also made important proposals in other areas. Speaking before the legislature in 1965, he called for the creation of a Fine Arts Commission to encourage cultural growth in the state, the enactment of tougher traffic safety laws, reorganization of the state water and mental health agencies in order to promote more efficient administration, and, once again, the repeal of the poll tax. He also cautioned the lawmakers that the federal courts had given the state an August, 1965, deadline to redistrict in accordance with the 1960 census.

It was also during his second term that Connally became obsessed with the idea of a four year term for the governor. He believed that a two year period was simply not long enough to accomplish anything, especially since the legislature only met biennially. He would, in fact, have liked to see annual sessions as well, but there was a great deal of opposition to this proposal from lawmakers who said it would make the governor too powerful. Yet, Connally's friends were able to put it through committee and get it adopted by the legislature. In November, however, it was rejected by the voters.

Even though Connally suffered a few setbacks, the overwhelming majority of his proposals breezed through the legislature, and much of what he achieved was extremely beneficial to the state and its people. With respect to the efforts of his friend Lyndon Johnson to improve the lot of those Americans who had suffered far too long from discrimination and poverty, however, the story was a little different. Connally was not necessarily opposed to the philosophy underlying the Great Society and the War on Poverty, but he did object to the element of federal control over state affairs that accompanied most of Johnson's programs. He believed that Washington bureaucrats could not possibly know or care as much about the needs of people in Texas as Texans did, and with that in mind, Connally used powers granted to governors in the original Economic Opportunity Act of 1964 to veto an eleven-county Neighborhood Youth Corps project, the darling of Sen. Ralph Yarborough and the Texas liberals. This led to a successful effort to remove the veto power from the original legislation and Yarborough claimed victory over the "forces of reaction." After that Connally never entirely overcame the image that he was indifferent to the social and economic needs of the poor, even though most Great Society programs eventually operated more or less successfully in Texas.

There was one incident in particular that damaged Connally's reputation with respect to social issues, one that he never lived down. In the summer of 1966, leaders of the immigrant farmworkers in the Rio Grande Valley planned a march of nearly five hundred miles to Austin to both dramatize the need for minimum wage legislation in Texas and demand a special session of the legislature to consider the issue. Connally hoped to ignore the marchers, but as they drew near to Austin, they began to attract more and more press coverage and received considerable encouragement from Senator Yarborough. Connally decided he must act.

Accompanied by Ben Barnes and Atty. Gen. Waggoner Carr, the governor intercepted the marchers near New Braunfels. He shook their hands, patted their backs, and told them that he sympathized with their problems; but he also declared that he would not call a special session of the legislature, and he was not going to be "home" if they called on him in Austin. He then went on to chastise the protesters for marching. Even though the group had been a perfect model of decorum, Connally told them he was afraid things might "get out of hand" and that they should disband. They did not, of course, and the only real outcome of the confrontation was to show the governor at his worst, seemingly unsympathetic to the plight of workers.

By 1967, having won reelection by an overwhelming majority the previous year, Connally found that he was bored with his job. He had discovered what all of his predecessors since 1876 had known – that Texas governors really do not have much power – and he was tired of both his administrative obligations and his ceremonial chores. He wanted to retire after his third term, but he hesitated because the thought that he might be succeeded by Preston Smith frightened him. The problem was much on his mind as he presented his third and final legislative program to the session on January 18, 1967.

The highlight of Connally's package on this occasion was his call for a convention to rewrite the Constitution of 1876, a document everyone knew to be hopelessly outmoded. He also called for approval of liquor-by-the-drink legislation, healthy appropriations for a world's fair in San Antonio (to be called "Hemisfair '68"), and measures to allow Texas to comply with such Great Society measures as the Highway Safety Act, the Water Quality Act, and Medicaid. The governor did not get everything he wanted; the proposed constitutional convention was rejected, liquor by the drink was defeated, and his recommended appropriations were slashed. In fact, the financial situation in the state became so critical that it required two special sessions before the end of 1968 to finalize a budget for that biennium.

By this time Connally had had all he wanted of the legislative process, but he still hesitated to announce his retirement in the face of

Preston Smith's incessant campaigning. It was not until the fall that Connally made his final decision regarding the governorship. Just after the National Governors Conference, Connally announced to a press conference held in Austin on November 10, 1968, that he would not seek reelection.

Regardless of Governor Connally's philosophy, he must be ranked as one of Texas' greatest governors for his achievements in the field of education and for his promotion of tourism. Both of these efforts have led to major changes over the last thirty years and have contributed substantially to Texas' growth and development. Connally cannot be blamed for the failure of his successors to build effectively on the foundation he laid, nor can he be blamed for the collapse of oil prices in the 1980s, which politicians of recent years have used to justify their penuriousness.

After leaving office in 1969, Connally returned briefly to private life, but Richard Nixon stirred the political world by naming him secretary of the treasury in 1970. Connally held this post for fifteen months before resigning, during which time he played a major role in formulating Nixon's dramatic anti-inflation program of 1971. These proposals included a ninety day freeze on wages, prices, and rents; cuts in federal spending and taxes; and the establishment of a "floating" dollar in world markets that ended the dollar's dependence on the price of gold. Later, during the Watergate scandal, Connally was accused of having accepted a ten thousand dollar bribe from a dairy industry official for recommending to the president that the administration raise federal milk price supports. Tried on the charge, he was found innocent.

Following his departure from the treasury post, Connally served Nixon as a special adviser. In 1972, he headed a group called Democrats for Nixon, and in 1973, shortly after delivering the eulogy at Lyndon Johnson's funeral, he announced that he was a Republican. Shortly thereafter, Vice President Spiro Agnew was forced to resign, and Nixon considered Connally as a replacement. However, the prospect of strong Democratic opposition in Congress convinced Nixon to appoint House Republican Leader Gerald Ford instead. Ford became president when Nixon himself resigned in August, 1974.

Connally retired to private life for several years following the Nixon debacle, but in 1980, he emerged once again as a candidate for president. He spent more than eleven million dollars in the early campaign but was unable to garner more than one committed vote. Eventually, the Republican nomination went to Ronald Reagan, who had assiduously cultivated Republican grassroots support through the years while Connally had been out of touch. Connally attributed his poor showing to the fact that people still associated him with Lyndon Johnson.

During the early 1980s, Connally devoted himself to private business and became involved in numerous lucrative land and oil deals. Thus, Texas and the nation were stunned when, in 1987, he filed for bankruptcy and disclosed that he had $93 million in debts and only $13 million in assets. His problems arose from the collapse of many of his oil and land investments that had been adversely affected by the economic decline of that period. To help pay their debts, Connally and his wife, Nellie, sold most of their personal possessions at a highly publicized auction in 1988. Connally then began a financial comeback and before long succeeded in recouping at least a part of his lost fortune.

Connally remained active in politics in recent years. He supported Sen. Bob Dole over George Bush for the Republican presidential nomination in 1988, and he chaired the election committee of former Houston mayor Fred Hofheinz, who attempted to unseat Mayor Kathy Whitmire in 1989. Just before the Persian Gulf War, Connally participated in a successful effort to secure the release of twenty-one hostages held by Iraq.

Still active in business, Connally announced his involvement in a venture to build and operate a Class I pari-mutuel horseracing track in Harris County in May, 1993. Unfortunately, he became seriously ill with a pulmonary ailment shortly thereafter and was forced to enter the hospital on May 17. He died on June 15, 1993, and was buried in the state cemetery in Austin.

Notes

1. James Reston, Jr., *The Lone Star: The Life of John Connally* (New York: Harper and Row, 1989), 290.

2. Ann Fears Crawford and Jack Keever, *John B. Connally: Portrait in Power* (Austin: Jenkins Publishing Company, 1973), 99.

Sources and Further Reading

Ashman, Charles R. *Connally: The Adventures of Big Bad John.* New York: Morrow, 1974.

Bartley, Everet R. *The Tidelands Oil Controversy: A Legal and Historical Analysis.* Austin: University of Texas, 1953.

Carlton, Don E. *Red Scare: Right Wing Hysteria, Fifties Fanaticism and Their Legacies in Texas.* Austin: Texas Monthly Press, 1985.

Caro, Robert. *The Years of Lyndon Johnson: Means of Ascent.* New York: Harpers, 1990.

Crawford, Ann Fears, and Jack Keever. *John B. Connally: A Portrait in Power.* Austin: Jenkins Publishing Company, 1973.

Davidson, Chandler. *Race and Class in Texas Politics.* Princeton, N.J.: Princeton University Press, 1990.

Green, George N. *The Establishment in Texas Politics: The Primitive Years, 1938–1957.* Westport, Conn.: Greenwood Press, 1979.

Green, James R. "The Role of Governor Price Daniel as a Legislative Leader." Master's thesis, North Texas State University, 1967.

Kinch, Sam, Jr., and Stuart Long. *Allan Shivers: The Pied Piper of Texas Politics.* Austin: Shoal Creek, 1973.

McBee, Roland L. "Beauford Halbert Jester." Master's thesis, University of Houston, 1954.

Phares, Ross. *The Governors of Texas.* Gretna, La.: Pelican Publishing Company, 1976.

Reston, James R., Jr. *The Lone Star: The Life of John Connally.* New York: Harper and Row, 1989.

CONCLUSION

T
he essays in this book deal only with the chief executives of Texas who are no longer living, but a brief reference to the five surviving governors – Preston Smith, Dolph Briscoe, William Clements, Mark White, and Ann Richards – is appropriate.

John Connally's successor, Preston Smith (1969–1973) of Lubbock, was much less dynamic and much more conservative than Connally. Thought by some to lack intelligence because he was such a poor speaker, he was, in fact, a cagey player in the political game and successfully maneuvered himself into position for election. During his tenure, conservative business interests controlled the state. With Gus Mutscher serving as speaker of the House and Ben Barnes ruling the Senate, little change or progress occurred except for the adoption of a state minimum wage. Smith's second term was marred by the so-called Sharpstown Affair, a stock scandal that destroyed Mutscher's career.

Although Barnes was never charged with any crime, his chances for becoming governor were ruined. Subsequent investigations eventually led to reforms in the legislature.

The election of 1972 brought millionaire, rancher-businessman Dolph Briscoe to the governor's mansion. Briscoe was a weak governor in the image of Coke Stevenson. His slogan was "no new taxes," and he kept his promise to the letter. During his tenure, a major effort was made to replace the antiquated Constitution of 1876, but with Briscoe offering no leadership, the attempt failed because of chaos and controversy in the legislature. Briscoe served for six years (1973–79), but was defeated when he sought renomination in 1978.

A new era seemingly dawned when Texans elected in 1978 their first Republican governor since Reconstruction. The victory of William Clements in that election has been attributed to overconfidence on the part of Democratic candidate John Hill, the well-heeled Clements campaign machine, which spent more than seven million dollars, and Clements's ability to appeal to the innate conservatism of the people.

Unlike Briscoe, Clements was outspoken and aggressive. He had opinions on all subjects and offered them frequently. Especially vociferous about the excessive cost of state government, he promised during the campaign to cut spending substantially but was unable to do so. Although few outstanding legislative achievements during Clements's first term can be directly attributed to his efforts, the diligence of certain leaders in the legislature eventually resulted in some positive changes in school finance and property tax laws. Some advances were made in crime fighting and education reform, issues that Clements strongly supported.

Mark White's (1983–87) defeat of Clements in the election of 1982 disclosed that the resurgence of a two-party system was not quite complete. White, a journeyman politician who tried to please everyone and thus pleased practically no one, placed the primary focus of his administration on education. The result was House Bill 72, arguably the most complex and controversial education law in the history of the state. H. B. 72 reorganized the state board of education, established a merit pay system, and, most controversial of all, required that students must have a passing grade in all subjects to be eligible for extracurricular activities. The reverberations of this provision are still being felt and the long-term effects of the law have yet to be assessed.

By 1986 Texas faced a financial calamity from the collapse of oil prices. In the emotion-charged atmosphere of a fiscal crisis, Mark White and William Clements squared off once again. In a mean-spirited campaign in which both sides spent millions of dollars, Clements was reelected. But his second term (1987–91) produced no more effective leadership than his first. He was succeeded by Ann Richards who defeated Clayton Williams in the 1990 election, a contest that featured some of the most bizarre developments in recent memory. Williams, who led Richards by a substantial margin in the early going, literally talked himself out of contention by his numerous gaffes and "politically incorrect" comments. Clearly, most people believed it was fortunate that Williams was not elected and had high hopes for Richards, but she experienced significant difficulties in establishing leadership and was defeated by George W. Bush in the Republican landslide of 1994.

Although these assessments of recent governors are preliminary, time will provide the perspective required to write more penetrating analyses. But for governors past, a general analysis is not difficult.

The most obvious flaw in the performance of Texas' politicians is to be found in their unwillingness or inability to lead. The office of governor in Texas is constitutionally weak. Hence, to be effective, a leader must be able to identify problems, explain them clearly to the people, seek out beneficial solutions, and implement them through the democratic political process. But for the most part Texas' politicians, past and present, have failed to meet this standard. Instead they have frequently catered to public opinion or attempted to manipulate it for their own purposes. The result is that Texas' leadership has often been attuned not to real needs but to such demands as those for weak government, tax avoidance, pay-as-you-go administration, discrimination, and avoidance of federal intervention, even when these demands were contrary to the public welfare. Moreover, in far too many cases, powerful business interests and wealthy individuals have been allowed to pursue their own agendas using the government as their vehicle.

This analysis leads one to the inevitable question. Did the people of Texas, in choosing their leaders, get what they wanted or simply what they deserved? This question may never be satisfactorily resolved. What is clear, however, is that largely because of the inadequacy of political leadership, Texas has never been well positioned to deal with the inevitable problems that have beset the state as it developed and matured from a raw frontier outpost into a complex modern society. As Texas approaches the dawn of the twenty-first century, its leadership offers only the same tired remedies of budget cutting and trimming services when conditions demand just the opposite policy.

Of course, Texas is not unique among the states for the poor quality of its political leadership. The difference between Texas and other states is to be found in the preservation of the myth of greatness. This is what makes Texas' historiography unique. It is time for the myth to be abandoned and relegated to the past. When it is, perhaps Texans will begin to make more realistic appraisals of their leaders of yesterday and more positive demands upon those of today and tomorrow.

INDEX